CULTS
LIKE
US

CULTS LIKE US

WHY DOOMSDAY THINKING DRIVES AMERICA

JANE BORDEN

ONE SIGNAL
PUBLISHERS

ATRIA

New York   Amsterdam/Antwerp   London
Toronto   Sydney/Melbourne   New Delhi

ONE SIGNAL
PUBLISHERS

ATRIA

An Imprint of Simon & Schuster, LLC
1230 Avenue of the Americas
New York, NY 10020

First One Signal Publishers/Atria Books hardcover edition March 2025

ONE SIGNAL PUBLISHERS / ATRIA BOOKS
and colophon are trademarks of Simon & Schuster, LLC

For information about special discounts for bulk purchases, please contact Simon & Schuster Special Sales at 1-866-506-1949 or business@simonandschuster.com.

The Simon & Schuster Speakers Bureau can bring authors to your live event. For more information or to book an event, contact the Simon & Schuster Speakers Bureau at 1-866-248-3049 or visit our website at www.simonspeakers.com.

Interior design by Hope Herr-Cardillo

Manufactured in the United States of America

1 3 5 7 9 10 8 6 4 2

Library of Congress Cataloging-in-Publication Data has been applied for.

ISBN 978-1-6680-0780-8
ISBN 978-1-6680-0781-5 (ebook)

For Robert and Victoria Borden
Thank you for encouraging faith and critical thinking, both.

When we see the roots of things, our suffering will lessen.

—Thich Nhat Hanh[1]

I think I can see the whole destiny of America contained in the first Puritan who landed on those shores, as that of the whole human race in the first man.

—Alexis de Tocqueville[2]

CONTENTS

CONTENTS

AUTHOR'S NOTE

Do you remember that cult?

You know the one: within months of founding their commune, half of them were dead. Wanting to escape public scrutiny and influence, the leaders had scored a patch of land and everyone moved. But wilderness life was harsh. Rules were strict. Their interpretations of God's word determined all social and legal systems, including radical opinions on marriage and child-rearing. Starting at age eight, children were taken from parents and raised by other caregivers in the community. Leaders demanded absolute obedience.

Grueling labor filled daily life. Those who failed to contribute met severe punishment. Conditions were poor and health suffered without adequate access to medical care. Leaders hid from their neighbors the alarming number of dead bodies by burying them at night. Eventually, the count of adult women shrank to four.

You probably know them best by their nickname: the Pilgrims. The avatar of our country's founding was a doomsday group. We've been iterating on its prototype since. We can't stop re-creating our first trauma, whether in religious movements that eventually go mainstream (such as the Quakers and Mormons); secular groups that devolve into abuse (like NXIVM and Amway); or zeitgeisty social movements (think eugenics or welfare reform). Myths about the Pilgrims persist, for example the Thanksgiving meal, the dour clothing and buckled shoes. But the continued manifestation of their foundational doomsday thought is largely unacknowledged.

The Pilgrims and the Puritans—known in their time as radical Protestants or "hot" Protestants—were apocalypticists. They believed the end of the world was imminent. On this violent "day of doom," the chosen few would be saved and their enemies punished. Most people today do not think a deity will descend from the sky, destroy an actual creature named Satan, and deliver a literal golden city to a chosen few. (About 20 percent of Americans do take the Bible literally.)[1] Yet everyone in the United States retains the societal DNA laid down when those ideas dominated New England.[2]

Puritan doomsday beliefs didn't go away; they became American culture. From our fascination with cowboys and superheroes to our susceptibility to advertising, and our allegiances to hard work and self-help, the United States remains a breeding ground for cultlike thinking. It informs our suppositions about American identity and our very understanding of the immutable self. It undergirds every vote, purchase, prejudice, and social media post. Like fish that don't know water, we swim through it without recognition.

Whenever the latest destructive cult dominates the media with sensational headlines, we cling to the comforting notion that its members are kooks and outliers. But beneath each group's unique and extreme characteristics are foundational ideas Americans already believe. Such indoctrination makes us credulous, renders us vulnerable to the exploitations of con artists, charlatans, and autocrats. We are all in the cult of America. This book traces the winding paths of certain tenets of American doomsday ideology from their arrival in New England in 1620 to today—or at least the high points—focusing especially on secular manifestations, spotlighting where they hide in plain sight. This is a tale of how religious radicalism became cultural orthodoxy—and how our indoctrination is used to activate us to behave in ways that benefit whoever pushes our buttons.

Beneath almost all apocalyptic thinking are notions of exceptionalism and, the flip side of that coin, persecution. *Trample me now, but one day you'll burn while I dance in the sky.* Pilgrim and Puritan discourse promotes the shining city upon a hill, the destiny of America to be special. Both groups fled persecution in England, where they endured derision from the public, and threats of execution by the crown.

Many of America's persistent philosophies—including individual liberties, limited government, and the Second Amendment—follow this paradigm, presupposing an evil "them" attacking a chosen "us." Why would Gadsden's flag read "Don't tread on me" unless he assumed someone trying to tread? America's early religious refugees did not in turn practice tolerance. The Puritan colony quashed dissent with particular zeal, banning Catholics and hanging Quakers. This irony persists today—the "them" attacking "us" on Fox News is as often "big government" as it is (Black and brown) immigrants.

However, there's a paradox in asserting no one can tell us what to do: it opens us to that exact result. The demagogue or cult leader's pitch warns of evil agents who wish to control us. Popular paper tigers have included "communists," our own psychological limitations, a "cabal of pedophiles" who run the government, and "woke" culture. How attractive it can be, then, when said leader offers to save us from that supposed persecution. If we follow their instructions—or buy their coaching sessions or supplements—we will receive a better life, either now on earth or everlasting, come doomsday. In an effort to dodge control, we fall under theirs.

In their pitch is always the specter of a thief: *They want to take your cigarettes . . . your inheritance . . . your guns.* But beware: when someone claims others aim to steal from you, the thief is usually the one talking. It's hard to remember that, though, when we've been primed to accept such belief systems. Granted, some of these thought tendencies predate the 1600s. Sapiens have apocalyptic text in our makeup; monotheism highlighted that text; and then America adopted it as the founding principle for a nation.

———

The word *cult* conjures a mental picture: a group of beautiful young people dancing trancelike in the sun, probably aspiring actors in Los Angeles who took a wrong turn at the beach and landed in an orgy. But *cult* is a slippery word. Originally, in Latin, *cultus* described any religion or religious practice. The word's meaning shifted in America around 1900, when it began describing "delusions, fanatics, enthusiasts, and imposters" and took on a decidedly derogatory tone.[3] Before long, the designation was used for all manner of new, nontraditional, or non-Christian groups within our borders. Some of the biggest targets of the era were Christian Science, the Jehovah's Witnesses, and, of course, Mormonism, all of which are now established and institutionalized religions.

Today, *cult* carries strong valences of deception, abuse, and charlatanism. This meaning coalesced in the late 1980s and early 1990s with the work of Robert Jay Lifton, a psychologist, who pioneered studies of thought reform (a practice colloquially known, if somewhat inaccurately, as brainwashing). In a 1991 paper, Lifton shared the following definition that remains gospel among anti-cultists: "Cults can be identified by three characteristics: 1) a charismatic leader who increasingly becomes an object of worship . . . ; 2) . . . coercive persuasion or thought reform; 3) economic, sexual, and other exploitation of group members by the leader and the ruling coterie."[4] Note that, by this definition, the Pilgrims and the Puritans weren't cults per se, since neither worshiped a charismatic leader (yes, Jesus was arguably one, but he'd been dead for sixteen hundred years). Instead, they were high-control doomsday groups that were exceptionally cult-*y*.

Many academics bristle at the c-word. During my research, one religious-studies scholar told me we shouldn't call them anything at all. I pressed until he offered the phrase *destructive group*. That's somewhat helpful, but not much. My definition is Lifton's plus a few additional characteristics: that the leader enjoys unchecked power, exploits people specifically by manipulating their latent beliefs and desires, and almost always exhibits some kind of narcissistic personality disorder; and that the group can be of any size. But if I typed all that every time I wanted to write *cult*, you would throw this book in the eternal Lake of Fire. So I'm sticking with *cult*.

I've never been in one myself . . . although, I was deeply involved in the improv-comedy scene in the aughts, the doctrine of which specifically required saying, "Yes." We also hugged each other indiscriminately, revered a bearded white dude, and passed out postcards that read "Don't think." My parents and sisters even had a conference call once regarding whether or not I was in a cult because I was at the theater every night, where I worked for free and spent money on a hierarchy of classes. Turns out, though, not a cult—because no one was manipulating my latent indoctrination in order to exploit me. The problem is the exploitation.

Destructive cults and extreme belief systems are not unique to America, of course. But Americans certainly tolerate them more both because of indoctrination and the First Amendment. There are an estimated ten thousand cultlike groups in America, about twice as many now as the estimate in the early aughts.[5] If they can secure church status, we don't even ask for taxes. Soon Americans will be tempted by even more of them.

Sociologists agree that cultlike thinking surges under certain circumstances: in times of technological revolution (social media has shattered traditional communities; AI is leading to mass layoffs), social upheaval (#MeToo; minority populations will soon be the majority in America), and crisis (climate change is arguably the biggest one humanity has ever faced). If we have any hope of saving ourselves from ourselves, we must understand apocalyptic thinking, where it comes from, and why we're addicted to it. Otherwise, we will continue to fall under the spell of extremism, whether religious, political, or economic. We will will keep walking into traps set by narcissists with an insatiable need for control and unconditional adoration. We will keep waking up in orgies wondering where we missed a turn and whose hand is on our thigh.

American culture today is awash with first-person accounts from survivors and deep dives into specific groups by journalists and documentary filmmakers. The onslaught of cult narratives is evidence that, as an organism, our nation endeavors to understand what's attacking it. We want to vaccinate ourselves. This book—a ten-thousand-foot view exploring the underlying cultural ideology beneath each flare of illness—is my contribution to inoculation.

Here's one last word-nerd factoid: typically, when we hear the word *apocalypse*, we envision a fiery battle or cataclysm that destroys the world. Technically, though, the word refers to a specific kind of text, one that contains a revelation. It derives from the Greek word *apokálypsis*, meaning "uncovering." What's revealed usually regards how, where, and when the world will end, yes, but the apocalypse is the document not the battle. Although this book is historic rather than prophetic, it is still an effort to uncover. It doesn't predict the end of days; it does aim to reveal certain patterns of thought. In that way, this book is *my* revelation. It is my apocalypse. Hear, ye, hear, ye.

WEEKEND AT BARTHOLOMEW'S

Once upon a time, there was a man hell-bent on ending the world. He had specific instructions from God outlining the steps to take. He came to America to do it. His name was Christopher Columbus.

By now, most know Columbus wasn't who history books said he was. Americans willing to pay attention have discovered Columbus wasn't all that motivated by adventure and progress, after all. Mostly, he wanted gold—and spices, mastic, anything to enrich his and Spain's coffers. The search consumed him. As it turns out, though, Columbus wasn't even who we rethought he was. It was natural to assume he sought wealth out of basic avarice. But no. In truth, he needed all that gold because it's expensive to bring back Jesus.

Columbus even had an itemized, second coming to-do list. First, expel all Muslims from the Holy Land. That's a big war—how would it be funded? Next, ensure the rebuilding of the temple in Jerusalem, an expensive architectural undertaking. Plus, convert everyone on earth to Christianity and rediscover the Garden of Eden, both of which would require multiple expeditions across the seas.

The list had been worked out by this guy Joachim de Fiore, a twelfth-century Italian abbot who interpreted the New Testament book of Revelation—that freaky, ultraviolent hallucination that prophesies the end of the world—to determine that certain boxes needed to be checked before Jesus would return. His work influenced the Franciscan order, which in turn influenced Columbus. In fact, it was a Franciscan monk who first introduced Columbus to Spanish Queen Isabella, who funded his travels. The budding explorer made the checking of said boxes his life's work. In a letter to King Ferdinand and his wife, Isabella, written on his way home in March 1493, Columbus predicted, "In seven years from today I will be able to pay Your Highnesses for five thousand cavalry and fifty thousand foot soldiers for the war and conquest of Jerusalem, for which purpose this enterprise was undertaken."[1] Although you probably knew about his cruelty to the Indigenous people he met and the disease-driven genocide he caused, you may not have known about the even bigger genocide he planned.

Almost all who carry out apocalyptic endeavors eventually place themselves at the center of the drama. So did Columbus, when he decided God had ordained him specifically to trigger the end the world. "Of the new heaven and earth which our Lord made," he wrote, "He made me the messenger thereof, and showed me where to go."[2] From his first voyage forward, Columbus signed his letters Xpo-ferens. His son Ferdinand explained in a biography that his dad was baptized Ypo Ferens or Christoferens, aka "bearer of Christ," and believed he was doing exactly what his namesake, Saint Christopher, did: carrying Christ across the waters. He only wound up in the Bahamas because he fell short of his grander plan to convert the Chinese.[3]

There is much we still don't know about the subject of all those children's songs and grade school plays. For example, he thought the world had a little tip at the top like a woman's nipple, which is where paradise was. If he were alive today, I imagine that would be on his dating profile. Mostly, though, I tell you all of this to highlight that the Americas have been a staging ground for Christian apocalyptic fantasy since long before the Puritans arrived.

Even though Columbus wasn't alone in these beliefs, he was in the minority. Apocalyptic thinking wasn't standard at the time. It wouldn't go mainstream until a century later in England, following the Protestant Reformation. From there, it would seed our shores.

———

In the late fifteenth and early sixteenth centuries, England experienced plague, smallpox, and economic crisis. Radical Protestants assumed God had engineered it all because England refused to purify the Church of England. They predicted

God's ultimate wrath was not only fast approaching but headed to England first. So they tried to outrun Armageddon.

Later, many would determine New England had been chosen by God specifically to play an apocalyptic role. But this wasn't always the case in 1620, when the Pilgrims emigrated, or during the 1630s, when Puritans boarded a succession of ships to Massachusetts. The devout on these ships mostly understood America as a convenient place to escape to. Their journey was less about coming to America than about leaving England behind, on account of the fast-approaching moment when flames would consume it.

Of course, they also fled England because they were being insulted, spat on, tried in court, executed. For example, during the five years of her short reign as queen, from 1553 to 1558, Mary I burned about 280 Protestants at the stake. But such persecutions did not deter the radicals. Rather, they proved the devotees were righteous and the state was complicit with the Antichrist.

It all began around the 1520s, when the Reformation led to a cleaving from the Roman Catholic Church, resulting eventually in a new branch of Christianity: Protestantism. Adherents argued that the practice of "good works" could do nothing to gain one entry into heaven because God has already determined who will and won't be saved before any of us has a chance to appeal it. Radical Protestants further argued that bishops were similarly useless as aids on the path to salvation. The Reformation aimed to return the church to its origins, to the way the apostles worshiped when Jesus was around (and right after he left). Once that had been achieved, plus a few other things, they figured Jesus would float on down, battle the Antichrist, and institute a thousand years of peaceful and prosperous rule by the Saints (aka the saved among the Protestants), after which he'd return again to judge everyone living and dead, before bringing heaven down to earth, where his chosen people would reign with him in New Jerusalem forever.[4] It's a mouthful.

These ideas shot through Europe. The speed was partly circumstantial: first, the printing press, and second, in 1527, Henry VIII wanted a new wife. When the Pope denied the annulment request, Henry orchestrated a religious coup, broke ties with the Catholic Church, and named himself the head of the new Church of England, which was Protestant. In the decades following, tides shifted back and forth for Protestants as rulers came and went. Complicating the relationship between them and the Church of England was the strain of apocalypticism that had taken root early in the Reformation. The basic idea: if Protestantism was the true church (that much was assumed), then whoever opposed Protestantism opposed God. Therefore, the Catholic Church must be what's prophesied as the evil geopolitical power "Babylon"; the Pope was surely the vague and shadowy Antichrist figure; both were being orchestrated by the devil; and soon this would all culminate in a fiery, world-ending battle.

While Elizabeth I (1558–1603), a Protestant, sat on the throne, this flavor of apocalyptic ideology went mainstream and spun out into several more radical strains. Soon, everyone was providing their own interpretations of the book of Revelation. My favorite among all the records of Pope-Antichrist accusations comes from the papers of John Chamberlain, a man-about-town in England, who wrote in 1609, "The Pope hath written to the French king complaining that our king misuseth him continually in table-talke and calls him Antichrist at every word."[5] *Guys, make him stop!!!*

The radical Protestants believed, as apocalyptic thinkers always have, that the world contained good and evil forces—and nothing else. You were on one side or the other. Just as there was no middle ground, neither could the two compromise or reach a détente. Eradication was the only goal and each supernatural side had pursued it since the beginning of time. With this in mind, radical Protestants determined that any surviving remnant of Catholicism within the Church of England was a "limb of the antichrist." Examples included certain prayers, articles of clothing, rituals, and clerical offices, or persons holding said clerical offices. All had to be eradicated. You don't want to accidentally conspire with Satan on account of your minister's vestment. Get that guy a new cape!

Still, most English were not on board with this fanaticism. The complaining extremists—those trying to *purify* the church—were labeled dissidents and, eventually, "puritans." It was not a compliment. Most mainstream Protestants found the radicals obnoxious and self-righteous. How arrogant is it to tell someone God abandoned him because of his cape?!

Even more extreme were the dissidents who eventually gave up trying to purify the church and aimed instead to *separate* from it. This was dicey, since the Church of England was the state. To separate was treason. The Pilgrims originated in a separatist group that worshiped outside of the small town of Scrooby, just northeast of Sheffield. (The sobriquet *Pilgrims* wasn't generally applied to Plymouth's founders until almost 1800.) With the authorities hot on their tail—literally; there was a boat chase—Scrooby-Doo and the gang fled to Holland, which offered liberty to a variety of religious freaks at the time. But after some years, they grew frustrated by, among other things, the impious and corrupting ways of their neighbors. So they left from there for America.

As for the Puritans, they only wanted to remove remnants of Romish popery from the Church of England, not toss the whole thing away. It was followers of this doctrine who fled to start the Massachusetts Bay Colony (MBC), where they believed they could create the purified church of their dreams. That's when they abandoned England to burn. They also hoped to trigger Jesus's return. They were people of agency. They wanted to help. John Winthrop, founding MBC governor, said they were partnering with God in "buyldinge his new Jerusalem," that they could lay a stone "in the foundation of this new Syon [Zion]."[6]

In this way, they could hasten the apocalypse—and get to the good part—by blotting out absolutely everything that did not fit their ever-shrinking view of righteousness. Whoever wasn't with them was against them. Historian and scholar Carla Gardina Pestana argues that Pilgrim governor William Bradford "thought anyone hostile to Plymouth itself risked God's anger."[7]

———

In 1620, the *Mayflower* landed on the northern tip of what we now call Cape Cod. Its passengers hadn't intended to settle there. They were headed for fertile land in Northern Virginia, where the *Mayflower*'s investors, a group of English merchant capitalist "adventurers," were confident they'd see a return on investment. But instead of hiring John Smith, of Jamestown fame, to guide them, the emigrants saved money by DIYing the trip with a map he'd published. Big mistake. To be fair, they didn't veer as much off course as you may think, since Northern Virginia extended pretty far north. The *Mayflower* had aimed for the mouth of the Hudson River. Imagine if Staten Island had been the birthplace of a nation.

The navigational flub resulted in disaster. By the time they hit land, it was already November—cold and too late to plant crops, but also too late for the captain and crew to keep sailing, since they were due back in England, and besides, the ship was low on provisions. A scouting party sought a settlement spot, dallying for five months anyway, while the sailors and remaining settlers held place offshore and grumbled. People started dying from the cold, the wet, and sicknesses associated with the cold and wet.

The immigrants eventually chose a spot that was already partially developed: an existing Native village on the mainland, emptied after an epidemic brought by previous western explorers had all but exterminated the Patuxet people. Naturally, the English believed God had left this just for them, along with the huge stash of buried corn and seed. They moved in and named it Plymouth. Still, they kept dying. By the end of winter, more than half of the group had expired. Not wanting their Native neighbors to ascertain their weakened and defenseless state, they tried to hide the bodies. There's even an account of settlers sitting up corpses against trees on the edges of the settlement, *Weekend at Bernie's*–style, with muskets alongside, mimicking active night watchmen. If this ever tricked their neighbors, it could only have been for a moment, after which, any Native onlooker surely reasoned, *Hey, free gun*.

Life was tough, but they felt they had God on their side. To be fair, not everyone in Plymouth was a doomsday prepper. Half of the *Mayflower*'s passengers were in it for a new opportunity, rather than a crusade. And several more ships arrived shortly after, bearing a variety of people, almost all Protestant, but of varying degrees of fanaticism. Still, the radicals were the dominant culture. This was especially true farther north, where the Puritans settled and developed Boston. They ran the churches; they held the power.

About a thousand people set sail on eleven ships to found the MBC in the spring of 1630. Within the first few months, almost a hundred of those settlers sailed back home, bad-mouthing the ministers. The MBC government claimed the defectors simply couldn't hack the hard work. As far as I can tell, both camps were right. Church government was punishing *and* demanded a staggering amount of labor from settlers. The colony's work ethic was as impressive as its economic output.

A persistent myth, supported by decades of misled historical scholarship, tells us that the Puritans aimed to detach from the cruel world of commerce and live a spiritual life unspoiled by worldliness. "You can still sometimes see that image in textbooks," Pestana told me, "but that's wrong." Plymouth and the MBC were economically active from the jump. They had to be. The MBC was a joint-stock corporation, meaning it had shareholders. It owed money to investors. And Plymouth had basically the same investment structure, though less formal. As early as 1624, Plymouth was described as a place where "religion and profit jump together."[8]

Within a decade of settlement, Massachusetts was producing an agricultural surplus, and that basically never stopped.[9] They became "almost the breadbasket," explains Pestana, for other colonies in the Atlantic, from Newfoundland down to the Caribbean. They also traded with Europe and the West Indies. Within a generation, they had dominated the Atlantic.[10] Of course, they shot to success in part due to the land they grabbed from Native peoples and the resources they extracted, especially timber. For that matter, as much as they lionized work, they were not totally opposed to slavery. In Plymouth, following King Philip's War in 1676, the locals availed themselves of Native-prisoner slave labor, and by that time a handful of purchased African slaves were also in the colony. As for the MBC, by 1644, Boston traders were actively engaged in trafficking.[11]

Even so, the secret to their economic success was in their religion. They believed having and pursuing a calling was the best way to glorify God. Ergo, work is holy. They also believed God made people specifically to glorify him, meaning there'd be trouble if they didn't. So *everyone* had to work. They didn't want to all get smote because Mahershalalhasbaz took too many pipe breaks.

Anyway, if work is holy, then idleness is a sin. A twelve-hour day keeps the devil away. They discouraged vagrancy and idleness by developing a strong education system and offering incentives to merchant entrepreneurs to establish business infrastructure. They also purged holidays from the calendar, which, whether intentionally or not, increased the number of workdays from 220 a year to 300. The New England colonies developed "a work regime that was truly historically aberrant."[12] It was an entire colony made of the kid who'd remind your teacher to assign homework over the weekend. Some scholars even believe "when they enshrined the Sabbath they did so, among other reasons, to stop their working themselves to death."[13]

Cultivating the land, in particular, was good, since they believed God impelled them to use the natural world for their benefit. Buttressing this was the more elemental and heartbreaking belief that nature is evil. This predates Protestantism, sure. But the Puritans upped the ante, thanks to their notion of predestination, which reasoned that anyone pre-chosen by God as saved had been given grace and contained no nature in them whatsoever. That's the hierarchy: holy grace above evil nature.

But, they reasoned, if you use the material world for a godly purpose (for example, your work), then you are *improving* the world and making it more godly. Not only *can* you extract what you want, you *must*. "Nature belonged to the gracious and could no more resist their control of it than Satan could resist Christ." This doctrine has become known as the grace-nature divide and has undergirded and justified centuries of runaway extraction economics.

Even though English royals were alarmed by some of the ideological developments in New England, they abstained from intervening in the settlements' religious practices for some time. They were dealing with their own crises, sure (for example, the execution of a king), but they also recognized that the ideology in New England was very good for business.[14]

Meanwhile, the Pilgrims and the Puritans waited for doomsday. It had to be soon. It just had to be—not least because they really wanted to see it. So common was the expectation, you could hear kids reciting these lines while they played:

With dismal chains, and strongest reins,
like Prisoners of Hell,
They're held in place before Christ's face,
till He their Doom shall tell.[15]

That is from "The Day of Doom," a long-form poem by the pastor Michael Wigglesworth. Dark stuff from a guy whose name sounds like a toddler in a tickle fight. It catalogues Judgment Day—when Jesus swipes everyone left or right—in gory, exhaustive detail. Published in 1662, it's a cosmic eff-you and I-told-you-so to the masses of those presumed damned. The Puritans *loved* it. The first eighteen hundred copies sold out within a year, remarkable considering New England's population was only about thirty thousand total. It's been called America's first bestseller. One in twenty New Englanders bought a copy.[16] Since books were treasures in the MBC and therefore shared within households, which typically numbered four to seven, my back-of-the-envelope math suggests "The Day of Doom" was read by about 30 percent of New England residents. For reference, as of 2021, 31 percent of Americans have read a Harry Potter book.[17]

New England was a culture of judgment, and "The Day of Doom" contains more than two hundred stanzas of people getting it. The poem is thrilling. *Will Christ pusheth the red button that drops them into the Lake of Fire—will he, will he??* (Yes.)

The Puritans were starved for entertainment. First, there was no theater in New England. Even dancing was disallowed because the only thing one could be exuberant about was God.[18] Then, into their boring Puritan days, Wigglesworth injected a gnarly horror story. In it, nature itself is so scared that mountains smoke, hills shake, animals flee into the sea, and the ocean roars, "forsakes the shore, and Shrinks away for fear." People read it and read it and read it again. Only one original edition has made it to the twenty-first century and its pages are so riffled and thumbed, they are barely intact.

Early Massachusetts Bay minister John Cotton believed the end would come shortly after 1655.[19] Cotton's son-in-law Increase Mather, also influential, was reluctant to assign a particular date, so simply said the cosmic battle would occur in the next several years . . . and then said, actually, in a few more after that . . . and, oops, but surely soon. Increase's son Cotton Mather, another significant minister in Puritan history, was willing to specify. First, he said the end would kick off in 1697. When it didn't, he recalculated to 1736, but then backtracked to 1716. All that year, people lost their minds, but were ultimately left perplexed. So he pushed it to 1717. Following that failure of prophecy, he grew more reticent, at least until 1727, when Boston experienced an earthquake, causing him to conclude the end had finally arrived. No subsequent predictions occurred because shortly thereafter he died.

In addition to fearing doomsday, residents worried God would punish the settlement if they didn't each stay in line. So they preempted the possibility. Punishment was central to the colony's theology and government, as well as to everyone's identity and understanding of their relationship with both corporeal and eternal life. Punishment was also New England's primary source of entertainment. The more humiliating, the better. In the 1620s, John Oldham was banished from Plymouth for insolence and dissension. But he came back. So they kicked him out again, this time through a spank tunnel. A guard of musketeers lined up in a row leading toward a waiting boat. Oldham was forced to walk through them, while each gave him "a thump on the breech with the butt of his musket."[20]

Common punishments for petty crimes were just as humiliating. Condemned Puritans were forced to stand on boxes in the center of town with notes pinned to them detailing their wickedness so everyone could stare in judgment. Bystanders could also toss detritus at any adjudged whose ankles were tied up in a bilbo, legs fastened in stocks, or wrists and neck locked in the pillory. Major BDSM vibes in early New England.

Fornication, that is, sex outside of marriage, was by far the most common crime. A Plymouth trial in 1671 investigated accusations made toward a woman named Mary. She confessed to fornicating three times and even shared specific dates, possibly America's first humblebrag. Court proceedings were a public spectacle here, conducted so in order to maximize humiliation and social control. She was fined £6. Two pounds per tryst: the cost of doing business.

Heftier crimes drew savage penalties. In addition to whippings, branding was common, the hot iron applied to the criminal's skin in the courtroom, just after sentencing. A for adultery, B for burglary, D for drunkenness. *M for that is Messed up.* Abel Buell took one to the forehead for counterfeiting money in Connecticut. He also had the tip of his ear clipped off and reattached. During its brief period of separation, the fragment was stored on his tongue. Some condemned criminals had ears cut off completely.

Gossiping, flirting, swearing, smoking, playing ball sports, doing almost anything on the Sabbath—all crimes. Skipping church or talking smack about the pastor were punishable. Even interrupting the preacher was considered a crime. Blasphemy called for the death sentence. America today has one of the highest incarceration rates in the world.

England's justice system was just as brutal, if not more so. However, New England didn't have much crime, comparatively. The colonies were not overrun with vagrants, sex industry, burglars, and bandits. Yet they still policed their citizenry excessively. This was not just a culture of punishment; this was a *high-control group*, meaning the power structure in the group regulated residents' behavior, beliefs, and information intake, all via high pressure to conform. Mandatory church attendance. All transgressions made public. Residents forced into informants: a New Haven woman was once reported by a servant who overheard her expressing disagreement with her minister.

They even turned policing inward.

————

Although no one could say *for sure* who had or had not been chosen, they felt pretty certain each person could discern the answer via extensive and exhausting trials of self-reflection. If, following such an exercise, you believed you had found grace within, you could be accepted by the community as "chosen" and granted membership in the church. Over the years, the trials grew more intense and entry harder to achieve, which was especially difficult on children.

High-control groups are often most damaging to youth. Discipline in Puritan homes was harsh and fear-based. Boston minister Cotton Mather wrote this in the introduction to a children's book: "They which lie, must go to their father, the devil, into everlasting burning; they which never pray, God will pour out his wrath upon them. . . . Are you willing to go to hell and burn with the devil and his angels?"[21] *Llama llama, childhood trauma.*

Around puberty, and sometimes earlier, Puritan children in New England were sent to live in other households, a practice the Puritans brought from England, where it was originally designed for kids to learn trades. In fact, the custom of moving children out to apprentice under different "masters" dates to the Middle Ages. But New England children moved to different homes even without educational goals, and girls did it as well as boys, although they could easily have learned housekeeping from their mothers. Some scholars argue the Puritans engaged in this practice to keep parents from indulging children with affection, lest they became spoiled, wicked, and disobedient. Puritans were so obsessed with obedience, as most high-control groups are, that rebellious children could even be sentenced to death.[22] Fortunately, no child received this sentence, but the fear it instilled and made commonplace was effective enough: "When children shall rebel against their parents, wickedness is excessively great. And such children do usually die before their time."[23]

Magistrates sometimes had to forcibly remove children from their parents to place them in other homes. Most parents, however, consented voluntarily to the practice, not least because failing to do so also risked their own salvation. If they gave their children too much affection, it was sinful because it showed love for a creature, which was dangerous, since you couldn't love anything as much as you loved God. For the same reason, widows were not allowed to grieve much, since doing so would suggest they had inordinately loved their spouses. Surviving diaries are full of worries over the sadness felt following the death of loved ones.

The endless and uncertain trials of reflection to determine their place among the saved, the extreme and shaming discipline at home, and the fear-based indoctrination in church produced tangible results. Scholars have deduced, after poring over diaries, that the second and third generations of New England Puritans exhibited during adolescence significant increases in melancholy, pathological abnormalities, nervous breakdowns, suicide, and insanity.[24]

But this all felt justifiable, considering the stakes: Jesus was watching, and if he didn't like what he saw, he could tear up his return ticket. With so much on the line, church members occasionally tried to optimize theology, leading to hot takes that challenged the status quo. Such proclamations were perilous, since opposition risked banishment, but dissenters prioritized salvation, which they believed depended on every minor point. And, anyway, if they were evicted, there was a lot of land in this new land. One could flee into pretty much any of it. New Jerusalem was always around the bend.

———

Some of you studied Roger Williams in high school. Others of you smoked pot; some of you did both. Williams is considered the father of the separation of church and state. His ideas influenced the Declaration of Independence and the Bill of Rights. He articulated what would later become the foundational American tenet of religious liberty. But in school, you probably didn't learn his motivation for keeping the state out of the church. That's not because you were stoned; most curricula don't include that he was trying to bring on the end of the world.

Williams believed the reformed MBC church had not gone far enough to purge itself of Catholic remnants, all of which was delaying Christ's return. He reasoned that if Jesus and the apostles didn't have an institutionalized church, neither should anyone. (For a time, the only person he'd pray with was his wife. In later years, he prayed alone.) He arrived in the MBC in 1631 and quickly began opposing its theocracy, arguing that the state had no jurisdiction over the church. He claimed anyone worshiping with an impure church, which was everyone, would receive the mark of the beast and be damned eternally. He basically told all of Boston they were going to hell.

Church leaders expelled him in 1635, but before they could toss him on a ship, he escaped into the woods, where he basically founded Rhode Island. His ideas were less about people having the right to do what they want and more about people not having the right to do anything that would stop the second coming. And, because apocalypticists have a serious case of Main Character Syndrome, the more he thought about it, the more he became certain of having a role in the center of the drama. By his own interpretation, he was one of the witnesses mentioned in Revelation, figures often understood as representatives of the church, and who the book of Revelation claims will have the power to send plagues and control weather. When he wrote in a letter, "Christ Jesus speaketh and suffereth in his witnesses," the subtext was *Christ speaketh through me. And maybe through this thunderstorm.*[25]

He also deduced a witness could carry out an ordained and prophesied task only if the witness had total freedom from the state. The origins of the Constitution's Establishment Clause and Free Exercise Clause are wrapped up in the mission of a man who believed he had been prophesied in Revelation to buck the authoritarian structure of his day in order to prepare the way for Jesus to drop the hammer.

Also, at one point, he supported forcing women to wear veils during worship. None of this sounds much like liberty to me. Then again *liberty*, at the time, was often shorthand for *religious liberty* or *liberty of conscience*. Both were defined as the ability to worship solo, beyond the literal or metaphorical walls of the Church of England. However, in turn, liberty could grant said petitioners the right to invalidate said church. Those seeking liberty, in other words, did not intend to grant the same tolerance to others. *I'm right, you're wrong, and that's coming from God, so believe me now or burn later.* Liberty! Put it on a bell.

Soon, he was joined in Rhode Island by Anne Hutchinson, a radical MBC resident who dared to criticize MBC church leaders and be charismatic enough to recruit others to her position. The magistrates responded in force. First, they tried, convicted, and banished her. Then, they founded Harvard. (Several motivations fueled the school's creation, but one was to indoctrinate youth in order to preclude dissent. This explains Harvard's motto, "Screw you, Anne.") Next, they cut the practice of questions and comments following sermons because it was "an occasion of much contention, vexation, and folly."[26] Finally, they forbade any town from accepting strangers unless or until those strangers had been vetted by council members or magistrates. Out of a paranoid belief that everyone was out to get them, MBC leaders made dissent impossible and, as a result, isolated themselves more than moving across an ocean already had.

And what choice was there but to banish Hutchinson and destroy her ideas, when another identity trait of God's chosen people was to destroy sin in others? It was a Puritan duty to self-righteously intervene. As minister Thomas Hooker argued, "What ever sins come within his reach, he labors the removal of them, out of the familyes where he dwells, out of the plantations where he lives, out of the companies and occasions, with whom he hath occasion to meet and meddle at any time."[27] If that sounds like *Taxi Driver*'s Travis Bickle no longer waiting for a real rain to wash the scum off the streets, you're right on the mark.

During and especially after that trial of dissenter Anne Hutchinson in the late 1630s, more than eighty families moved to Williams's fledgling settlement. A few had been excommunicated, but most moved voluntarily, either in solidarity with Hutchinson or out of general frustration with church leaders. Another bold-name dissenter, Samuel Gorton, wound up there, along with Baptists, Quakers, and, eventually, Jews. A lesser-known dissenter, Richard Borden, turned up in Portsmouth, Rhode Island, at least by 1640, when his son, my great-great-etc-grandfather John entered the world, meaning my first American ancestor was either in cahoots with these radicals or had fled his own excommunication. Yes, I want that on a T-shirt.

The unrest and court proceedings around Hutchinson's rabble-rousing became known as the antinomian controversy. The word *antinomian* literally translates to "anti-law." The Protestants were anti–Catholic law. The Puritans were anti–Church of England law. Hutchinson was anti–MBC law. Reform itself was a way to battle the Antichrist. Protestantism by nature bucks authority, splinters off, and enterprises itself again and again. Williams, Hutchinson, and their sympathizers weren't alone. Thomas Hooker also led people out of the MBC and into the Connecticut Valley, in 1636, when he believed the end imminent. And in 1638, John Davenport and his followers founded New Haven. *You get a church, and you get a church, and you get a church.*

————

Some of the Puritans' controlling doctrine and behavior started at the jump, but much of it developed beginning around the 1640s and 1650s, when founders and elders became rigidly determined to hold what they'd built and developed—that is, when they became corrupted by power and refused to relinquish it. The Puritans came here as dissenters, but ended up as rigid and intolerant as the leadership they'd fled, arguably more so. Their lofty ideals twisted over time. For example, as more community members developed the inner conviction of being saved, ministers feared their leadership would lose authority. In response, they started preaching uncertainty. *Actually, God is hardly saving anyone at all, so you're probably not among them—there's wickedness in you somewhere, just keep looking.* Membership in the church became almost impossible to attain.

Elders devised other ways to hoard power. By the 1650s, in Sudbury, just west of Boston, twenty-six sons had aged into adulthood, but still not received the land their fathers were to pass down. If you didn't have land, you couldn't get married and therefore couldn't leave your parents' dominion. And there was no more land in the settlement to claim. These sons were trapped and powerless. In some cases, fathers aimed to preserve the free labor of their sons (either on their own land or on the land of others to pay down debts). Inevitably, these delayed marriages led to an outbreak of fornication. In response, leaders relaxed the laws governing premarital sex rather than grant earlier independence to the next generation—just as leaders of high-control groups almost always change rules rather than cede power.

In high-control groups, unchecked hunger for power can never be sated; its ultimate destination is violence. Granted, most cults implode or dissipate first. Yet the Puritans did arrive at such a terminus: the Salem witch trials of 1692 and 1693. Some scholars believe the craze developed specifically in response to the MBC's strict patriarchal structures. "The hysteria began with the most powerless among the powerless."[28] Accusations were lobbed by children, females, and servants, that is, exactly those most controlled by the colony's system of family governance.

Ultimately, nineteen were hanged, one was pressed to death with stones, and five died in custody. I described violence as a high-control group's "ultimate destination" because it typically develops just before a group expires. It is not a coincidence, in my opinion, that the witch trials in Salem occurred around the time the Puritan experiment in Massachusetts ended. England had just recently revoked and replaced the colony's original charter. In a few more years, the Puritans would blend in with the larger British colonial culture, in part because of fears regarding the dangers posed by theocratic rule (for example, killing twenty people for being witches).

———

Robert Jay Lifton, the leading modern scholar of coercive groups, developed eight criteria of "thought reform," eight indicators that a group psychologically controls its members: information and communication are controlled; perfection and purity are demanded; sins and faults are openly discussed and excoriated; doctrine and leadership are ultimate truth and beyond criticism; personal experiences are subordinate to ideology; language and thought-terminating clichés are used to force conformity; everyone in the outside world is evil; and experiences are orchestrated to appear spontaneously mystical. The Puritans meet at least the first six. By now you know where this is going: another word for a high-control group is *cult*.

The Pilgrims' and the Puritans' cultlike ideology today manifests as commonplace secular belief. It is at the heart of American culture. I find seven of their credos to be most pervasive and problematic and I've devoted a chapter to each: our innate desire for a strongman to fix our problems and punish those who aggrieve us; the temptation to feel chosen, which justifies acting on our base desires; our knee-jerk anti-authoritarianism and anti-intellectualism; our impulse to buy and sell salvation on the open market; the belief that hard work is holy, while idleness is a sin; how quickly and easily we fall into us-versus-them thinking; and, finally, an innate need for order, which makes us vulnerable to anyone screaming, "Chaos!" and then offering control. Throughout, I also explore an eighth credo, the aforementioned grace-nature divide, which distinguishes and creates a hierarchy between humans and the rest of the planet. Along the way, I share case studies of cults, specifically so you'll see the ideology at play in a context typically considered wacky and outlying, and then see that same idea propelling a variety of major movements in American history.

Some of these modes of thought arrived with the Puritans. Some have been with our species as long as we've stood erect. All make us more vulnerable to our fears and to bad-faith actors. Admittedly, I'm using "we" when I really mean "most." You, reader, may not feel you fall prey to each of these listed tendencies (although, I challenge you to check again after finishing the book). Still, I will most often speak of "us" because "we" are in this together, "this" being the cult of America.

———

The sixth stanza of "The Day of Doom" reads like a twisted "'Twas the Night before Christmas."

They rush from Beds with giddy heads,
and to their windows run,
Viewing this light, which shines more bright
Than doth the Noon-day Sun.[29]

When, what to their wondering eyes should appear? Not Santa with a sack of firewood and antibiotics, but Jesus come to judge. After that, it gets dark fast. Bodies spew from the ground and sea, reincarnated only in order to be damned. The Pilgrims and the Puritans believed almost all humans had been created just so God could watch them grovel before tossing them into fire where, for eternity, he would listen to them scream. But before that judgment, Jesus pulls up everyone going to heaven—so they can witness and help. Their first heavenly reward is to watch their friends and family beg for mercy.

Finally, at the end of the poem, we learn what waits for the Saints in heaven: never ending hymns and rest, getting to see God, and the absence of distress. That information is revealed in five verses. The entire poem is 224 verses. You tell me whether they were more interested in hell or heaven.

CHAPTER 1

THE QUICK AND THE DEAD
ON STRONGMEN AND PUNISHMENT

"We dedicate this service now to the tackling of the beast and the dragon that gave it power behind the entire momentum of rock music on this planetary home."

A mysterious cassette tape recording containing those words has circulated nationally among underground DJs and music aficionados since the late eighties. The speaker, a woman, really hates rock 'n' roll.

She explains that "fallen ones" are trying to subdue the "light bearers" via the "syncopated rhythm" and "the misuse of the four-four time." She calls on "ascended masters" to take action: "Bind the fallen ones, all the promoters of rock music, the composers, and those who execute it." All must be bound—a kind of spiritual neutralization, a thwarting of someone's ability to do harm—because rock music is "the great anti-freedom force on the planet."

Then the voice, the curator of the unseen events taking place, plays her followers a long montage of rock music. Counterintuitive, yes. But she wants them to practice fighting it. Listeners can shield themselves from the syncopated rhythms, she advises, if they sit sternly with spines erect, arms folded, and feet flat. During the tail end of the presentation, clips play of "Better Be Good to Me" by Tina Turner, Van Halen's "Hot for Teacher," and Madonna's "Lucky Star."

How much this woman loathes rock 'n' roll is equal and inverse to modern DJs' love for the recording, and that is because, following the music montage, a man takes the stage and names names. He calls for the specific binding of almost seventy different artists. It's a who's who of eighties pop. There are obvious offenders—Prince, Kiss, and Elton John—as well as surprising entries, such as Diana Ross and Phil Collins. Some artists are mentioned twice: Christine McVie gets name-checked even though Fleetwood Mac has already been bound; Michael Jackson is bound as a solo artist, as is his collaboration with Paul McCartney, who has no solo entry, although John Lennon does (perhaps for trying to imagine there's no heaven).

But the speaker can be forgiven these missteps, since he clearly has no idea what he's talking about. For example, he says, "David *Boowie*," "Cyndi *Looper*," and "*Jack* Cougar Mellencamp," malapropisms that lend a childlike innocence to what is in fact a call for cosmic violent judgment. He believed these artists were responsible not only for physical and sexual perversions, but even murder. He had seen the devil and it was Mike Jagger from the Rooling Stoons.

This recording is titled "Sounds of American Doomsday Cults, Vol. 14," and it's been sampled by Negativland, Throbbing Gristle, and Fatboy Slim, among other musicians.[1] But its name is somewhat cheeky, since there are no Volumes 1 through 13, and anyway, it was simply ripped from the cassette "Rock 'n' Roll Exposé #1," dated 12-15-84, one of thousands of recordings distributed in monthly mailings to global members of the Church Universal and Triumphant (CUT). The woman on the tape is Elizabeth Clare Prophet, the leader of CUT, which numbered fifty thousand members at its height. (She died in 2009 after a long struggle with Alzheimer's.)

Her daughter, Erin Prophet, who's now a scholar of new religious movements and medicine at the University of Florida, told me that Elizabeth's fear of rock 'n' roll was authentic: "She thought the syncopated rhythm would prevent you from raising your Kundalini energy, so you couldn't ascend." Elizabeth's church lives on, espousing a mishmash of Eastern and Western traditions. The goal is to balance your negative karma down to at least 49 percent, at which point you become immortal. But doing so requires the aid of ascended masters, a group of beings who have already reached immortality. "The idea is that the more you listened to [rock 'n' roll] or engaged with it or moved your hips and body to it," Erin explains, "it was going to prevent you from having contact with God and the masters, who would just sort of go away and leave you."

The "masters" include Jesus and Buddha, as well as such semi-divinities as El Morya (previously embodied as Saint Thomas More), Serapis Bey (once a high priest on the doomed island of Atlantis), and Saint Germain (the master of the Age of Aquarius and the sponsor of the United States of America, who was once also the prophets Samuel, Merlin, Christopher Columbus, and Sir Francis Bacon).

The masters communicated with human beings through messengers. Elizabeth Clare Prophet was one of them. So had been her husband, Mark Prophet, who founded the church, originally called the Summit Lighthouse, in 1958 (after falling under the influence of other New Age groups, themselves impacted by the Theosophy and I AM movements). He died in 1973, and Elizabeth ascended, relaunched the church with a new name, took it global, and served as its sole messenger.

"She's got her eyes closed and she's just talking for like an hour or more, supposedly getting these messages from beyond," her son Sean told me. He was once a high-ranking member in the church. As the head of media, he says he recorded "tens of thousands of hours" of his mother, including "Rock 'n' Roll Exposé #1." He eventually left and found success as a TV editor. He is also an outspoken critic not only of CUT and cults, but of all religion (his sister Erin considers herself agnostic). "It was pretty phenomenal," he says about his mother. "She was a performance artist in some ways."

But one belief in particular made Elizabeth Clare Prophet a national media sensation: her prophecy that the Soviets would drop nuclear bombs on America on March 15, 1990. Church members felt such cataclysms were inevitable whenever earthly karma from evils, such as rock 'n' roll and abortion, accumulated to a breaking point. Such disasters rebalance the world—in spite of the fact that, or perhaps because, millions perish. In this way, Elizabeth predicted the nuclear attack would only be the kickoff. In short order something more classic would follow, like a continent-splitting earthquake or biblical flood, "that would wipe out most of the survivors, leaving us free to start our own civilization," Erin writes in her memoir, *Prophet's Daughter: My Life with Elizabeth Clare Prophet Inside the Church Universal and Triumphant*.[2]

This is always the case with doomsday groups: followers believe they have been chosen to survive an inevitable disaster—one delivered specifically in order to save the chosen from evil. Evil, in this case, is everyone else: those who didn't listen to the chosen and, especially, those who persecuted the chosen. Fortunately, that means they needn't feel bad for everyone else, since the afflicted clearly had it coming.

———

CUT members thought they were the light-bearers destined to witness the "golden age," rule theocratically as instruments of God, and repopulate the earth. But Elizabeth was too savvy to take her doomsday prophecy wide—to draw attention and risk ridicule. Even church members didn't know its specific date was March 15. She told her global membership only that March and April were a "danger period."[3] Still, that vague pronouncement led thousands to travel to Paradise Valley, Montana, to be with her at the church's headquarters. On the night of March 14, they exercised what they believed was only a drill. When the next day passed without consequence, she owed no explanations. But word eventually leaked that her prediction actually had been specific.

A couple of months later, Elizabeth appeared on ABC News' *Nightline* with Ted Koppel. The host introduced the segment dismissively, saying, "This quite frankly is one of those stories you save for a slow day . . . and even then you wonder whether it merits the attention."[4] During the interview, he twice calls it all "nonsense," and as a sign-off, adds, "I'm not sure how much we've learned, but, uh, it was interesting." Granted, it had been twelve years since nine hundred died in Jonestown, and Waco hadn't yet blazed into the American imagination, but still, I'm not sure by what standards CUT's behavior wouldn't merit attention. The group had spent $25 million on materials alone to build the biggest private bomb shelter in the United States, outfitted to house 756 people for several years. A month prior, an accidental fuel leak at the site had dumped thirty-two thousand gallons of diesel oil and gasoline into the Montana wilderness just north of Yosemite Park. And in the summer of '89, two church members had been arrested for purchasing weapons under a false name, which revealed a plan to arm at least two hundred members, including with military-style semiautomatic weapons and armor-piercing rifles.[5]

On *Nightline*, Elizabeth joined the conversation via broadcast from the church compound. She is firm, somehow both calm and fiery, and displays the confidence and charisma that helped her build an international organization. But she does not tell the whole truth, evading questions by changing the topic or launching criticisms of the media. Sometimes she lies outright.

Koppel mentions her failed predictions of nuclear warfare and she replies, "Absolutely not. I've never predicted a nuclear attack." This is only true if one argues that because there were *so many* predicted days, there couldn't possibly have been any single one. The first was October 2, 1989. Elizabeth heard El Morya say an attack was likely on or after this date. She told her followers that they wouldn't die as long as they completed their shelters by then. But when members overseeing construction determined the work wouldn't be complete, Elizabeth asked El Morya to hold off the karma. Naturally, he complied. Erin then got new messages—she was now receiving dictations too, at Elizabeth's behest—including a vision explaining that "during a twelve-year period beginning April 23, 1990, we would see retribution upon mankind . . . including a cataclysm maybe even worse than the flood of Noah."[6] (I wonder if El Morya was actually predicting Vanilla Ice.)

During the Koppel interview, Elizabeth also prevaricates when she says, "No one has to come and live with me to be a part of my church," which is technically true but fundamentally false. Only "permanent members," about a quarter of her total following, were required to live at the Montana compound. This status required them to give all assets to the church—without any kind of safety net, to be clear, and indeed dozens were kicked out swiftly and with only bus fare, sometimes for nothing more than criticizing Elizabeth. However, later, if someone wanted to secure a spot in the fallout shelter, they were indeed expected to move to Montana *and* to sign away their assets. Many members were left penniless following the failure of the prophecy. Some had accrued substantial debt and even written bad checks to local businesses, totaling, Erin reports, $100,000, including $35,000 to a local grocery store. Church members' debt put a lumber company out of business.

The pattern of church equivocation continued during an *Oprah* interview that pitted Erin against her sister Moira, who had been removed from the church and begun speaking against it. There was also a group appearance on *Donahue*. Highlights include the outlandish incongruence between the subject matter and Phil's folksy nature, for example, when he says, "And lookee here, church members have guns too."[7]

Elizabeth and high-ranking church members also lied to reporters, and the federal government, when they denied she had prior knowledge of the plan to procure weapons. Erin writes in her memoir that her mother fully understood the plans and the money source—and anyway had already been hoarding weapons since 1973. Still, it does seem weapons were intended for self-defense. Sean only remembers guns being utilized to hunt. Erin insists the stockpiles were not for use against neighbors desperate for food during nuclear fallout (in fact, she claims the group had extra rations in storage so they could help neighbors). Rather, the guns were protection from the predicted bands of militias that would rove America after the government fell and anarchy ruled. By all accounts CUT was indeed a peaceful group, as members claimed again and again. But even this is wobbly.

The group may not have exhibited violence, but it certainly *wished* it against the hedonistic world in general and against certain enemies in particular. "My mother would say things like 'I demand the instantaneous final physical judgment of this person,' meaning they would die," explains Sean. He recalls that she used this decree—decrees are CUT's form of prayer, a kind of high-speed monotone chant—against Gregory Mull, a former member whom the church battled in court from 1981 to 1986. First, the church sued him, claiming he owed money. He countersued, arguing he'd been permanently scarred due to his involvement with the sect. "Gregory Mull, for sure. She wanted him dead," Sean adds. "She thought she had the power to somehow spiritually order his death."

Ironically, during the protracted court proceedings, Mull was diagnosed with multiple sclerosis. He died three months after a jury awarded him $1.5 million in damages. "So some people said that we decreed him to death," Erin told me.

Of the general practice of decreeing for a negative outcome, she shares, "My mother started doing it in the late sixties. Not everybody liked it or wanted to do it, but it kept taking on a bigger and bigger part of our prayer work as time went on." As high-control groups and cults age, punishment is increasingly used as a tool for conformity. Fear keeps people in line and leaders in power. When Moira began attacking the church in the press, Sean says, Elizabeth delivered the same invocation—*I demand the instantaneous final physical judgment of this person*—even wishing death on her daughter.

And on the morning of March 25, 1990, she went further. (She and Erin now believed bombs would fall on March 26.) In the past, although Elizabeth *expected* the rest of humanity to be destroyed in a cataclysm, she nevertheless had her congregation ask El Morya to hold back the violence. But by that morning, something had changed. She instead prayed *for* the bombs to drop. She used her power, which she believed was immense and supernatural, to call for carnage.

First, she convinced a reluctant Erin and Sean to give such a prayer with her. "My mother, my sister and I stood in that serene forest on a crisp spring Montana morning, and we actively prayed to God for a judgment that could lead to the deaths of billions of human beings," Sean writes in his book, *My Cult, Your Cult.* "To disobey her was to disobey God. I didn't believe I had a choice." Sean thinks his mother felt *she* didn't have a choice either, that destruction was God's will, and she was the instrument of that will. But, he says, she confused the will of God with her own: "The world persecuted God's messenger, and so she felt that in order for divine justice to be done, the world must be destroyed."[8]

It sounds like the kind of grievance narrative often motivating desires for divine punishment. I asked Sean if there was anything his mother had believed she was owed but didn't receive or believed had been stolen. He pointed immediately to the Gregory Mull trial. "They attacked her spiritual authority," he said.

The trial was nasty. Her ex-husband divulged during testimony that he'd had an affair with Prophet while she was still married to Sean and Erin's father—behavior she regularly castigated from her soapbox. Mull's lawyer mocked Prophet and her group, referencing at one point their belief in past lives by asking Prophet's then husband if he believed he was Captain Cook. The media published every delicious detail, painting the church leader a hypocrite and a joke. Sean says his mother was different after the trial. The feeling of persecution changed her.

Just before noon on March 26, 126 people went underground for what they thought was another "drill." But by that night, when still nothing had happened, Elizabeth gathered the entire group and had them all pray together for the bombs to fall. No one objected. They swung their ceremonial swords and chanted, "Beloved Mother Mary, let the right arm of your Son Jesus Christ descend in vengeance for the evils continuing in the earth!" And "Blue lightning bombs descend! Blue lightning bombs descend!" And "Archangel Michael, let the bombs descend!"[9]

They decreed over and over and over. Prophet's voice rose in time until she was shouting at the top of her lungs. Afterward, as Erin writes in her book, "few people spoke about what we had done: praying for the destruction of our country. Some tried to say that it never happened but others could not forget."[10]

Elizabeth Clare Prophet *did* want violence, vengeance against those who failed to see her. She just wanted someone else to deliver it. That desire, as we will explore, is one of America's most enduring legacies.

I n the mid-1960s, at Morningside College in Sioux City, Iowa, Robert Jewett and John Shelton Lawrence discussed the Vietnam War. They wondered how and why the nation could tolerate such extreme violence. Then they made a startling discovery about narratives of violence in popular culture. It eventually became their 1977 book, *The American Monomyth*.[11]

Basically, Jewett and Lawrence noticed a storytelling pattern in film, television, and comic books, wherein an Edenic community is threatened by some kind of evil, which law enforcement and government are either powerless or unwilling to stop, until a loner arrives to rescue the community—through violence. This hero is opposed to violence, mind you, but something always forces his hand, meaning that when he does accept his solemn duty to rain terror, the choice is justified. What's more, his violence has scalpel precision. There are never innocent casualties. If you die, you deserved to. Therefore, this violence is cleansing. Therefore it is righteous. Once the community has been redeemed, the hero disappears from whence he came.

To name a few examples: *Star Trek* (on other planets, Kirk and Spock save communities that can't help themselves); *Death Wish* (Paul Kersey redeems New York City from muggers when the cops won't); *Star Wars*; *The Matrix*; *Air Force One* (the president saves Eden); *Independence Day* (the president saves Eden from aliens); *The Lion King*; *Lean on Me* (a principal saves a school—by purging half of it); *The Birth of a Nation*; every Western; almost every film starring John Wayne, Clint Eastwood, Chuck Norris, Sylvester Stallone, Arnold Schwarzenegger, or Steven Seagal; *Braveheart*; the *Shaft* franchise; *American Sniper*; *Jaws*; nearly every disaster film; the *Jack Ryan* franchise; the *Jack Reacher* franchise; the *Kangaroo Jack* franchise (just kidding); most video games, starting with *Space Invaders* in 1978 and including all first-person shooter games; and almost every film in every superhero genre ever made.

In this monomyth, as they call it, tropes abound. The police chief is clumsy and overweight. The senator conspires with the villain. Cities are full of vice, while rural areas are populated by good and simple people. Women are either lustful temptresses or weak pacifists. The hero, meanwhile, is lonely and selfless, and despite how many women throw themselves at him, he never wants the girl (even when she is his wife). This last one is an ideology also echoed by Charles Manson when he said, "I don't need broads. Every woman I ever had, *she* asked *me* to make love to her. . . . I can do without them."[12]

The authors trace the local origin of this ubiquitous myth to a collection of early American writings known as "Indian captivity narratives," a genre developed during the Puritan era, in which settlers who had been abducted by Native tribes recounted their harrowing journeys and rescues. In these stories, the violent means by which captives are saved also redeems the larger community and cleanses the wilderness. The monomyth as we know it today, however, really took shape in the 1920s and 1930s, with an explosion of cowboy Westerns and the development of superheroes. But all of those were just more recent spins on a much older tale. The true origin of the American Monomyth is the story told in the very last book of the Bible: Revelation.

In most of the New Testament, Jesus is a gentle lamb. Sure, he knocks over the odd table in the temple, but usually it's *bring me the children* and *don't stone sex workers*. Then, out of nowhere, in Revelation, Jesus becomes a merciless punisher. The story—which in reality is a work of anti-Roman war propaganda written around 90 CE—is wildly, enthusiastically, euphorically violent. Here's how it goes.

While its author, John, is "in the spirit," that is, an ecstatic state of altered consciousness, he sees himself being taken up into heaven and shown a "revelation" of the future.[13] There, God sits on a throne with a scroll in hand, its contents waiting to be revealed . . . except it can't be because no one is worthy of breaking the scroll's seven seals. Bummer. John weeps. But wait! Suddenly standing there is a slaughtered lamb, aka the crucified Messiah, aka Jesus.[14]

Who, me? A lowly and technically deceased ruminant? If I must. The dead lamb takes the scroll from God—don't ask how—and is deemed worthy. Everyone and thing in heaven rejoices and the party gets started.

The lamb/Jesus starts opening seals, one after another, each accompanied by terrifying events, for example famine, pestilence, war, earthquakes. After the seventh and last seal, angels blow trumpets and the performance escalates. A mixture of hail, fire, and blood rains down, a mountain falls from the sky, a third of the sea turns to blood, and a third of all sea creatures die. Shortly thereafter, a bottomless pit is unlocked and locusts with human faces and women's hair fly out under order to torture anyone lacking God's seal, but not enough to kill them because that would be too kind. We are just getting started.

Four angels, who had been hanging out for eternity waiting for the call to murder, are now released to kill a third of all humankind. More earthquakes occur, including one that takes out seven thousand people at once. And a giant dragon swipes its tail through heaven, sending a third of all stars to earth (pretend you know nothing about the size of stars). Eventually, it's harvest time. An angel with a sharp sickle is instructed to reap the grape harvest of the earth. The grapes, of course, are people, the wicked ones to be precise. He gathers this grisly crop, tosses "the vintage of the earth" into "the great wine press of the wrath of God," and the press produces so much blood that a river as high as a horse's bridle flows for two hundred miles.

The violence goes on after that . . . but why? How do you heighten from horse-high blood flood? Maybe giraffe-high blood flood? Resurrect-the-wicked-and-make-them-synchronize-swim-in-their-blood flood? The specificity of it makes me wonder if there had been some battle, after which Roman soldiers boasted that the blood had risen to their horses' ankles—and then John caught wind of the brag and thought, "Ankles? Hoho, just you wait!"

Eventually, in John's vision, he also sees the Whore of Babylon (aka Rome) judged, Satan bound in a pit, and Jesus ruling for a thousand years, after which *another* battle consumes the earth, the devil is thrown into the Lake of Fire, the dead are resurrected, and Jesus judges everyone to receive either eternal life or damnation. He, who in his lifetime wouldn't throw a stone at a prostitute, now sentences countless humans to violent, unending torture. Finally, after it's all over—after righteous violence has redeemed the world by cleansing it of evil, thereby rescuing the chosen—Paradise can return. New Jerusalem literally descends from heaven. It's an actual city and John gets a VIP tour. It's made of gold but it's clear as glass (so it's clear gold, which is not gold, but OK), and the walls are jasper but covered in various jewels. The gates, as you know, are pearls.[15]

Revelation is not simply the title of this work. It's the title of a genre. Many works in the genre were produced during the first and second centuries, times of great economic and martial strife, which are always marked by increases in end-time thinking and the accompanying visions of how it will go down. But of the revelations produced around then, only John's has stood the test of time. First, its vague and coded language—likely employed to save himself from Roman retribution, via plausible deniability—has allowed groups throughout history to plug their own enemies into its narrative. It's beloved mostly for its violence. One persecuted group after another has found solace in visions of its own oppressors squished inside the winepress. We are vengeful creatures, we humans, we grapes of the earth.

Famed eighteenth-century minister Jonathan Edwards said, "The sight of hell-torments will exalt the happiness of the saints forever."[16]

Still, in the years after John wrote his hallucinatory screed, plenty of early readers were like, *No thanks*. Plus, Revelation is basically only in the Bible by accident. Because the author's name is John, some early Christians mistakenly believed it was written by John of Zebedee, to whom is attributed the Gospel of John and who was one of Jesus's disciples. That guy is a legend! They figured anything he wrote ought to be in the Bible, no matter how freaky. But Revelation, it turns out, was written by a dude named John of Patmos. Oops.

This John had fled the war in Judea, the one that started in 66 CE, when a few occupied Jews fought back, and ended four years later when Rome sent sixty thousand troops to absolutely crush Jerusalem in response. By 66, John was on the island of Patmos, where he'd been exiled for following Jesus. (He was an OG Jew for Jesus.) There, he wrote his durable fantasy of rescue and revenge. John was living through a time when the Jewish people suffered devastating cruelty at the hands of Roman soldiers and governors. But soon, John and the rest of Jesus's followers believed, the Messiah would return—would literally come out of nowhere—to save them and punish their bullies, Rome.

We know his story is about Rome because John left rather intentional clues. For example, the beast has seven heads, one for each of Rome's emperors up to that point. Plus, the whole 666 thing. John writes, "Let anyone with understanding calculate the number of the beast, for it is the number of a person."[17] In Jewish numerology, 666 spells the imperial name of Nero, the cruelest of the emperors. There are many more clues, but I'll share just one: many scholars believe the "mark of the beast" is a reference to "the images and names of Roman emperors and gods stamped on coins."[18] Jews hated Roman money and often refused even to touch it—when your God has made idolatry his top pet peeve, how can you carry and value pictures of his competition?

Because the book of Revelation and the Gospel of John differ wildly in language and style, modern scholars have long agreed the two can't have been written by the same person. But even seventeen hundred years ago, at the time of the Bible's canonization, some people were suspicious. For that matter, there were also scholars then who considered Revelation "unintelligible" and "irrational."[19] But it was canonized anyway, in part because this one power player pushed it through, with a boost from the misinformation regarding its author. He did so because the narrative served his own political goals, which is exactly how people have continued to use this freaky fantasy since.

———

If this story originates in first-century Judea, how did it become American? It happened the same way these kinds of stories always develop: in the wake of a promise broken. These are grievance narratives.

During the Puritan settlement and even dating back to Columbus's explorations, America became synonymous with New Jerusalem. They believed God had promised it would be where Jesus returned to judge the quick and the dead and then reign forever with his chosen people, that is, Puritans in America. Then, this promise of America as privileged and perfect went secular, where it fueled a host of ideologies, including those supporting westward expansion.

By the late nineteenth century, many saw the American West as the new promised land. Enter the Homestead Act of 1862, which offered up to 160 acres of land to anyone over twenty-one in exchange for nothing more than a filing fee and willingness to live on and cultivate the land. Eventually, 500 million acres were dispersed. Much of that land was already occupied by Native peoples, of course, but settler ideology held that land could only reach its highest potential if agriculturally developed. So when the new colonial government removed Indigenous people, it claimed it was for the land's sake, so it could be developed into farms.

However, not all Western land was arable. And people knew this: the Great Plains used to be called the Great American Desert. By coincidence, however, certain recently developed areas had then seen increases in rain—which led climatologists to theorize that "rain follows the plow." The Department of the Interior used this motto in booster campaigns following the Civil War, encouraging people to head west. Railroad companies also encouraged the expansion. One Union Pacific Railroad ad painted Western settlers as a kind of chosen people, "the advance column of civilization . . . a peaceable, even-tempered race, who hate war, love peace . . . honor their wives, raise honest children, live within their income, and grow rich out of Kansas soil."[20] Droves of people moved west just in time for the fantasy to shatter. The economic panic of 1873, the depression of 1882–1885, and the panic of 1893 devastated many homesteaders who were already struggling to grow food with very little water. In short, Western settlers experienced the cultural equivalent of what's known in cult studies as a failure of prophecy: a promise broken.

The term *failure of prophecy* is best known from a 1950s research study of a UFO cult in Illinois known as the Seekers. Its leader, Dorothy Martin, said her extraterrestrial contacts told her most of the world would be destroyed in 1955: "There will be much loss of life, practically all of it. . . . The world is in a mess. But the Supreme Being is going to clean house by sinking all of the land masses as we know them now and raising the land masses from under the sea."[21] Fortunately, she said, their group would be rescued by a flying saucer beforehand, on Christmas Eve 1954. *The world is overrun with evil, but a hero's coming out of nowhere to redeem it with violence.* Sounds familiar.

After the event failed to occur, researchers witnessed group members struggling to hold two beliefs at once: their belief in the prophecy of a cataclysm, and their belief in their eyes and ears, which saw and heard no sign of saucer or flood. The researchers coined this psychological struggle *cognitive dissonance.* To relieve the tension of this dissonance, some members chose reality and left the group. But many instead relieved dissonance by digging in their heels—by rationalizing reality until it supported prophecy. They readily accepted Martin's claim that the group's steadfastness had persuaded God to stem the flood and save the world.

Although this research has received a fair amount of criticism over the years, its basic arguments remain: we humans typically prefer to explain away pesky evidence rather than change our beliefs. The degree to which one has invested in a set of beliefs will largely determine how willing they are to argue away reality in the face of disconfirmation. If, for example, it's the middle of the 1800s and you left everything behind on the East Coast to move your family west to homestead on a plot of land in Kansas, which is now all you own in the world, you're pretty invested. When it all goes to hell, will you accept your mistake, cut your losses, and leave? Or will you fall for a second prophecy that promises rescue?

The vigilante narratives of the time, which developed into the Western genre, offered true believers such an alternative, a subconscious mythic prophecy that guaranteed homesteaders relief. The burgeoning genre, spread via Wild West shows and dime novels, galloped in on a white horse to mythically massage fears and frustrations. *No, no, it is not wrong to believe the prophecy of Western riches. It's the politicians and big-city financiers who let you down.*

It's the ne'er-do-wells who've descended on your struggling communities and overwhelmed your police forces. Your beliefs are not the problem; evil is. Here's a six-gun vigilante to save the day.

Then came the Dust Bowl in the 1930s, a far more devastating and undeniable failure of prophecy that resulted not only from drought but more specifically from that ill-advised land cultivation, which left topsoil vulnerable to drying out and being carried by wind. But by then, the American Monomyth was deeply entrenched in our national psyche.

———

Following the failure of prophecy in the Church Universal and Triumphant, after no bombs fell in March 1990, Elizabeth Clare Prophet told her followers that their mobilization in response to the predicted nuclear crisis had been enough to stall the attack. Nevertheless, she reminded followers that the window for potential worldly disaster had been prophesied to last until 2002—so, wink wink, don't stray from the flock. Even so, she lost a third of her followers.[22] Those who remained prepared even more feverishly for the end.

And, of course, John of Patmos also experienced a failure of prophecy. Jesus had told his followers he would return within their lifetimes. It had been about sixty years. Jesus still hadn't returned. Jews still suffered persecution. Instead of the Kingdom of God descending from heaven, the Romans ruled supreme. The prophecy had failed. Jesus's followers needed a new one. So John delivered it.

On September 17, 2021, former United States national security advisor Michael Flynn spoke at a Christian Right conference in Iowa, where he led the congregation in an unusual prayer. "We are your instrument of those sevenfold rays and all your archangels, all of them," he said, leading a call-and-response. Later, he used the phrase *in the name of your legions*.[23] Suspicious evangelicals perked up their ears. "Sevenfold rays"? "Legions"? Blog posts and podcast chatter followed. Was Flynn conspiring with the devil to dupe good Christians into joining Satan's army?

Flynn replied on Telegram that it was simply a prayer about his namesake

Saint Michael, and everyone should calm down.[24] They did not. Then an anti-fascist activist named Jim Stewartson sourced the prayer: it had been cribbed almost verbatim from Elizabeth Clare Prophet at the Church Universal and Triumphant. Under a side-by-side video comparison of the two prayers, one user responded wryly, "She recited it from memory. He had to read it." (In fact, she spoke extemporaneously . . . unless you believe the archangel Michael delivered it through her.) Flynn's evangelical and QAnon contingents accused him of occultism and Satanic collusion. Whether or not Flynn had knowledge of the prayers's origin, he and Prophet do share an agenda: theocracy.

"I remember being a child, wanting the golden age to happen, when God would be in charge of America—you know when *we* would be in charge of America," Sean Prophet recalls. "We thought we were the chosen people who were destined to rule America. It was never very well thought through. It was just this vague idea that there would be this purging and cleansing and then everything would be made right." His mother preached that evil forces were cooperating to destroy democratic government. In fact, it was *she* who aspired to that.

Both Flynn and Prophet have proselytized their autocratic dreams. A few months after the January 6 insurrection in 2021, Flynn launched the ReAwaken America Tour, taking his Christian Nationalist movement on the road. The events hosted speakers and attendees who believed the Big Lie, that Trump had won the election but been kept from office by a conspiracy. They not only wanted Trump back in office, they wanted a Christian nation. A 2022 poll conducted by the University of Maryland found that 61 percent of Republicans agreed: they supported declaring the United States a Christian nation.[25] Jewett and Lawrence could have predicted both of these movements—because, they argue, the American Monomyth has a tranquilizing effect on those who consume it, which leads to a lethargic approach to democracy. Drawing on psychological understandings of how myth affects the unconscious, they argue that the story of the selfless violent redeemer exerts tangible behavioral effects on its audiences, teaching them to "applaud passively from the grandstand, convinced they are too impotent to cope with evil." In effect, the myth exchanges "a sense of communal alarm and obligation for a fantasy of Edenic resolution achievable only by superhumans."[26]

No wonder Americans are tempted by the monomyth! Not only have we been unconsciously indoctrinated by it for centuries, the narrative also conveniently relieves us of individual responsibility for community success. But unlike most myths, which support the foundational philosophies of their host communities, the American Monomyth undermines our nation's founding ideology, democracy. It subconsciously encourages the public to forgo the messy, laborious, and painstaking process of cooperation and compromise by instead waiting for a superhero—and then granting that figure unlimited and unchecked power. It creates a passive public desiring a totalitarian leader. When parents complain that comics rot their kids' brains, they're actually kind of right.

———

We see this pattern in American history again and again. In the 1980s National Security Council member Oliver North schemed to sell weapons illegally to Iran in order to fund the Contras in a guerrilla war against Nicaragua's socialist Sandinistas. Although Congress had voted against it, North and his NSA and CIA collaborators decided they knew better. During his testimony to Congress, which he agreed to in exchange for immunity, North basically explained he had been willing to get the job done and by any means necessary. He seemed disdainful of inefficient and menacing government oversight, scornful of checks and balances against the executive branch, and proud of his crusading role. He even cribbed a line from a Clint Eastwood Western while under oath when he said, "I came here to tell you the truth—the good, the bad, and the ugly."[27] Viewers ate it up. *USA Today* hosted a hotline on the topic. While 1,756 callers wanted North in jail, 58,863 said he should receive another medal.[28] A *Newsweek* columnist deemed the hearings "Jimmy Stewart cast in 'Rambo Goes to Washington.'"[29]

Fifteen years later, a 2002 cover story appeared in the wake of America's response to 9/11. Germany's *Der Spiegel* depicted five American national-security players as recognizable Hollywood-blockbuster crusaders: Secretary of State Colin Powell is Batman, Secretary of Defense Donald Rumsfeld is Conan the Barbarian (with a bloody sword), Vice President Dick Cheney is the Terminator, National Security Advisor Condoleezza Rice is Xena Princess

Warrior, and President George W. Bush is Rambo, replete with muscles and an automatic weapon. The (translated) title reads "The Bush Warriors: America's Battle against Evil." The article is castigating. Nevertheless, the U.S. ambassador to Germany was dispatched to order thirty-three poster-sized copies of the cover from the publication, reporting that "the president was flattered" and everyone on the cover wanted a copy.[30]

When teenage vigilante Kyle Rittenhouse was acquitted in 2021 on all charges after shooting three people and killing two of them at a police-brutality protest in Kenosha, Wisconsin—with an AR-15 the prosecution argued he wasn't legally allowed to possess—the far right lionized him as a hero who had taken the law into his own hands to protect and defend innocent Kenoshans from marauding rioters. At least four Republican lawmakers said they'd like to give him an internship.[31] Tucker Carlson wondered on air why people were surprised that "seventeen-year-olds with rifles decided they had to maintain order when no one else would."[32]

Speaking of the guy who ruined bow ties for me, on one of his streaming programs in 2021, Carlson interviewed a New Right blogger named Curtis Yarvin, who believes we should bring back a kind of monarch, one who would "reset" American government by dismantling it and taking all the power for themselves. Yarvin has even spelled out exactly how someone could do it, including a tactic that goes by the acronym of RAGE—retire all government employees—which was name-checked by 2022 Arizona Senate hopeful Blake Masters. Yarvin's ideas have also been supported by tech billionaire Peter Thiel and Ohio senator turned vice president JD Vance, who referenced Yarvin in 2021, when he suggested that if Donald Trump wins another term, he should "seize the institutions of the left," remove "every single mid-level bureaucrat," and "replace them with our people," whether or not the Supreme Court tries to stop it.[33]

Our latent indoctrination into Puritan doomsday ideology is a pilot light that flares into extremism. Polling in 2023 of GOP caucus goers determined that Trump's most autocratic statements make some voters *more* likely to support him, including 19 percent in response to his claim that he'd have "no choice" but to jail his opponents if reelected. (And 43 percent said that statement didn't matter to them one way or the other.) Also, 55 percent increased their support in response to his interest in rooting out the "radical left thugs that live like vermin."[34]

In March 2021, on the heels of the January 6 insurrection, pollsters found that 15 percent of Americans agreed that "things have gotten so far off track, true American patriots may have to resort to violence in order to save our country." By the fall of 2023, that number was up to 23 percent—the first time polling had found one in five Americans condoning political violence.[35] We're conditioned to believe violent punishment will solve our problems—is the only way to solve our problems. Another 2023 poll found that 33 percent of Republicans and Republican-leaning independents felt Trump's efforts to overturn the 2020 election "are not relevant to his fitness for the presidency."[36] A 2021 study determined that 26 percent of the U.S. population are "highly right-wing authoritarian."[37] At the 2016 Republican National Convention, Trump spoke of a nation under various threats and said, "I alone can fix it."[38]

People want a strongman to punish those they believe have taken what was rightfully theirs: power. The book of Revelation and the American Monomyth are grievance narratives. In the former, the Romans are ruining everything. In the latter, it's usually corrupt bureaucrats or women. Michael Flynn's ReAwaken America Tour also demonizes immigrants, homosexuals, and medical care professionals supporting vaccines. They must be demonized in order for us to stomach the violence against them. In the first acts of monomythic Hollywood films and TV, audiences see images of others sinning—whether the bogeymen are criminals in vigilante films, Native Americans portrayed as savages in Westerns, or promiscuous urbanite women in disaster films—so that viewers are "mythically prepared for the punishment that inevitably follows." This allows us to enjoy the violence and identify with the saved. In this way, the monomyth "offers a moral confirmation of the audience's righteousness, since only the virtuous survive."[39]

There's an attraction to being chosen. It comes with honor and pride, sure, righteousness. But, perhaps more tantalizingly, it comes with the promise of reward. We are chosen to receive something. When one feels special, or is told they are special, or soaks up four hundred years of cultural identity as special, one expects to *receive*.

Sometimes those promises are blatant, such as the Homestead Act's. Sometimes they are assumed, as with Michael Flynn's. And sometimes they are created by a self-assuming divinity—a kind of cosmic confirmation bias, as Elizabeth Clare Prophet had. But always, the promise is assumed to have come from elsewhere, to have been bestowed on us by some greater power, whether country or God. When the prophecy fails, when there is no reward, we perceive a grave injustice. We believe someone robbed us. They must be punished. So we empower a strongman, who shows up, promising to cleanse us of the threat and thereby deliver that original reward, whether it's wealth, safety, power, or superiority.

Associated Press journalists who attended one of Flynn's ReAwaken America events described it as having a "message of a country under siege."[40] Erin Prophet writes in her memoir, "Mother took Jesus's words to the Pharisees, 'ye are from beneath, I am from above,' and applied them to people she knew . . . unbelievers who deserved to die in the holocaust she was prophesying."[41]

Sean Prophet told me, "My dad would've fit right in with the QAnon people, the MAGA people. This is the same recycled stuff from my childhood."

Apocalyptic ideology makes us fearful, ready to believe that the only thing that can stop a bad guy with a gun is a good guy with a bigger gun. But vigilantism increases violence, never diminishes it. "My mom thought she could judge the whole world and had the authority to call down a nuclear war that would kill billions of people," Sean says. "What's the check and balance when someone thinks they have divine backing? At what point does it stop before you kill everyone in the world or try to?"

CHAPTER 2

FATHER KNOWS BEST
ON PERFECTION AND BEING CHOSEN

John Humphrey Noyes really wanted to bone his sisters. He claimed it would bring them closer to God. Noyes's brother once quoted him as arguing that "the fellowship of brothers and sisters is fundamental and eternal" because it concentrates the perfection of God's people. By *fellowship*, he didn't mean spaghetti dinners in the church basement. He argued God had started it, anyway, by inbreeding the ancient Jews into a perfect race. Case in point, Abraham married his half sister and that guy fathered a nation (and three religions). Noyes devised his own incest plan based on the assumption that he and his family were the chosen people of their generation. He went on to say that sibling sex "approaches nearest to the fashion of God himself whose life ever turns in upon himself."[1] Honestly, it sounds like he wanted to have sex with himself. And now, sadly, I'm thinking of all of the ways he must've tried.

As for his five sisters' roles in this pursuit of perfection, Harriet, at least, would surely have been down. She worshiped him—not only as a brother and figurehead of their group, the Oneida Bible Communists, but as the guy ordained by the Holy Spirit to deliver them to the promised land. Still, we can't know if they crossed that sibling taboo—nor can we know whether or not Noyes made good on his desire to impregnate his daughter, Constance—because records from the Oneida Community, which numbered three hundred at its height, bear no mention of such copulations.[2]

On one hand, the records that remain are voluminous, and remaining diaries and letters declare all manner of other nontraditional behavior occurring between the 1841 founding of the group and its dissolution, in 1880. So it seems we'd know if sibling incest happened. On the other hand, in 1947, officers of the Oneida Limited Company—by then a $3.5 million silverware corporation and respected national brand trying to bury its cult origins—secretly filled a truck with the community's collected archives and burned them at the dump.[3] Considering how much of their freaky activity has *not* been lost to history, it's tempting to assume the nature of what was destroyed.

Anyway, Noyes did have sex with his nieces, and often. In fact, uncle-niece pairings were common in the community (and were even legal at the time). He also personally "initiated" all young Oneida women into their sexuality. Noyes believed he was literally perfect, which to him meant free of sin. Most Christians would argue there has only been one human free of sin, Jesus of Nazareth, which maybe suggests Noyes's opinion of himself. To be fair, though, he argued anyone could be perfect, could live sin-free simply by accepting Christ's grace. He didn't invent the idea. A strain of theology bubbled at the time, aptly titled perfectionism. The Great Awakening and the Second Great Awakening had inspired believers away from the helplessness and pessimism of predestination (the idea that God had already chosen whom he would and wouldn't save) and toward the promise and optimism of grace by human agency (the idea that people could save themselves by accepting God).

When this can-do self-determined spark hit the fuel of the Protestant work ethic, it lit a fire that burned so brightly it has been energizing America since. Inherent in the belief of being chosen is the promise of perfection. As Americans, we have often felt it our purpose and duty to achieve perfection within ourselves, our nation, and the world. We feel we are required to impose this vision.

In the early days of the perfection movement, Noyes added his own hot take: if it's true that we now have the capacity for such purity, then the second coming of Christ must have *already* occurred. Now, he claimed, heaven was simply waiting for us. How to get there? Become perfect. And hurry up: God is waiting. Even though Noyes didn't proclaim the *end* to be nigh, he did preach the time was nigh. Cultlike thinking demands and lives off expediency. If the work can be done whenever, what's to stop followers from procrastinating? A cult agenda is like a fire sale at a mattress store: you must act now.

Noyes believed one of the fastest routes to perfection was sex, and the act should be shared widely. "All experience testifies . . . that sexual love is not naturally restricted to pairs," he wrote, while arguing that all carnal deviancy stems from the unnatural and illegitimate law of monogamy.[4] If people could simply sleep with whomever they like, he argued, then masturbation, prostitution, and adultery would cease to exist. By solving one problem, he could solve countless more. I have heard this argument my whole life from alpha males at parties using psycho-philosophical babble to get into my pants.

Believing the Almighty had already granted eternal life, which was ours for the taking, Noyes and his followers aimed to create New Jerusalem in their little community in Putney, Vermont. In fact, Noyes decided God *wanted* them to bring heaven to earth. So, in May 1846, Noyes and his wife and another couple began to swing. The community practice of complex marriage was born. Six months later, two of his sisters and their husbands and another couple joined. Although nothing is less sexy than a manifesto contract, they all signed one saying property was no longer the only thing communal.

This, Noyes believed, had ended time as they knew it. In 1847 he told the rest of his followers that they'd become immortal, of which he was certain, since no one in their community had died. Granted, they'd only existed for a few years . . . but in that time other people in town had died . . . also some in their community had gotten sick, but then recovered . . . so *you* do the math. The next step after immortality, he reasoned, was the imminent delivery of New Jerusalem, which he was bringing down himself. God provided the layup, but he made the dunk.

Perhaps high on being immortal, he confided in a local noncommunity friend that he and a few other couples were sharing spouses.[5] Shortly thereafter, the Vermont State's Attorney's Office sent a sheriff to arrest him on October 26, 1847. Within a year, the group had been run out of town. But they quickly resettled in Oneida Creek, New York, where they soon numbered eighty-four and built a big mansion to live, work, and fornicate in.

Noyes likened Jesus's healing energy to a kind of electricity. At the time, scientists and thinkers were still exploring the newly harnessed life force. Noyes figured Jesus had electricity and passed it to humans when they opened themselves to it. Humans could also pass this energy to one another, he reasoned, and at no time more potently than during sex.[6] Charging oneself with Jesus juice, the theory went, could also stave off death. The community members were eager to begin their sexperiment. All they needed now was a protocol.

If you fancied someone and wanted to connect your battery to theirs, you filed an official request through the community matchmaker. This served two purposes: first, allowing the recipient to accept or deny via a third party, and second, allowing Noyes and other leaders to control community members by keeping tabs on who jump-started whom. For example, when two people requested one another too often, they were censured for "sticky love," for a selfish and unholy attachment to only one person. Aside from occasional heartbreaks resulting from tearing two lovers apart, complex marriage was largely successful, although two major problems did arise.

First, the young guys were a lot to handle. Noyes compared their relentless juvenile appetite to an "untamed lion" and declared a need to protect the young women from "spiritual collapse."[7] Therefore, the original plan to pair off youngsters with one another was sidelined for the practice of ascending fellowship, which Noyes launched in 1851. For the young members' introduction into the "social life"—and by *social*, he didn't mean ice cream parties in the rainy-day playroom—boys were paired with older women and girls with older men until each had been appropriately educated. "We are all brothers and sisters, and the wiser ones lead the less wise through ascending fellowship into love," wrote community member Jessie Catherine Kinsley.[8]

This all fit neatly into the group's notions of strict hierarchy. Those at the top brought up those at the bottom. Since John Humphrey Noyes was at the very tip-top, he figured he should personally initiate all of the girls. Or, perhaps, he simply created a justification for his desire to take every virgin in his cult. And I do mean *girls*, since they passed this milestone at puberty, and the average age of puberty onset in the community seems to have been thirteen.[9]

The older women got a much better bargain. Plus, their pairings with young men, who had trouble controlling the seeds of their amorous fruit, were additionally advantageous for the community, since the women were beyond childbearing years. This brings us to the second problem arising from complex marriage: babies. The Oneida Community was flush with desire, not cash. Their first go at sustenance had been orchards, but they didn't have the climate for it. After several other endeavors, they entered the silverware business—which survived the group's dissolution, made its way into bridal trousseaus across the country, and grew into one of the most successful businesses in America.

But before all that, they were mostly broke. And children are expensive. Noyes announced to the men that if they really loved God, they wouldn't ejaculate. He stole the idea from a rival commune, called it male continence, and compared it to visiting a waterfall. "If he is willing to learn, experience will teach him the wisdom of confining his excursions to the region of easy rowing, unless he has an object in view [propagation] that is worth the cost of going over the falls."[10] The community said OK and merrily merrily merrily merrily didn't go all the way.

If male continence was awkward for men, it was often a relief for women. Not only were they encouraged to have and enjoy sex, while being granted the privilege of consent (though, presumably no one rebuffed Noyes), they also enjoyed the freedoms accompanying birth control. They worked alongside men, read books, and pursued hobbies. And those who did have kids benefited from communal childcare. Oneida women were also free of their era's restrictive clothing. Several even held intellectual positions. Decades later Noyes became a bit of a hero among New York City's underground birth control activists.

Still, the feminism argument is complicated. Scholar (and Oneida descendent!) Ellen Wayland-Smith makes clear, in her book *Oneida: From Free Love Utopia to the Well-Set Table*, that Noyes deemed women inferior. (He cared for their well-being in more of a paternal way—and took credit for any benefits resulting.) Further, communal child-rearing had its deficits. Children lived with their mothers only until one and a half, when they were weaned and moved into the children's house. Some parents and children wanted more time together, but were criticized for being too selfishly attached (not coincidentally similar to Puritan practices). Oneida diaries are full of heartbreaking accounts of mothers and children kept apart as punishment.

There were a few holes in the male continence net. During the twenty-one years of its practice among about two hundred adults, the community experienced thirty-one unplanned pregnancies.[11] Jessie Catherine Kinsley, whom I quoted earlier, was one. In 1857, her mother realized she was pregnant. Although she couldn't be certain which male had followed the falls over continent's edge, she had suspicions. Then, when Jessie Catherine was seven, community member Eleazer Hatch suddenly announced his paternity. Her mom was unsure, but went along with it so Jessie could have a dad.

Forgive my cynicism, but when it comes to male continence, I assume Noyes intended the practice for everyone else, but secretly ejaculated where and when he pleased. The powerful characteristically assume that rules don't apply to them. And since this protocol was born of necessity, it's hard to take its stated religious underpinnings in earnest. So imagine my lack of surprise when I read that Kinsley eventually came to believe her father was Noyes. She writes of an incident occurring sometime around her twenty-first birthday, when she sprained her ankle. While she received medical care, Noyes popped by to "offer sympathy." Upon seeing her bare foot, he remarked, "Why, you have my riding toe." I don't know what a riding toe is and neither does Google, but presumably it's hereditary because, she writes, "then followed inquiry, and an enthusiastic acceptance of the *thought* that I *might* be his daughter." *Well, it's hard to say—I ejaculate in so many people—but sure, it's possible.*

Later, on his deathbed, he called for her to see him. She writes that she "stepped around the bed and clasped his head in my arms and kissed his cheek, and said, 'Dear, dear, Father!' He gave me such a happy, grateful look."[12]

Sounds like John Humphrey Noyes engaged in incest after all. Am I suggesting he intentionally made surreptitious babies with whom he could fornicate thirteen years later, in order to impregnate them as well, to grow closest to achieving his ultimate dream of procreating with himself? Yes, I am. He did father eleven children *on the record*, not even including those who didn't survive. And he did literally express a desire to make a baby with his daughter, Constance.

More than anything, he was a man who loved himself. Perhaps he wanted to turn in upon himself the way God does because he believed he *was* God. He believed he could bring immortality to his group by making many many more of himself. In some ways, that's the same reason anyone has children. But he was unique in wanting to concentrate his own blood, to get closer and closer to re-creating *himself*—creating man in his image.

This is precisely what he did in 1869, when he recruited certain members of the group to create with him a master race.

To a certain degree, a lot of American Protestants were playing God in the nineteenth century, especially in the North, in that they were rabid social reformers: think the abolition, temperance, and anti-poverty movements. Collectively, these efforts became known as the Social Gospel. It's almost the opposite of Puritan doomsday belief and yet directly descends from it. This theological one-eighty resulted from three circumstances. (I'm a theology nerd, but you may not be, so I'll try to get through this in a few paragraphs.)

First was the gradual, Great Awakening–fueled shift I already mentioned from powerless predestination toward the agency of saving oneself via grace. Second, although early Puritans thought they had to wait for Judgment Day, following generations viewed the rewards they had since received—a new nation and unimaginable prosperity and comfort—as evidence that God wanted humans to *help* him bring about the end of the world.

The third part of this theological turnaround resulted from a contemporary shift in prophecy interpretation. Puritans had understood the events in the book of Revelation as literal and occurring in a certain sequence: first Jesus returns and puts an end to human history, then some amount of people live through a thousand years—a millennium—of peace and prosperity. Next comes the great judgment. Finally, New Jerusalem descends from the sky, literally, as a city. This belief system is known as premillennialism (Jesus comes *before* the thousand years), a doctrine alive and well among fundamentalist and evangelical Christians today.

But many others believed all this prophecy was surely allegorical. Lady-haired locusts wouldn't ravish fields, and glittering streetlamps wouldn't fall from clouds. Rather, it was just good metaphorical storytelling. Ergo, if the great cosmic battles are only a metaphor, then Jesus won't literally fight them.

Instead, his second coming would probably happen *after* the millennium (which may or may not be exactly one thousand years). And the New Jerusalem he brings won't have walls made of clear gold, but will simply be heaven on earth, free of sin and evil. This belief system is postmillennialism (Jesus comes *after* the millennium) and became dominant in liberal Protestant churches, think Episcopalian and Presbyterian.

From there, postmillennialists were like, *Hold on . . . You guys, this is kind of a stoner thought, but stay with me. God has given us a new nation, and exceptional wealth and power—sounds like we already* are *approaching the millennium. And if that's true, wait for it . . . What if we can bring it on* ourselves? *Whoah, dude, whoah! If we keep spreading Christianity, eradicating sin, and improving life for all of God's people, we can deliver* ourselves *to New Jerusalem!!* Horace, pass the joint.

Congregationalist pastor Joseph Bellamy wrote in 1758 that "true Christians" were expected to "be workers together with God."[13] In the early nineteenth century, Beverly, Massachusetts, Congregational minister Joseph Emerson wrote, "The wonderful and amazing events that will introduce the Millennium will be principally effected by human instrumentality."[14] And Charles Grandison Finney, leader of the Second Great Awakening, explained in 1835 that if churches worked hard enough, they could bring about the millennium in as few as *three years*.

Naturally, this all dovetailed with another strain of thought that developed shortly after the Puritans arrived in New England, which held that God intended *America* to be the site of the second coming. Clearly, the reasoning went, the chosen people living in the chosen nation bore heavy responsibility in the pursuit of the City of Gold, metaphorical or not. During the (first) Great Awakening of the 1730s and 1740s, Jonathan Edwards saw the incredible interest in revivals as a sign of the millennium's approach—toward America. Lyman Beecher, Presbyterian minister (and father of *Uncle Tom's Cabin* author, Harriet Beecher Stowe), preached in Plymouth, Massachusetts, in 1827 that it was "the purpose of God to employ this nation in the glorious work of renovating the earth."[15] And in 1980, during his GOP presidential nomination acceptance speech, Ronald Reagan said, "Can we doubt that only a Divine Providence placed this land, this island of freedom, here as a refuge for all those people in the world who yearn to breathe freely?"[16]

Premillennialists don't care about progress because the world is about to end anyway. But postmillennialists think progress is nothing short of a path to heaven. From the late eighteenth century to the early twentieth century, postmillennialism and progress were conjoined twins, together becoming the nation's dominant religious ideology *and* civic ideology. UC Berkeley scholar Ernest Lee Tuveson argues in his seminal 1968 book, *Redeemer Nation: The Idea of America's Millennial Role*, that most of the attributes of nineteenth-century notions of progress had already been present in millennialist thought two hundred years prior.[17] The abolition movement, the temperance movement, the anti-poverty movement, efforts to improve technology for the masses, and public education—whether funded and instituted by churches or governments—all have roots in postmillennialism, in efforts not only to help those in need and right egregious wrongs, but literally to accelerate the return of Christ.

Reformers believed that freeing people from slavery and alcohol would prepare the afflicted for conversion by giving them agency—one couldn't accept God's grace without the choice and mental capacity to do so—and the more souls converted, the closer to the kingdom everyone grew. The American Temperance Society, the American Tract Society, and the American Anti-Slavery Society were all launched by churches, which additionally came to embrace scientific advancements. Social reform leader and protestant clergyman Josiah Strong wrote, "Science, which is a revelation of God's laws and methods, enables us to fall into his plans intentionally and to co-operate with him intelligently for the perfecting of mankind, thus hastening forward the coming of the kingdom."[18] Social reform movements aligned nicely with other means of progress, during a time when the country experienced rapid advances in knowledge, reason, science, technology, manufacturing, wealth, and convenience.

For example, apocalypticists understood the scripture "Many shall run to and fro and knowledge shall be increased" as a signal that our heavenly reward would be marked by advances in transportation and the spread of information.[19] Other common prophecy interpretations included the ideas that, in the millennium, people would live longer, the population would increase, and

barren land would be made fruitful.[20] All of that was already happening in the
civic realm. Railroads put down fifty thousand miles of track between 1830 and
1860 alone. Between 1840 and 1860, the population leapt from 17 million to
31 million and the production of cotton cloth jumped from 300 million yards
a year to 1 billion yards a year.[21] Myriad advances suggested that the human
race, whether guided by Providence or not, could progress to unknown heights,
which would only be realized if we continued our efforts. What else was waiting
to be discovered and developed? They had to go go go to get to God.

However, some who were lit by this can-do attitude preferred to pursue the
greater good only by example. The middle of the nineteenth century also saw
a rash of commune experiments. If the communes of the 1960s and '70s were
connected by the antiwar and civil rights movements, the groups in the mid-
1800s were linked by the aim to perfect, to create heaven on earth.[22] By seques-
tering themselves from the rest of society and its deeply entrenched systemic
sins, they could experiment. They could upend traditional American notions
of commerce, labor, family units, and property ownership, often in socialist or
communist ways. While national reform movements struggled to help those at
the bottom of an increasing wealth gap, communes did away with the gap by
sharing everything. Many, including the Oneida Community, believed they were
not only advancing members toward New Jerusalem but had actually built New
Jerusalem itself. I can't imagine the chutzpah required to start a town and then
claim it's heaven. Noyes even had his followers vote, at one point, to officially
affirm "the Kingdom of Heaven has come."[23]

There were also the Shakers, whose leader, Mother Ann Lee, came from
England in the 1780s. They practiced equality of the sexes—unsurprising, perhaps, considering she believed she was the second coming of Christ—and peaked
in the middle of the nineteenth century with eighteen major communities all
over the East and Midwest. The utopian experiment with the most cachet was
probably Brook Farm, though it lasted only six years in the 1840s in Massachusetts. Ralph Waldo Emerson famously visited for a spell. And Nathaniel
Hawthorne and eventual *New York Sun* editor Charles Dana were original
shareholders. Dana once wrote, "Our ulterior aim is nothing less than Heaven on
Earth, the conversion of this globe."[24] All experiments with communitarianism

struggled to survive. Although they had an outsized influence on arts and letters, they were ultimately visited by few Americans.

Unlike the communitarians, the Social Gospel reformers toughed it out in open society, where they aimed to reach many more people (sounds a lot like the separatists versus the Puritans of sixteenth-century England, eh?). But they were no less ambitious. This nation's duty, reformers believed, was nothing short of redeeming the world, and progress was the means. But they faced a major hurdle. How could God's nation erase global sin when it hadn't absolved itself of the glaring sin of slavery? How could God bring heaven to earth when the Antichrist was still in the American South? This was part of the motivation behind the call for abolition. Many in the Social Gospel movement assumed slavery was the last hindrance to Jesus's return—and that the Civil War would be the battle of Armageddon itself.

In 1862, Julia Ward Howe, who ran in Boston's reformer circles, published the "Battle Hymn of the Republic." Its lyrics marry the Civil War with the book of Revelation and recall that infamous horse-high blood flood: "Mine eyes have seen the glory of the coming of the Lord: / He is trampling out the vintage where the grapes of wrath are stored." It goes on, "As he died to make men holy, let us die to make men free." Some Bible mathematicians even determined the Antichrist's prophesied reign would end in 1866.

But after the war, life, crime, and sin marched on. The Civil War was a failure of prophecy. So, as always happens in that scenario, the prophecy shifted and morphed. Enter World War I—*the war to end all wars*, an unmistakable reference to Armageddon, full stop, no matter how numb we have become to the phrase. (Note that in 2023, Donald Trump referenced the upcoming election by saying, "2024 is our final battle.")[25] In a 1919 speech supporting America's entry into the League of Nations, President Woodrow Wilson spoke of the "moral obligation that rests upon us not to go back on those boys, but to . . . make good their redemption of the world."[26] Small thing, though: World War I didn't save the world either. Neither did World War II, or any conflict the nation has involved itself in while paternalistically claiming to rid or save the world from evil. The prophecy always fails. Yet the prophecy endures, shifting and morphing as it sheds its skin and slithers on.

This is merely paternalism, of course: a few people determining what's best for everyone else and acting on it. Often, though, "what's best" is only what's best for the powerful people who make the decisions. Pairing such paternalism with the powerful's unconscious (and sometimes conscious) biases would ultimately lead to messianic expansion and the extermination of people based on race or presumed hereditary traits. Father doesn't always know best.

O f North America's physical features, wrote some Anglo-Saxon, "It is a wonderful provision for the intelligence, sagacity, energy, restlessness, and indomitable will of such a race as the Anglo-Saxon—a race that masters physical nature without being mastered by it—a race in which the intensest home-feelings combine with a love of enterprise, advent, and colonization—a race that fears nothing, claims every thing within reach, enjoys the future more than the present, and believes in a destiny of incomparable and immeasurable grandeur."[27] I found that quote in Tuveson's *Redeemer Nation*, but can't discern who wrote it or when. It's as if a ghost returned to wipe the attribution the way people scrub social media posts.

Of all there is to unpack here—for example, "claims every thing within reach" is intended as a compliment—I want to focus especially on the idea that America was naturally designed for people of Germanic origin. This belief was common at the time. Here's its supposed logic. The blessing of the Reformation was launched in Germany. Martin Luther himself believed Germans were the true Israelites descended from Adam. Then the heart of that movement moved westward through France and the Netherlands, and eventually into England (whose Anglo-Saxon people trace ancestry to conquerors from what is now northern Germany). There, residents nurtured it and then carried it farther westward to America, where its protection continued in the development of the Commonwealth of Massachusetts.

Exodus states, "Wheresoever the children of Israel dwelt, there was light." Therefore, God's chosen believed that "succession to the spiritual, cultural, and political leadership of the world followed the solar cycle of the sun from east to west."[28] They felt it natural that they continue moving westward, beyond the Mississippi, through the Great Plains, on to the Pacific and . . . to infinity and beyond! Case in point, the Philippines. Following the Spanish-American War, America annexed the country rather than grant it independence. In 1900, Senator Henry Cabot Lodge urged the Senate to keep the Philippines, by noting that westward progression had come almost full circle from "whence our far distance ancestors started on the march which has since girdled the world."[29]

Now, add to this another convenient justification masquerading as genetic proof: the Anglo-Saxon myth. As the idea goes, Germanic people are naturally conquerors, and therefore, God chose them specifically to spread his word. In an epic history of the German people, written by a diplomat to the Grant administration, the author argues, "The truculent German, Germann, Herr-mann, War-man, considered carnage the only useful occupation, and despised agriculture as enervating and ignoble. . . . Thus they were more fitted for the roaming and conquering life which Providence was to assign to them for ages."[30] No principal in any grade school has ever witnessed a more infuriating excuse.

Purveyors of this theory—Anglo-Saxons, themselves, naturally—did not praise the conqueror's proclivity to massacre and were careful not to claim God approved of it either. They simply argued that such an imperial spirit had powerful silver linings, that the same traits that drove Germanic people to conquer—specifically courage and an obsession with freedom—also made them the perfect defenders of true Christianity. If other character traits were morally questionable, they were nevertheless convenient for God's plan and therefore, justified. By the turn of the twentieth century, it was already "an old platitude" that the Reformation had not only been a revolution against Roman theology but "an insurrection of all the branches of the great German race against an alien domination."[31]

These beliefs not only suggested Anglo-Saxon conquerors could do whatever they wanted, but allowed them some hey-it's-not-my-fault humility along the way. This smacks of the bumbling-jerk dad in sitcoms—Herr-man

Simpson?—whom we're nevertheless directed to adore. Whatever the motive, the connection between conqueror and redeemer is clear. *We are but a vessel. God wants us to cover and thereby save the continent, on our way to also redeeming the world.* What could go wrong?

———

In an 1830 congressional address, Andrew Jackson shared his moral mission to expand westward. He argued the nation had already brought cultivation and democratic civilization to land previously covered with boring, gross forest, and look at it now!—an "extensive republic, studded with cities, towns, and prosperous farms, embellished with all the improvements which art can devise, or industry execute."[32] Those who believed this nation was intrinsically better than any other would certainly want to build more of it.

George Bancroft, author and political appointee under multiple presidents, wrote even more candidly in 1834 of the benefits of American colonization when he called the land of precolonized New England "an unproductive waste," the soil "lavishing its strength in magnificent but useless vegetation."[33] Now, however, Bancroft argued, the country was happy and glorious—and all because of "Providence." Worth was tied to use. This imperialism, masked as God's plan, promised that more glory, resulting from industry, waited for America in the West. This campaign would eventually take its name from an 1845 article in the *United States Magazine and Democratic Review*, arguing for "the fulfillment of our manifest destiny to overspread the continent allotted by Providence."[34]

This plan faced a major hurdle, of course: the rest of the continent was already populated. So Andrew Jackson subdued and moved them to reservations. This consequence of American millennialism would ultimately result in the development of another uniquely American messianism. In 1889 a member of the Paiute nation named Wovoka fell into a coma and saw a vision. As a child and young adult, he had worked for a Presbyterian farmer in Nevada, who taught him Bible stories. Wovoka also brushed up against the Mormons and the Indian Shaker church. These influences combined with his ancestral theology to develop a new belief system that swept through reservations in the

West from California up to Canada, through Idaho, Utah, and Arizona, over to Oklahoma, and most enthusiastically in the Dakotas.[35]

In Wovoka's vision, he died, met with God, and received a revelation: in two years, God would return the land to its prior state before white men arrived. Native people's ancestors would resurrect, game buffalo would return to the plains, and white people would be buried thirty feet underground. He also learned how to bring this all about, by practicing a ritual called the Ghost Dance. During his vision, God asked Wovoka to share the message and dance with others. Word traveled fast.

Reservation life had been crippling. There was little game to hunt. Much of the land was too arid to farm. Droughts, in particular among Lakota camps in South Dakota in 1889, resulted in creeping starvation. Years later, Oglala Lakota leader Red Cloud explained Native attraction to Wovoka's teachings: "Someone had again been talking of the Son of God, and said He had come. The people did not know; they did not care. They snatched at the hope. They screamed like crazy men to Him for mercy. They caught at the promises they heard He had made."[36]

Apocalyptic thinking typically blooms among the persecuted, like a fungus decomposing their dejection, pain, and fear. Wovoka was ultimately seen as a messiah himself, a Native Jesus. He inflicted stigmata wounds on his hands and feet. People traveled from distant tribes to learn from him.

A *New York Times* reporter wrote in November 1890 of a scene in Pine Ridge of 182 Sioux dancing in a circle around a tree, while another four hundred watched and chanted. "The dancers held one another's hands and moved slowly around the tree. . . . The chant was incessant and monotonous. 'I see my father, I see my mother, I see my brother, I see my sister,' was [my guide's] translation of the chant, as the [dancers] moved laboriously about the tree. . . . [My guide] says the dance which the spectators were then witnessing had been going on all night."[37]

According to a separate eyewitness account from Pine Ridge, which also appeared in the *New York Times*, the ritual could last for three days, during which none of the dancers ate or drank. This witness relayed that the purpose of the fasting and the incessant movement was to lose consciousness so they could meet with God and then, upon waking, share what they had learned. "All their tales end with the same story about the two mountains that are to belch forth mud and bury the white man, and the return of good old Indian times. . . . When they cannot lose their senses from exhaustion, they butt their heads together, beat them upon the ground, and do anything to become insensible, so that they may be ushered into the presence of the new Christ."[38]

All of this concerned white settlers, particularly those near the Lakota in South Dakota, where the movement had grown especially intense and somewhat less restrained. Although the Lakota's approach was not militant—they believed God wanted them to wait in piety until he removed the white man himself—it was particularly fervent. And they did believe their ceremonial white shirts could later be worn as armor in battle, since the Ghost Dance made clothing impervious to bullets. Settlers understood this to be a hostile attitude, and the phrase *hostile Indian* had been European Americans' most motivating fear since the sixteenth century.

Reservation agent Major James McLaughlin called the movement "the 'Messiah' craze" and determined to arrest Sitting Bull, a Lakota leader, for allowing the religion to spread.[39] The botched effort on December 15, 1890, which left Sitting Bull and eight Hunkpapa dead, would set in motion a chain of events leading to the massacre at Wounded Knee Creek on December 29. I won't recount the whole affair; I'm telling a story of the Plains Native people, not the 7th Cavalry. But I will at least argue that what happened that day was darker than actions taken by any cult leader against his followers, and resulted in the deaths of between 250 and 300 people, more than half of whom were women and children, including unwounded infants left to freeze in the arms of their dead mothers.

For decades afterward, historians argued that the day's aggression had been fueled by the 7th Cavalry's desire to avenge Custer's death fourteen years prior and, more generally, fears of Native insurrection. But recent scholars have noticed in the events patterns of certain Christian orthodoxy that seeks to eradicate heresy wherever it exists. This argument suggests settlers aimed to extinguish the Ghost Dance movement and assimilate its practitioners for the same reason the Puritans hung Quakers and expelled Roger Williams, and for the same reason they criticized the Church of England, leading them to flee to America in the first place.

After years of policing ejaculation, the Oneida community launched a baby-making experiment. In 1869, fifty-three specially chosen women signed a pledge promising "that we do not belong to *ourselves* in any respect, but that we *do* belong first to *God*, and second to Mr. Noyes." They also relinquished control over procreation partners.[40] Thirty-eight men also signed a pledge, and over the course of ten years sixty-two supposedly superior children were born (or fifty-eight, depending on the source). Noyes fathered ten of the babies himself (or nine, depending on the source), and another nineteen were related to him. Remember his idea that one became closer to God by plugging into Christ's electrical battery? He believed that once this divine current had permeated people completely, they would become immortal. As such, the field of genetics turned on a light bulb in his head. Surely "electrical, spiritual conductivity" was a heritable trait.[41] So he bred a colony of superconductor babies, little invisible antennae sprouting from their heads. Amazingly, none of this is more far-fetched than theories from supposed scientists in that time period's burgeoning field of eugenics—scientists who would help pass laws that sterilized between sixty and seventy thousand Americans.

Darwinism hit the scene, and the field of genetics was blossoming, all suggesting that some human characteristics were fixed and couldn't be changed. People began to wonder, Exactly *what* traits? And did any of them lead people toward those social ills the reform movement up north had been working so hard to assuage? By the turn of the twentieth century, some philanthropists were "tired of giving to homes for cripples and aiding paupers."[42] It seemed the beneficiaries were not improving, but were fixed in a way that continued to burden benevolent societies and taxpayers. More alarmingly, they had children who continued the pattern. Charles Davenport, the father of the movement, opened Cold Spring Harbor Station in 1904 with a grant from the Andrew Carnegie Institution, and immediately started collecting "data." He asked schools, hospitals, mental words, and the like for the family trees of those in their care.

He deputized field researchers to visit families and determine if multiple generations exhibited alcoholism, criminality, pauperism, feeble-mindedness, or other specters of social decline then being pathologized by doctors and scientists.

In 1911, Davenport published *Heredity and Eugenics*, writing, "The fundamental fact [is] that all men are created *bound* by their protoplasmic make-up and *unequal* in their powers and responsibilities."[43] From this conclusion grew a movement dedicated to the removal of unequal protoplasm, achieved by marriage restriction, quarantine during reproductive years, or sterilization. All of these were considered preventative medicine. In addition to protecting future generations from "imbeciles" (scientific term) eugenicists felt that such "morons" (scientific term) needed our help, simple-minded as they were. It was really for their own benefit that "idiots" (scientific term) be put in homes and kept from breeding. This sinister paternalism presumably extended to ding-dongs and nincompoops too.

Davenport's studies delivered, no surprise, exactly the assumptions of the researchers and hopes of wealthy reformers. The hypothesis determined the science. Take the Kallikaks. A field-worker traced the line of a struggling eight-year-old girl back to her great-great-great-grandfather, who had come from a "good" family but then had an illegitimate child with a "feebleminded" young woman he met in a bar during the American Revolution. Later, he married a woman from another "good" family, and they bred lawyers, doctors, educators, and judges. Meanwhile, the tavern girl's line filled the area's "hovels" and tenements.

Yeah, obviously. She was a poor single mom when women had few prospects. In retrospect, it's clear these problems were environmental. But this was before B. F. Skinner and behaviorism. A gross misunderstanding of genetics swept the nation.

Eugenics was not just a science but a fad and a household word. It had powerful supporters, such as Alexander Graham Bell, John D. Rockefeller Jr., Margaret Sanger, and Teddy Roosevelt (some early supporters, including Bell, later renounced their affiliation, but Roosevelt was a long-hauler). It became a panacea for every social ill at a time when America was determined to bring society closer to perfection. Scholars tend to agree the eugenics campaign grew out of that secular-millennial reform movement we discussed earlier. The Social Gospel began as an investigation into the causes of social ills, then shifted from focusing on individuals (in this case, "social degenerates," who, if their nature was genetic, couldn't even be reformed) to focusing on society (which *could* be reformed by removing certain genes from the pool). Many saw such goals as additionally helping "defects" themselves, in a this-is-for-your-own-good kind of way.

The movement told the same story as John the Baptist did in the book of Matthew, as Michael Wigglesworth so evocatively depicted in his epic dooms-day poem, and as countless American Monomyth narratives have portrayed in American movie theaters: that a savior will separate the wheat from the chaff. Turn-of-the-century scientists—the superheroes of their day—played God's part for him, removing the supposedly unfit with literal surgical precision. An Indiana State Board secretary situated the problem in terms of good and evil: "It is impossible to calculate what even one feeble-minded woman may cost the public, when her vast possibilities for evil as a producer of paupers and criminals, through an endless line of descendants, is considered."[44]

Further, just as the American Monomyth—along with all cult ideology—leads to autocratic thinking, so did eugenics. Leaders of the crusade found naïve "the popular notion that everyone ought to participate in government." They found unscientific and dangerous the hope that "the American environment and education would open opportunities so that even the lowliest could rise."[45] Ultimately, even if unconsciously, the eugenics movement was about power and not wanting to share it.

If it all began with what some argued were noble (if incredibly misguided and paternalistic) motives, it went out in racist flames. Anti-immigration nativists saw an opportunity in eugenics to keep out immigrants, who would "lower the average of our people."[46] Davenport and others jumped on the bandwagon, believing that the prevalence of nativism would grow eugenics into the popular campaign they'd always hoped it would be. At this point, many social-reformer supporters tried to pull out.

In line with the Anglo-Saxon myth—that this race's industrious liberty-loving nature was inextricably linked to American ideals and it was therefore the chosen race to dominate America itself—nativists fomented fear of "inferior stock" filling the gene pool. Francis A. Walker, a Civil War general and census director, noticed the birth rate among so-called "native" (read: Anglo-Saxon) Americans had declined during the same period in which more than 5 million immigrants had arrived. He did some math, freaked out, and told anyone who'd listen that if these trends continued, immigration "amounted not to a reinforcement of our population, but to a replacement of native by foreign stock."[47] The so-called "replacement theory" is, of course, alive and well, including among tiki-torch bros who marched in Charlottesville in 2017; in Tucker Carlson's rhetoric; and in the manifesto of the perpetrator of a 2022 Buffalo, New York, massacre, in which thirteen were shot, eleven of whom were Black. A 2022 poll found the replacement theory was believed by half of Americans.[48] In December 2023, Trump said immigrants are "poisoning the blood of our country."[49]

Davenport once published a harebrained explanation of American genetic geography: the Puritan genes spread west, defining the nation's character, while the great statesmen of Virginia descended from dandy British royalist aristocrats, and the criminals and indentured servants among our original settlers resulted in the inferior people of Indiana, and the hills of Kentucky and Tennessee.[50] Sadly, he wrote nothing about the origin of Florida Man.

By the late 1910s and early 1920s, the science was falling apart. But in many ways, it was too late to stop the train. New intelligence tests—the precursors to IQ tests—allowed eugenicists to assess and label anyone.[51] *Run for your lives.* Thirty-two states ultimately passed sterilization laws, the first being Indiana in 1907. Somewhere between sixty and seventy thousand Americans were sterilized, more than twenty thousand in California alone (although Virginia, North Carolina, and Georgia all performed more per capita). In 1927, even the Supreme Court determined that sterilization could continue "for the protection and health of the state," in the *Buck v. Bell* ruling.[52] Although this decision was weakened by adjacent subsequent cases, it's never been overruled.

By the thirties, though, eugenics had been completely discredited by scientists. After the public learned what Nazis had done with the practice, it was hardly spoken of again. Still, it's never gone away, because neither has the desire among the powerful to "perfect" society, that is, conform it to their own narrow views of righteousness. Paternalism is the exercise of power but also an *effect* of power, in that power literally disables people from seeing perspectives other than their own. The psychological effects of power are key to understanding our nation's obsession with achieving perfection. Fortunately, they're also fascinating.

For example, studies suggest power diminishes empathy. The experience of feeling power causes a person to focus attention on themselves. Since attention is a limited resource, that person necessarily focuses less on others. This is a problem because it is the act of mirroring another's expressions, positions, and gestures that creates the experience of empathy. (For example, if I *hypothetically* received Botox injections that resulted in me appearing slightly scared every time I tried to raise my eyebrows, I would, in turn, scare anyone I talked to.) When we focus less on others, as a result of power, we literally lose the ability to connect with each other.

Power, of course, is often related to wealth. One study asked participants to view images of children suffering from cancer. Then it measured responses in the vagus nerve, the body's largest nerve bundle, which in part evolved to help us care for one another. Activation in this area is associated with increased altruism and cooperation. Those who grew up poor showed a strong vagus-nerve response. Those who grew up with wealth, prestige, and education exhibited little response.[53]

Another result of power? It causes us to do whatever the hell we want. We all have a little cult leader inside of us; it's called the ego. The experience of feeling power lowers one's inhibitions, concurrently expanding the spectrum of what one considers appropriate behavior and leading one to act more impulsively. Since the powerful are rarely checked, they get away with this behavior, which makes them feel more powerful, a self-perpetuating cycle. This is the science behind the phrase "power corrupts" and is why some cult leaders develop from annoying if relatively harmless narcissists into megalomaniac financial and sexual predators. This is possibly how John Humphrey Noyes came to rape every preteen girl in his community, while justifying it to himself and others.

Dacher Keltner—who conducted some of the studies I've described—is a psychology professor at the University of California, Berkeley. He believes power causes people to develop "narratives of exceptionalism." These narratives support powerful people's disinhibition, while maintaining outrage when others exhibit the same behaviors. Science has proved the obvious: double standards. He also discusses narratives of exceptionalism in relation to the eugenics movement, and argues that such thinking still happens today. One of his studies found that the wealthy and powerful are more likely to believe that "a person's standing in society . . . is determined by genes and is thus rooted in biology."

If power affects humans physiologically, you better believe its absence does. Powerlessness attacks the nervous system. It triggers the stress response and its resultant release of cortisol. When such a response becomes chronic, it damages veins and arteries, the nervous system, immune response, the digestive tract, and DNA. It also results in literal brain damage, particularly to the parts we use to help us plan and pursue goals.

Being subordinate increases our vigilance to threat, a brain drain that results in diminished "rigor of thought and quality of decision making." In one study, more than a thousand children received brain scans early in life, at which point the results were similar for poor and wealthy children, and also at age eleven, when poorer children's brains were then 5 percent smaller. Specifically, the stunted regions included areas that enable reasoning, language, academic work, and stress regulation. As a result, they can't perform in school as well as their wealthier peers. And once again, we are in a self-perpetuating system that maintains the sovereignty of a few.

Powerlessness even damages DNA, specifically the telomeres, strands that hold chromosomes together and thereby contribute to cell health. The result: shorter lifespans, specifically by six years for anyone who grew up poor during the first twenty-five years of life. Keltner believes powerlessness is "the greatest threat outside of climate change facing our society today."[54]

I'm sharing this research because, during the eugenics movement, those relegated to reformatories, prisons, hospitals, and asylums were typically not genetic "defects" but simply poor and powerless. Meanwhile, the eugenicists—that is, people who believed they were chosen by God, whether God is a paternal figure in the sky or a genetic twist of fortune—wanted to replicate traits *that ultimately resulted from power*, not genetics. That is, eugenicists only replicated their own power, which of course they were already doing in a variety of other ways. The practice of eugenics has only ever been redundant. But the effect was the extermination of people deemed unchosen, all under the legitimizing veils of secularism and science.

It's important to remember there was vocal resistance to eugenics among the general population. For that matter, many Americans were horrified by the manifest destiny–driven removal and extermination of Native communities. Plenty thought the Anglo-Saxon myth was baloney. (One anti-immigration leader wrote to another that their biggest obstacle was the "sentimental humanitarian attitude" held by many Americans who believed our country should be an asylum for the downtrodden and oppressed.)[55] And the last generation of young women in the Oneida community "found the memory of John Humphrey Noyes nothing short of loathsome."[56] Nevertheless, the beliefs behind all of these movements and practices helped chart the path of our nation's development—and lately, they've been back at the drawing board.

———

Pronatalists are, generally, pro birth. They worry about declining birth rates in industrialized countries. They want to ensure the next generation contains enough taxable workers to pay for future retirees. They fear that smaller generations will result in less innovation and global competitiveness, and ultimately economic and cultural stagnation. But while some in the movement lobby for child tax credits and affordable childcare, others challenge rights to abortion and contraception, and try to pull women from the workplace. Pronatalism is typically accompanied by a certain flavor of fearmongering that, like the eugenics movement or the plot of the 2006 Mike Judge film *Idiocracy*, suggests that when desirable people don't have babies, their superior genes will be swallowed up in the general pool by the genes of "others." Once that happens, the story goes, it's the end of democracy, civilization, and global stability.

The movement is not new, but it is on the rise. It's received ample attention since 2021 footage resurfaced of vice president JD Vance claiming people without children are miserable and shouldn't be leaders. And it has big supporters, including Elon Musk and Marc Andreessen, among other wealthy elites, especially in venture capital and tech. According to *Business Insider*, PayPal cofounder Luke Nosek hosted at his home a pronatalist discussion titled "The End of Western Civilization." The movement's goals dovetail with recent tech developments in genetics, in particular as applied to the fertility market, in which Peter Thiel, Steve Jurvetson, and OpenAI founder Sam Altman have all invested.[57]

Hopeful parents exploring IVF have long been able to scan embryos for genetic factors associated with mortality or morbidity. New technologies allow for risk assessment of outcomes such as anxiety, mood swings, and brain fog. Via the use of polygenic scores, genetic tests claim to predict risk factors not only of diabetes, cancers, hypertension, and coronary artery disease, but income, intelligence, and educational attainment. These developments are fraught with all of the ethical quandaries you might expect of them. There are also unanticipated but measurable consequences. "For example," the *New England Journal of Medicine* points out, "if an embryo is selected on the basis of the polygenic score for educational attainment, the risk of bipolar disorder is increased by 16%."[58]

Unsurprisingly, there's a large overlap between pronatalists and adherents of longtermism, the purportedly humanitarian movement arguing that as important as it is to care for the people of today, it's also and maybe more important to care for humans of the future—like, hundreds of thousands of years into the future. To do so, as global populations increase (remember that only wealthy nations shrink), will require huge technological advancements. Elon Musk donated $1.5 million to the now-defunct Future of Humanity Institute.[59] Peter Thiel has donated heavily to the Machine Intelligence Research Institute.[60]

However, the Carnegie Council for Ethics in International Affairs calls longtermism "a Trojan horse," writing, "we worry that these legitimate concerns can easily be distorted and conflated with personal desires, goals, messianic convictions, and the promotion of deeply embedded political agendas and corporate interests."[61] Further, the authors argue, tech leaders are hypocritically unlikely to support research into the potentially harmful effects on the current society of products that are already in place and making money.

Some in the center of the Venn diagram of pronatalism and longtermism argue that the future world will need a lot of big ideas to care for future people—and therefore we should be concerned that the people currently contributing big ideas to society are least likely to procreate. The father of longtermism, William MacAskill, expressed in his best-selling book *What We Owe the Future* a fear of "technological stagnation" resulting from declining birth rates. Therefore, he floated the idea of breeding some amount of the population to have "Einstein-level research abilities." A former colleague of Musk's claims the mogul "urged 'all the rich men he knew' to have as many children as possible."[62]

This branch of pronatalism is modern-day eugenics. Once again, the wealthy and powerful impose their visions of perfection on others—just as Noyes and the Social Gospelers did, just as the Puritans did. We are culturally indoctrinated to believe that perfection can and should be achieved and that efforts to do so are therefore justified, even if they infringe on the rights of everyone else. The proponents' image of perfection is, of course, themselves, the presumed chosen. They aim to remake the world in their image. At the first Natal Conference, in Austin, Texas, in December 2023, one speaker seemed to argue they could overpower liberals and progressive ideology if they "seize the means of reproduction," that is, if they all made more of themselves: "We can use their visceral hatred of big families to our advantage."[63]

And always, they express a sense of urgency. One enthusiastic breeder, who works in VC and private equity, told *Business Insider* in 2022, "I do not think humanity is in a great situation right now. And I think if somebody doesn't fix the problem, we could be gone."[64] There's that cult watch again, always striking at now o'clock. First comes the claim of a problem and then the panicked call of danger.

But what if there actually is no problem? Many demographers suggest immigration will do what it's always done, allow for the redistribution of workers from overpopulated countries into developed countries with declining birth rates. This begs the question, Exactly what kind of people are pronatalists hoping to create? Besides, the ecosystem called earth is groaning under the weight of our progeny. To survive as a species, we have to make fewer of ourselves than we traditionally have. Instead of worrying over breeding more workers, why can't we problem-solve a new way to fund Social Security? That is exactly the kind of big idea pronatalists claim they want to engender and safeguard.

Big ideas come from anywhere, assuming, as we've learned from powerlessness research, that the thinkers grow up in communities free of crime where their basic needs are met and they feel empowered. If today's quote-unquote elites continue to hoard the world's resources, then, yes, all of tomorrow's big ideas probably will come from their own privileged progeny. That doesn't mean the best way to secure future big ideas is for elites to procreate more. The entire premise is a false syllogism.

Certain pronatalists and longtermists share the paternalistic belief that the world will most benefit from elites, whether they're choosing what we develop, where we go, and how we live, or literally populating the world with more of themselves. Former longtermist turned critic of the movement, Émile P. Torres has said, "The longtermist view itself implies that really, people in rich countries matter more."[65]

Yes, intelligence is to a certain degree hereditary; no one needs a scientific study to be convinced this is true. But it's only one factor. Common sense also tells us that one can only pursue the limits of one's brain power—or artistic expression, athletic ability, etc.—if given the opportunity to do so, which requires not only the expense of education but also the most valuable resource of all: time. This, of course, is the same reason wealthy elites stop procreating in the first place. Children are expensive and require time, both of which rob parents of opportunities to continue developing their minds and abilities—that is, to exercise the privilege they enjoy. If these elites of Western civilization were as smart as they claim to be, they would solve the problem alarming them by giving their money to paid family leave, daycare funds, universal pre-K, and college scholarships, not to mention by lobbying to raise the minimum wage, institute universal healthcare, and improve public education. This would also be a way to care for people today, by investing in community, instead of messianic individualism seeking technological magic bullets that turn innovators into heroes and celebrities.

There's a thought puzzle common in some pronatalist circles, that asks whether the future will be better served by improving educational outcomes for people ranking in the top 0.1 percent of intelligence or the bottom 10 percent. The answer, they argue, is to help those at the top because those advancements will stretch the limits of human intelligence on the whole and thereby carry civilization itself into a more advanced future. OK. I understand the argument. But explain to me why we have to choose. These VC and tech titans have enough money to educate the bottom and top percentiles, and to help current people and future people. These zero-sum choices only exist because they created them. My nine-year-old saw me reading an article with "Elon Musk" and "babies" in the title and asked what it was about. I explained pronatalism, and she replied, "They probably just want there to be more people to buy their products." I've never been more proud.

The problematic wings of the longtermist and pronatalist movements conveniently provide arguments for why powerful people should hold more power, excuses for hoarding resources. Similarly, eugenicists believed "an ideal democracy was a government in which the competent understood and guided the incompetent," which is merely a justification to hold power.[66] And John Humphrey Noyes believed the spiritually advanced should train the spiritual initiates, which was a justification for rape.

Buying into such ideologies absolves them of culpability or guilt. And undergirding such ideologies is the belief that they are God's elect. Americans have been indoctrinated to see ourselves as a chosen nation of chosen people. Many believe their calling is to achieve perfection, whether that is God, status as the leading nation in the world, or being the most superior race. Since only they can understand perfection, they must impose it on others, whether sinners, the rest of the world, or supposedly inferior people. They will get the job done. They will stick their noses in your wars, your wombs. Really, it's for your own good.

But who is actually choosing the chosen people? Social reform or effective altruism, eugenics or pronatalism—they are all ways of *playing* God. There's an urge for people in power to become godheads, whether that means starting a cult that worships you, determining who is or isn't born in some latter-day Garden of Eden, or being the benefactor of humanity current or future. An obsession with one's own DNA is nothing less than an act of self-worship as the god one believes oneself to be.

Some tech giants even try to achieve godlike immortality. Larry Ellison, Sergey Brin, and Jeff Bezos invested heavily in the 2010s in biotech companies "they thought could help them defy death."[67] On the light side of this movement is biohacking, a collection of techniques one can use to optimize health and performance—to constantly strive toward perfection. On the heavy side of this movement is tech mogul Bryan Johnson, who has spent millions of his fortune on Project Blueprint, a personal initiative that aims to slow or reverse aging. In 2023, Johnson, in his mid-forties, received transfusions of plasma from his seventeen-year-old son. The process resulted in a tidal wave of vampire memes, but no detectable benefits.

But even if *they* can't live forever, at least their supposedly superior genes can. Elon Musk, an avid supporter of pronatalism, has been candid, according to a one-time colleague, about "populating the world with his offspring."[68] He was once described by former partner Grimes as obsessed with Genghis Khan, the thirteenth-century Mongol ruler who was so powerful and prolific that 8 percent of men in that area today are believed to be his descendants.[69] Musk has fathered twelve kids and counting.[70]

The desire to replicate the self is also a commonality among cult leaders and other elites. Warren Jeffs, former leader of the fundamentalist Church of Jesus Christ of Latter-day Saints, purportedly has at least sixty children. Malachi York, founder of the Nuwaubian Nation (see chapter 6), might have up to three hundred. Jeffrey Epstein had plans to seed the world with his DNA by impregnating up to twenty women at a time, continually, until, presumably, he ran out of sperm. It's almost like they have a parasite pushing them to replicate again and again; the parasite is unchecked power.

———

Historical accounts often paint John Humphrey Noyes as a man devoted to his faith. Perhaps he was. That doesn't mean he didn't also engineer reality to justify his most base desires. His ego had no boundaries. He described God as one "whose life ever turns in upon himself," but it was Noyes who turned in upon himself, consuming all he wanted, pulling more and more into him. He created God in *his* image, one he could more easily achieve. In a way, social media has allowed all of us to fashion ourselves as gods; seeking worship via likes, comments, subscriptions, and shares; approaching perfection via angles, filters, and photo editing. One wonders how JHN might have captioned a selfie. #HideYourDaughtersHideYourWives.

But he did not rule forever and ever, amen. Prominent anti-obscenity crusaders finally closed in. After reading in the *Syracuse Standard* of his imminent arrest, Noyes fled to Canada on June 22, 1879. The ensuing power struggle never resulted in a suitable successor (the children of the inner circle had been sent to college—rookie mistake—where they fell for Darwin and started doubting JHN's teachings). Ruling from Niagara Falls, Noyes ended complex marriage on August 28, and announced the community would adopt traditional marriage customs.

It was messy. Who should marry whom when they had children with different partners, and with which families should the children go? Also, with private families came the need for private property. So on November 20, 1880, they created a joint-stock company, Oneida Community Ltd. Members were given shares, depending on how long they'd been in the community and how much property they'd originally brought with them. This Ltd later became synonymous with the silver company, which after some initial fits and starts skyrocketed to success, enjoying decades of stability and profits. According to the company's archives, by 1983 more than half of all flatware bought in the United States was Oneida.

As for Jessie Catherine Kinsley, she married Noyes's right-hand man, Myron Kinsley, which was basically arranged by Noyes. Based on her memoir, they seem to have been happy, in spite of the large age difference. She writes that her husband, "twenty-two years my senior, used to tell of trotting me on one knee." At her funeral, someone said her life was "a lasting spring," a phrase from one of her favorite verses of Shakespeare (*Henry VIII*), describing a land, created by Orpheus's lute, in which plants and flowers always bloom, like a kind of Eden, a New Jerusalem.[71]

In a 1921 speech given by Oneida descendants George Wallingford Noyes and Hilda Herrick Noyes during the Second International Eugenics Conference, they echoed that old maxim about the path of Germanic providence, but now they brought the path of righteousness right to their doorstep. They spoke of the fortitude of the English Puritans. From that group, they argued, the New England pioneers selected themselves out for greatness. From them came the American Revivalists, an even more righteous group. From them came the perfectionists . . . and on to the Oneidans . . . and eventually, the babies of Noyes's eugenics experiment. All the while, they argued, each descendent had been bred closer to perfection.

John Humphrey Noyes built a Tower of Babel trying to reach God and immortality. For the record, everyone in his community died. But their genes live on. Presumably, so do their riding toes.

CHAPTER 3

DON'T SPREAD ON ME
ON REBELLION AND ANTI-INTELLECTUALISM

"If you are so utterly stupid that the early planned extermination of over one-half of the world's population—(embracing some four hundred million educated men and women, including you and your loved ones and about six hundred million less cultured humans)—means nothing to you, then do not waste your time reading the rest of this announcement."[1] That's how one of America's most successful hoaxes in history began—with a basic, pick-up-artist neg.

If readers of this 1940 pamphlet had questions, though, there was no one to ask. Such literature claimed to be authored by a secretive group, the Sponsors, whose noble mission necessitated anonymity lest efforts to save humankind be foiled by the architects of said tyranny, the shadowy Hidden Rulers. The latter supposedly comprised a global group of families who'd accrued outrageous wealth and power and secretly ruled the world for most of history. But then (purportedly) some disobedient among them allowed education and "Christian religion" to spread, which affected the minds of their unknowing subjects, who were thereby transformed into "right-thinking people."

This spelled trouble. The Rulers strived to eradicate these right-thinking people in some hodgepodge manner, but couldn't smite them all. Therefore, "The only method left to the world's Hidden Rulers—if they are to succeed in retaining their control over the world and its people—is to exterminate all people who are either educated or religious." The remaining "one thousand million" would be enslaved.[2]

But, *fear not*, the literature asserted, readers could fight back. They could join a global, epic, and imminent good-versus-evil battle to save the world and institute a golden age of peace, prosperity, and equality . . . unless, that is, they were too utterly stupid to care. All of this was spelled out in *Mankind United, A Challenge to "Mad Ambition" and "The Money Changers,"* a textbook of sorts that began circulating in San Francisco in 1934. It's impossible to know how many members ultimately fell into Mankind United, or how much money it raised, but authorities estimated the number of loyal followers at 14,000, with the total number who participated in, explored, or were recruited by the group over the span of about a decade reaching 250,000 total, an astonishing reach for a time before TikTok and cable TV.[3]

Followers were told to believe the group's leaders, superintendents, had been chosen by even higher leaders, the Sponsors, after extensive training, to spread their information to the public. Beneath superintendents were bureau managers, captains, lieutenants, and finally, enrollees. Supposedly, divisions dotted the globe, all building armies of right-thinking people. But in reality, the Pacific Coast division, with bureaus throughout California and Oregon, was the only one. And its leader—who went by the aliases the Voice of the Right Idea, Dept. A, the Speaker, the Voice, and Church Trustee—was the only superintendent. He, of course, had engineered the entire scheme. When the FBI took him and eleven Mankind United members into custody on December 18, 1942, it did so under his real name, Arthur L. Bell.

There's no way Bell believed the bunk he peddled (not least because he seems to have personally spent all the money raised). He claimed the Sponsors often teleported him from one part of the globe to another, that they had created seven doubles of him so he could be in more than one place at once, and that he often left club meetings by traveling through the ceiling. He promised members that once the organization finally vanquished its foes, every family would get air-conditioning and a swimming pool. It was too fantastical, too conveniently black-and-white, too well designed to trigger fears and monetize desires.

For example, the Hidden Rulers supposedly controlled "every political party, government, industry, and public utility in every civilized nation in the world" and deliberately orchestrated "all revolutions, wars, and poverty," planned to "exterminate all people who are either educated or religious," manufactured devices that could vibrate millions of people's eyeballs out of their sockets, and elected an executive board whose members dedicated their lives and talents to these goals.[4]

As if superrich people would lose time organizing all of that! They're too busy enjoying their yachts, jets, and, I don't know, cloned pets. Still, every successful conspiracy theory contains kernels of truth. Bell claimed that Hidden Rulers had carefully selected all of the world's leaders and dictators. And yes, the wealthy have always had an outsized influence on elections and coups. Bell also explained—during the middle of the 1930s, when Americans struggled through the Great Depression—that a group of evil rich people had been responsible for all depressions, specifically so they could swoop in and buy land, properties, and farms from the afflicted at cut-rate prices. This his followers had just witnessed when, after the 1929 crash, oil baron J. Paul Getty scooped up real estate and oil stocks for pennies on the dollar and stock speculator Joseph Kennedy Sr. hoovered up real estate at bargain prices. It's even been argued that Kennedy's speculations contributed to the crash, off of which he made even more money.

This economic aside doesn't even include Mankind United's terrifying prescience about human eradication, which was beginning to be conceived by the Nazi Party just then coming into power across the Atlantic.

The movement's central argument—that a coalition of powerful and evil people conspired against good hard-workers—found fertile soil in the minds of the afflicted and suffering because it's comforting to blame an antagonist. The existence of an adversary provides us with agency to improve our lives. If we have someone to fight, we have a course of action. And if this enemy is also evil? Now our actions are not only self-interested, but also serve mankind—without the nuisance of remorse! This is the comfort of black-and-white thinking.

Fortunately, the textbook, pamphlets, and meetings had a clear and concise plan . . . which they promised to share just as soon as the organization had accrued enough warriors and money. After all, if they played their cards too soon, the Rulers might foil their plans and all would be lost. But wouldn't you know, the Sponsors kept pushing out the date of action. There never seemed to be enough warriors and money.

Meanwhile, Bell motivated his followers with an especially fat and delicious-looking carrot: the dream of wealth with little labor. Whenever the Sponsors deemed the world ready, "the Institute's well-guarded sixty-years of discoveries and carefully prepared recommendations will be freely offered to the human race," literature promised. There would be jobs for all, and at only four hours a day, four days a week, and eight months a year. Also, the Sponsors promised technological advances that could produce a hundred times more food and clothing than could ever be consumed by the global population and without exhausting the planet's resources. The excessiveness of the claims recalls late-night infomercials.

That's not all they'll get, Carol.

Tell us, Jim!

The Sponsors also planned to institute a new currency, which would allow every employee to receive at least $30,000 a year ($655K today)!

That's incredible, Jim.

Wait, there's more!

Everyone was also promised a house—with an air conditioner, television, radio, vegetable garden, playground, swimming pool, fountain, and mini waterfall.

Jim, this sounds too good to be true!

Carol, it is!

The Sponsors would also disband all of the world's armies and navies.[5] And all jealousy, fear, and hate would cease to exist as would, in their absence, almost all physical and mental diseases, bringing an end to premature death.

Wow, Jim. Our phones are ringing off the hook! What will all this cost?

Oh, Carol, they'll pay and pay, but never fill the hole in a grifter's heart.

Bell sold his apocalyptic message to people who had few other options. The FBI would later determine, "Most of the [Mankind United] members were either elderly persons, or individuals who had suffered severe economic reverses."[6]

But the outbreak of World War II was bad for business. Since being anti-war was kind of the Sponsors' whole thing, Bell had to instruct his followers to oppose the conflict. He advised them not to purchase war bonds and to avoid the draft. He claimed the Pearl Harbor attack was a conspiracy involving the FBI. In December 1942, the FBI took fifteen bureau managers and Bell into custody under the wartime Sedition Act for "intent to interfere with the war effort of the United States and undermine the morale of the armed forces."[7] It was the first time those Mankind United "bureau managers" ever heard Bell's real name.

Following a five-week media sensation of a trial in Los Angeles in 1943, Bell and six others were sentenced to five years in federal prison for sedition; the other five took lesser charges. (All were eventually acquitted due to a successful argument that the jury lacked gender diversity.) Around that same time, Mankind United members were suddenly required to donate 50 percent of their salaries—gross, not net—to something called the "50-50 fund." Bell had another plan up his sleeve.

Little is known about the man himself. Most of it was learned during the FBI probe and in later bankruptcy court proceedings in 1946 and 1947. Additionally and blessedly, a young academic named H. T. Dohrman, with a grant from Harvard, spent two years conducting field research in the forties, attending court proceedings and group meetings; poring over files, documents, and transcripts of the various hearings and committee meetings and reports; and interviewing dozens of members and former members, eventually even scoring an interview with the Voice himself.

As a teenager, Bell went west to live with relatives in San Francisco. There, through an aunt, he became involved with Christian Science and, later, also took a shining to the utopian novels of Edward Bellamy. He plucked ideas from both while developing Mankind United, as well as from the middle-class promises of Upton Sinclair's 1934 California gubernatorial campaign.[8] Little of what Bell presented was original. But he made it irresistible to contemporary struggling Americans.

A handsome man, he always had and spent cash. He frequented the best restaurants and hotels, usually under a variety of pseudonyms, and had apartments in San Francisco and Los Angeles, and mansions in West Hollywood and Burlingame.[9] During the government's fact-finding process, committee chairman and California state senator Jack B. Tenney estimated that between 1934 and 1944 Mankind United pulled in $4 million ($88.4 million today).[10] And that was all before Bell tricked the government into incorporating the group into a church, and then turned the remaining organization and followers into a full-fledged cult.

Cults and conspiracy theories are kissing cousins: they share DNA, often look alike, and sometimes get married. Our modern tendency to see and believe in conspiracy theories is actually a remnant of a handful of evolutionary advantages held by our forebears. The conspiracy-theory theory posits that early humans who exhibited hypervigilance, a focused attention on the what-ifs and maybes, died less, thereby dominating the gene pool. But a by-product of hypervigilance in these areas is a tendency to see patterns, discern motives, perceive threats, and ascertain alliances where in fact there are none.[11] A tendency toward conspiracist thinking is one of the costs of evolutionary success. Next time you're tempted to call conspiracy theorists stupid, consider that they might instead be too smart.

They may not take that as a compliment, though, particularly in America, where we tend to scorn intelligence—a knee-jerk reaction central to our specific brand of conspiracism. Although conspiracist thinking dates to our earliest days as a species, we nevertheless have our own flavor. Whenever you hear of a heroic rebellion against a coalition of intellectual elites colluding to harm good simple folk, you're witnessing America's finest conspiracy theory at work. And it was absolutely influenced by those doomsday-preaching Puritans.

If you think only a fraction of Americans believe conspiracy theories, know that in June 2020, 22 percent agreed with the statement that "there is more to [conspiracy theories] than the official accounts of the events."[12] In 2022, 41 percent of American adults read this statement—"Regardless of who is officially in charge of the government and other organizations, there is a single group of people who secretly control events and rule the world together"—and said it was either probably true or definitely true. Another 18 percent reported being unsure.[13]

Americans love a conspiracy theory. Our favorite flavor has three defining characteristics: the alleged conspirators are unfathomably powerful and typically world leaders, they're brainiacs who prey on the less intelligent, and there's something we can and must do to stop them. The first comes to us by way of the Antichrist.

For all of the Protestant obsession with that figure, you may be surprised to learn that his name barely appears in the Bible. But enthusiastic interpreters of Bible prophecy see him everywhere nevertheless and have put together an enduring character profile: just before the end-times, a charismatic genius will rise to power, who will excel in politics, economics, and the military, but who is secretly greedy, ambitious, and lawless. What he really wants is power and control, to rule "over every tribe and people and language and nation."[14] He will do so by uniting all nations and religions, a coalition that will signal a time of unprecedented peace (and is why conspiracists see evil in the United Nations and the Council on Foreign Relations). But don't be fooled by the peace. Ultimately, he is out to destroy. It's simply his nature. He exists only so God can prove that evil will be conquered.

Protestant reformers and the Puritans among them, who settled in New England, believed the Pope was the Antichrist. Over the years, Stalin and Barack Obama have also been charged, as shifting fears and desires create new bogeymen. Even Oliver Stone's 1995 film, *Nixon*, implicates "the beast," some unknown, but powerful American political machine. In a 1996 interview, Stone said, "Call me wrong, but we have John Kennedy suspiciously killed, we have Robert Kennedy suspiciously killed, we have Martin Luther King suspiciously killed, and we have Nixon suspiciously 'falling on his sword.' . . . Between 1963 and 1974, these four men all ran up against the Beast and were removed or killed as a consequence."[15]

So, we have an evil force that will join together nations in order to control all of humanity—one has to be pretty smart to pull that off. Not coincidentally, intelligence and wit are character traits the Puritans somewhat despised, which brings us to the second defining characteristic of American conspiracy theories.

Anti-intellectualism had already been a Renaissance-era meme: fools were lionized over wise men because being simpleminded at least precluded one from deceit. This had deeper roots in the conflation of the "New World" with Eden, of the "simple" native life with how Adam and Eve presumably lived.[16] The Puritans in New England ran with it, made it a dominant part of their culture, and valued simplicity of dress, manner, and especially thought and speech. As John Cotton preached, "The more learned and witty you bee, the more fit to act for Satan will you bee."[17]

These ideas have serious staying power. Speaking of geniuses in 1844, Henry Ward Beecher said, "They are to be known by a reserved air, excessive sensitiveness, and utter indolence; by very long hair, and very open shirt collars; by the reading of much wretched poetry, and the writing of much, yet more wretched; by being very conceited, very affected, very disagreeable, and very useless."[18] I have so many questions. How does Beecher know how bad that guy's poetry is? Is he reading it and, if so, why?

Suspicions ran deeper to include a general disdain for all elitism. Writing of Puritan understandings of Satan, one scholar notes, "Above all, the devil accomplished his wiles in the guise of a princely gentleman—suave, sophisticated, cultured, aristocratic, accustomed to power and authority."[19] At the time of their egress, the Puritans fled not only the Church of England but also the sinful life of manners and wealth allowed to develop under its hegemony, all of which they believed God would imminently smite. Once, as a clever way of wondering whether one was going to heaven or hell, Cotton Mather said, "to Heaven or to Europe."[20]

Some scholars argue that this self-righteous attitude toward the Old World merely masked an inferiority complex: if Puritans were less cultured and stylish, they could at least consider that virtuous. They were creating a new identity for themselves—as a new community—by defining themselves in opposition to something else, in this case their bully. Regardless, the Puritans couldn't fully insulate themselves from what they fled. "The unrelieved hell of European civilization" crossed the Atlantic, arriving in the colonies in the form of East Coast metropolitan development.[21] Divisions grew between the now prosperous coastal settlements and the newer frontier, between city and rural folk, rich and poor. The latter in each pair feared that Europe's evil ways were infecting America.

The threat of European corruption became a bugbear of Benjamin Franklin's. At the end of the Revolution, he wrote, "The people of the Trading Towns may be rich and luxurious, while the Country possesses all the Virtues, that tend to private Happiness and publick Prosperity. . . . We may hope the Luxury of a few Merchants on the Seacoast will not be the Ruin of America."[22] Decades later, Ralph Waldo Emerson shared his belief that Europe extended to the Alleghenies, while America lay beyond them.

These ideas partly fueled manifest destiny—*We came here to start fresh! Oops, all the stuff we built got corrupted. We'll move to "new" land and try again! Oops again. But this time, we can outrun the devil! Oops* . . . all the way to California. It was a chase for the paradise lost, a desire to return to Eden, which many believed was stolen by the Antichrist and his [insert historical-figure minion]. This would fuel pastoral dreams among city dwellers for centuries, eventually leading countless cubicle-bound Manhattanites to add farm pics to Pinterest pages.

The scholar Charles Sanford, author of *The Quest for Paradise: Europe and the American Moral Imagination*, calls this the "cult of the simple" and cites it along with Puritan values as the origins of "a traditional American impatience with speculative thought, with rigorous analysis, with precise use of terminology and language as tools for communication, with difficult new art forms, with efforts to understand increasingly complex public issues and governmental operations on other than moral grounds."[23] Books bad, Jethro good. But what do I know . . . I'm just a caveman lawyer.

We see it all over pop culture. Ever notice that comic book villains are brainiacs whose superior intelligence has corrupted them irrevocably *and* allowed them to devise innovative ways to destroy the world? Sure, plenty of superheroes are also superintelligent, but the character trait isn't literally in their names, as it is for villains such as Egghead, the Brain, Brain Storm, Brainiac, Mister Mind, Mad Thinker, M.O.D.O.C. (Mental Organism Designed Only for Computing), and the Riddler. In reality, of course, villains are rarely known for intelligence, as evidenced by the character traits embedded in the names of these very real organized crime members: Joe Bananas, Big Tuna, Willie Potatoes, Louie Bagels, Chicken Man, the Hump, and Butterass.

Now, if a global power ring of evil intellectuals is out to get us, are we going to sit back and take it? No way, this is America, you sissy. Here's that third characteristic of American conspiracy theories. We are rebels, a nature baked into our Protestant origins. The Reformation was "fundamentally a religious revolt against authority"—against papists who controlled the Church of England, and therefore the monarchy, all of which disallowed the Puritans from worshiping and behaving as they wanted to.[24] Even founding father John Adams viewed the Reformation as having freed people from "a wicked confederacy."[25]

Protestantism is by nature schismatic and has continued to fracture through history, with each new sect or denomination accusing its precursor of tyranny. Even during the first days of English settlement, the Puritan Congregationalists in the MBC were not alone in dissent. The Quakers were so fractious they attended Congregationalist services just to stand and shout at random times, intending to disrupt and generally be knobs. Speaking of knobs, Quakers also protested by taking off their clothes. Called "the practice of going naked," it was intended to shame Puritans who, Quakers said, hid beneath the metaphorical dressings of authority, status, or wealth. In short, every new sect believes its predecessors are going to hell while it's getting it right, so it may as well pull out its tits.

By the middle of the nineteenth century, largely as a result of the Second Great Awakening, the colonies experienced an explosion of schisms and sects—think the Shakers, the Church of Latter-day Saints, and the Seventh-day Adventists—all claiming authority and distinguishing themselves from dominant faiths. A more recent and extreme example is the Worldwide Church of God, which began as a radio ministry in 1934, experienced a major fracture when the leader's son left to start a new church in 1974, and within thirty-five more years had produced four hundred different offshoots. Catholicism is conformity and canon; Protestantism is rebellion and re-creation.

Certainly, the American Revolution was a complicated affair. Plenty of colonialists didn't want it. Even among those who did, many nonetheless considered themselves English. There were as many motives as there were men holding guns. But it would be silly not to consider one of those motives to be a deeply entrenched, culturally defining, and potentially unconscious American impulse to rebel against authority. Sanford argues that the association of the Church of England with unreformed Catholicism eventually led to the *substitution* of England for Rome as the seat of the Antichrist. Then, once traditional European enemies France and Spain were no longer threats to the colonists, England became the sole force constraining colonial freedom. American individualism developed out of an "inner necessity to assert [oneself] against cramping restrictions of any kind, especially those associated with an authoritarian, older civilization."[26]

Years later, while designing our new government, the founding fathers argued continuously over whether or not to have a central federal government and, if so, how much power to give it. Detractors argued that any kind of centralized power could easily be commandeered by aristocrats, who were, the argument went, just hanging out looking for a chance to control everyone, as that was their nature.[27]

———

Because these fears are deeply ingrained in us, they are often employed to manipulate us. The call to rebel against a group of elites preying on good simple folks has been the rallying cry of demagogues since the dawn of our nation. It's also how Trump convinced a crowd to storm the U.S. Capitol on January 6, 2021. Almost always, there is some truth behind the call. Intellectuals *can* be uppity. Banks *do* sometimes fleece customers. The government *has* made decisions that benefit billionaires at the expense of farmers and blue-collar workers. And social liberals *have* attended satanic blood-sacrifice ritual marriages to the beast. Jk about that last one, but some certainly feel that way—and voter feelings are all that matter to a demagogue, who stokes fears, bends the truth, or outright lies, and builds fanatic followings instead of platforms.

As bad as things are, the demagogue says, and as rigged as the system is, there is something we can do about it, but you have to act now. And you have to vote for me. Unfortunately, they are usually out for their own gain and willing to deconstruct any political norm or power system in their way. In his book *American Demagogue: The Great Awakening and the Rise and Fall of Populism*, J. D. Dickey argues that American demagoguery was born during the Great Awakening itself, when fiery orator George Whitefield took his galvanizing calls for repentance to the people, pulling audiences of twenty to thirty thousand people, especially along the frontier. He lit them up, called them to action, and in so doing forever reshaped church and political life in America. That illustration of people power was lost on no one.

Whether populist, demagogue, or both, Huey Long, Father Charles Coughlin, George Wallace, Joseph McCarthy, Richard Nixon, Pat Buchanan, and, of course, Donald Trump have all sought their own gain by pushing our evil authority–fearing, anti-intellectual, rebellious buttons. Poet and culture critic Kevin Young writes, "What Donald Trump the candidate promised was not freedom for but freedom *from*."[28]

Even mainstream politicians rely on a certain populist trope, endearing themselves to voters by feigning to be outsiders unpolluted by the elitism ruining Washington. The gymnastics required to re-create oneself as just a regular guy are perhaps most thrilling in George W. Bush. You can't get more inside than having a father who was literally in the White House for twelve years. Unless, perhaps, you also have a degree from Harvard Business School. And co-own a Major League Baseball team. And were a member of the Skull and Bones secret society during your studies at Yale. Nevertheless, his folksy nature and, in particular, his public-speaking flubs—including the most famous, "They misunderestimated me," and my favorite, "Rarely is the question asked: is our children learning?"—made Bush the guy in the contest with whom voters would rather get a beer. Or single-malt scotch.[29]

Who are we without someone to fight? The dualistic nature of apocalyptic thinking demands an antihero. From the birth of New England, America's fledgling colonies saw themselves not only as the hero—literally rescuing the world's one true religion—but as the persecuted little guy, the scrappy kid fighting a Goliath bent on our destruction. If evil is outside of you, you have something to fight. You have something to do about your predicament. If evil is outside of you, it's not inside of you. You have hope of destroying it without destroying yourself.

As we'll explore later, the United States government itself eventually became the evil enemy, that simpleton-preying Antichrist against which we must rebel. That belief has been utilized not only by grifters and demagogues, but also racists, paranoid gun-toting secessionists, and sometimes all of the above. But first, let's look at what else these beliefs have spawned: some spectacular American conspiracy theories.

Perhaps it's not surprising, as a gaffe-y kind of guy, that in March 2022, President Joe Biden accidentally "confirmed" one of the biggest conspiracy theories in American history. While the Business Roundtable's CEO quarterly meeting occurred in DC, the White House hosted a briefing for them on the war in Ukraine. It was pretty standard White House stuff, and at the end, Biden said, "Now is a time when things are shifting. We're going to—there's going to be a new world order out there and we've got to lead it. And we've got to unite the rest of the free world in doing it." Presumably, to Biden, the words *new*, *world*, and *order* are just two adjectives and a noun. But to countless Americans, those words make the title of a secret organization of the globe's most powerful elite, which is busy developing an international government to control and enslave the entire human population.

These conspiracists believe most world leaders are already involved. And, wouldn't you know, the Business Roundtable's CEO quarterly meeting included some of the most powerful on the planet, for example, the leaders of Amazon, Apple, U.S. Steel, General Motors, JPMorganChase, Bank of America, FedEx, Exxon, ConocoPhillips, and Cargill. Within hours, the phrase *new world order* was trending on Twitter. On March 22 alone, Facebook posts containing it racked up more than 278,000 reactions. (Much closer to an *actual* conspiracy is the Business Roundtable organization itself, founded in 1972 to increase corporate influence in politics, which was right around the time the modern lobbying movement got underway, resulting in decreases in environmental regulations, corporate tax rates, and labor reforms.)

So what? you might be thinking. Surely Biden couldn't be expected to know every rabbit hole in America's meadows. Then again, the New World Order theory has been around for more than three decades. Infamous televangelist and onetime presidential candidate Pat Robertson even wrote a best-selling book promoting it. Adherents claim crises such as 9/11, COVID-19, and mass shootings are actually false-flag events orchestrated by the cabal to disrupt resistance and sow unrest. Biden may as well have said, "Thank you for attending this Illuminati meeting. Next, we head to a pizzeria basement for the chemtrail training."

This modern iteration of the New World Order conspiracy was launched in a speech by President George H. W. Bush, given before a joint session of Congress on September 11, 1990, one year after the Berlin wall fell and in the middle of the Persian Gulf war: "Out of these troubled times, our fifth objective—a new world order—can emerge: a new era—freer from the threat of terror, stronger in the pursuit of justice, and more secure in the quest for peace. An era in which the nations of the world, East and West, North and South, can prosper and live in harmony."[30]

He repeated the phrase in the State of the Union in January, at a press conference in August, in a speech to the UN in September, and in his 1991 State of the Union. Periscopes popped up out of the conspiracist depths and put their gunners on high alert.[31]

Why else, conspiracists argued, would the Great Seal of the United States, which has appeared on the back of the $1 bill since the 1930s, read "New World Order"? First of all, it doesn't. That's a mistranslation of *Novus Ordo Seclorum*. The guy who designed the seal in 1782, Charles Thomson, pulled the phrase from Virgil's *Eclogues*. The whole phrase, *Annuit Cœptis Novus Ordo Seclorum*, is more accurately translated to "He [God] has Favored our Undertakings [of] A New Order of the Ages."[32] He was referencing the kind of freedom recently detailed in the Declaration of Independence . . . *unless, gasp, Virgil was himself a member of the New World Order working to enslave the ancients?!*

Regardless, following Bush's speeches and especially after Robertson's aforementioned 1991 book—a deeply antisemitic conspiracy-theory catch-all that connected the cabal to the coming apocalypse—America's fever dreams coalesced on the New World Order. Ever since, it has been the official bogeyman. But, of course, this bogeyman has always existed; he just occasionally changes masks.

———

Freemasonry, so iconic a conspiracy bubble it inspired the classic "Stonecutters" episode of *The Simpsons*, came to the colonies in the 1730s and quickly exploded in popularity. Benjamin Franklin and George Washington were members. The organization, which began as a stonemason guild in the Middle Ages, morphed into a kind of brotherhood promising members access to mystical knowledge that would spark a new Age of Enlightenment, but which one could only reach after varying levels of initiation. Interest in such organizations is largely driven by the desire to learn what secrets wait in the farthest of the back rooms. I've never been a Freemason, but I have been in a secret sorority, and can say with certainty that what's in the back room is usually cocaine.

Members also seem to have joined for the benefits one gets from being in any elite secret society: privilege, access, and favors. Accusations of more sinister conspiracies abounded nevertheless, not least because many members were in or tied to the government, including, ultimately, sixteen U.S. presidents, Ronald Reagan being the most recent. Clearly, conspiracists reasoned, they were plotting across Europe and America to control the globe and everyone on it. Fears of government infiltration are always with us. During times of elevated anxiety, it bubbles over. Cue the Red Menace.

In 1950, at a random fundraiser at a Republican women's club in West Virginia, Joseph McCarthy kicked off his Red Scare tour when he waved a piece of paper, claiming it bore the names of 205 Communists moonlighting in the State Department. The Associated Press picked up the story, at which point McCarthy was unable to produce a single name or this inflammatory piece of paper. Nevertheless, he spent the next four years calling everyone in the government a pinko and trying to catch them all in some dark Pokémon game. He claimed a group of powerful Communists from around the globe were already taking over China and the Soviet Union and were now coming for the rest of us.

Most in government barely tolerated McCarthy. Eventually, the Senate censured him for bringing "dishonor and disrepute" to the institution, and stripped him of his chairpersonships.[33] His behavior grew even more erratic as his drinking increased—to more than a quart of liquor a day—and he died suddenly at the age of forty-seven of a "liver ailment," while still in office.[34] But the damage was done. Many Americans assumed that strong concerted forces—whether Communists, industry barons, Jews, or some combination thereof—pulled strings behind the curtain in order to gain power and wealth, while ruining good simple folk. (Again, that *is* happening now, but the forces are less cinematic: corporate leaders who successfully lobby government for the right to increase their salaries while decreasing worker pay and increase their profits while spoiling natural environments.) McCarthy simply stoked an existing fire.

Something that sounds like a conspiracy theory but is 100 percent real: the candy Junior Mints helped fund a right-wing anti-Communist extremist movement that is still around today. Junior Mints were manufactured by Robert Welch, a prodigy who used his success and money in the candy business to fight the pinko conspiracies he perceived everywhere. He believed staunchly conservative President Eisenhower was secretly a Communist, that the burgeoning Civil Rights Movement in the South was a proxy war funded by Communists in order to create a "Soviet Negro Republic," and that Communists had put fluoride in public water supplies to undermine Americans' health (which you may recall General Jack Ripper ranting about in *Dr. Strangelove*).

In 1958, Welch launched a right-wing political advocacy group called the John Birch Society. The most successful anti-Communist organization in American history, its membership reached one hundred thousand people before shrinking in the late 1960s. But it's still around today, and claims personal responsibility for Trump's 2016 election. "The bulk of Trump's campaign was Birch," a former CEO of the organization told the Associated Press in 2024. "All he did was bring it out into the open."[35] It's worth noting that today's John Birch Society members also believe conspiracies about the Rothschilds, Davos, and the New World Order. The last thing I'll say about this group is that Welch also created Sugar Daddies, my favorite candy as a kid, which I only realize now has a wildly inappropriate name.

By the 1950s, Americans were already wary of powerful international collectives, having experienced a proliferation of global organizations and think tanks, including the Council on Foreign Relations in 1921, the United Nations in 1945, and NATO in 1949. Such a collective of international leaders is exactly how the Bible says the Antichrist will rise to power. And these groups were just the beginning. The World Economic Forum, known for its annual meeting in Davos, launched in 1971, the Trilateral Commission in 1973, NAFTA in 1994, and the annual UN Climate Change Conferences in 1995—they have all been targets of conspiracy theorists trying to stop Satan's minions from enslaving mankind.

In the middle of the 2009 UN Climate Summit in Copenhagen, radio host and peddler of destructive lies Alex Jones said this to his listeners: "Do you understand how diabolical this is? It isn't a bunch of idiot tree-huggers that mean well and just got their science wrong. . . . They came up with this idea to exterminate, and reduce births. . . . It is life and death! . . . Do you like being sterilized? Do you like being killed?! . . . This is the New World Order crashing the gates."[36] Trump, who has been a guest of Jones's, has increasingly employed the specter of a globalist cabal in campaign rhetoric. In 2024, the *New York Times* reviewed years of Trump's emails to supporters and public statements by Republicans in Congress. The investigation marked a "meteoric" rise in the use of conspiratorial tropes, from about thirty in the mid-2010s to more than three hundred in 2023. They often reference "the man behind the curtain," a "billionaire puppeteer," or, when writing more specifically, George Soros.[37] The nonagenarian financier has donated billions to liberal causes. But it's no coincidence that he is Jewish.

Antisemitism is like a tattoo on the body of conspiracy theory: it's always there, is a handy way to identify conspiracist rhetoric, and has kept quite a few conspiracists from gainful employment. The word *cabal* itself derives from the Jewish mystical practice Kabbalah—and *cabal* first appeared in usage around 1610 or 1620, at the height of the Reformation, as the Pilgrims were packing their trunks.

The eight-hundred-pound gorilla in the room of antisemitic conspiracist thinking is *The Protocols of the Elders of Zion*. It's a totally fake and plagiarized document purported to be a stolen set of notes from a global meeting of powerful Jews who were collaborating to control the world and enslave humanity in a police state. In reality, it was written by Russia's secret czarist police, working under Nicholas II, partly in response to Marx's *Communist Manifesto*, in order to create a scapegoat for the empire's economic problems and point the finger away from the Romanovs. But as we've learned from the internet, lies spread faster than truth. *The Protocols* first appeared in the 1890s. It disseminated through Russia and found its way to Western Europe and the United States in the late 1910s. Despite being exposed as plagiary in 1920, it kept circulating. An American edition was published in 1927 under the sponsorship of Henry Ford. One publisher estimates it's had at least eighty-one printings total.

This alleged organization of powerful Jews aiming to enslave or exterminate all of humanity surfaced in the 1980s under a different name: the Zionist Occupied Government (ZOG). ZOG, a bogeyman developed by the white-power movement, was supposedly a Jewish-run organization that also controlled the banks and the U.S. government, and used its influence, along with puppets in the media and academia, to try to eradicate the white race. I use the past tense there because ZOG eventually morphed into the New World Order.

One of the most recent and vocal supposed whistleblowers was Sherry Shriner, who died in 2018 but whose YouTube channel still has more than thirty thousand subscribers. As Arthur Bell did, she also turned her following into a cult. She preaches that a race of shape-shifting reptiles, most of whom are descended from Satan and comprise the New World Order, are planning to bring the Antichrist to power and . . . say it with me now . . . exterminate or enslave us all. In fact, she argues, most famous people have already been enslaved and are kept underground while their clones on earth execute the reptiles' plan.[38] One of her most popular videos, "When Clones Malfunction: The Fakes among Us," is clearly just a montage of people who happened to faint on camera.

Enslave or exterminate: just as Arthur Bell argued in his Mankind United textbook. That's always the endgame. Whether they're using radio waves, fluoride in municipal water, or microchips, the goal is to get rid of us all so they can take the world's riches and resources for themselves—"them" always being murky, difficult to name, and apparently unsuccessful for centuries, but all-powerful nevertheless. Alex Jones has argued the New World Order will exterminate 80 percent of the globe's population, way more than Mankind United's predicted 50 percent, in some form of conspiracy-theory inflation. And popular and prolific conspiracist Jay Hanson has said the elites will depopulate "most of the planet," and "the global genocide will be rationalized as a second chance for humanity—a new Garden of Eden—a new Genesis."

A lot of conspiracy theorists do have good intentions. They believe they're helping people by spreading truth. They feel they have to because those truths are being suppressed. Because the [insert power group] doesn't want you to know . . . because their plans are evil . . . because *they* are evil. But the only truth underlying any of this is the deep-seated conviction that *someone* is evil because vanquishing that kind of wickedness is easier to imagine than battling systems, biases and, scariest of all, the self.

If the only people harmed by this kind of thinking were the conspiracists themselves and their families, that would be tragedy enough. But these ideologies have much larger and more far-reaching consequences. At the center of a Venn diagram of rebellious anti-elites, political extremists, and conspiracists sits the modern white-power militia movement. It launched in the late seventies in response to the failure of the Vietnam War. The movement's de facto leader was Louis Beam, a veteran of that war, who attributed America's loss to a corrupt government that hamstrung soldiers from winning, abandoned prisoners of war, and denied a proper homecoming to those returning. In addition to his anti-Communism and racism, Beam also returned home with proficient military training and a U.S. government–sized chip on his shoulder. Active especially in his home state of Texas, he became increasingly involved with a resurgent Ku Klux Klan—KKK activity has swollen following every major American war—where he worked to radicalize members further into paramilitary factions. He aimed to continue the war, to, as he wrote, "bring it on home."

By the early nineties the Southern Poverty Law Center estimated the movement had ballooned to 5 million (a number including nonmember sympathizers). Whereas earlier white-power movements in American history, most notably the KKK, purported to support and serve a stronger (white) state, this modern iteration has aimed its arsenal of stolen weapons directly at the U.S. government (or, more specifically, at the alleged group of elites using our government as a puppet). An irony in the movement's growth out of the Vietnam War is the glaring and very real conspiracy within the U.S. government *against* Black soldiers fighting in the conflict. The Vietnam draft disproportionately pulled Black men from poor communities and specifically targeted those who had been involved in race riots. Once in ranks, Black soldiers received more courts-martial and fewer promotions.

Regardless, Beam focused on returning to a supposedly Utopian time before the war—before the economic downturns of the seventies, the oil crisis, the farm-foreclosure crisis, and the civil rights and women's rights movements— when jobs were plenty and the dominion of white men went unchallenged. Not only, members felt, was the government not protecting this supposed Eden for its people, it was actively conspiring against it. In 1983 Beam and the Aryan Nations World Congress declared war on the United States—or, rather, on the Zionist Occupied Government, which purportedly controlled the U.S. (and the United Nations, banks, and a number of journalists and academics).

"America's political leaders, bankers, church ministers, newsmen, sports stars and hippies called us baby killers, and threw chicken blood on some of us when we returned home," he wrote. "You're damn right I'm mad! I've had enough! I want these same traitors to face their enemy now, the American fighting man they betrayed, all three million of us." He saw loss of civilian lives as a necessary tactic. Any weapon would do. "A sword in the year of our Lord 1981 can be an M-16, three sticks of dynamite taped together, a twelve-gauge, a can of gas, or whatever is suitable to carry out any commission of the Lord that has been entrusted to you."[39] They saw themselves as the kind of monomythic warriors studied by Robert Jewett and John Shelton Lawrence. After a massacre of Communist demonstrators in Greensboro, North Carolina, in 1979, the movement put out pamphlets calling one of the shooters "Greensboro's answer to John Wayne."[40] Ironically, while conspiracists in the militia movement claim a shadowy cabal uses extreme power and weapons to control them, they are themselves secretive and use extreme power via weapons to commit violence, one of the most blatant forms of control one can exercise. In that way, we manifest what we fear into reality. We become the enemy we claim to hate. Or maybe we invent the enemy in our image to justify acting on our impulses.

———

Eden dreams, particularly when paired with preparation for battles against a super state, dovetail neatly with apocalyptic thinking. The white-power movement dreams of what would follow an epic battle, namely a white homeland. Others simply want to overturn the U.S. government. Still others believe battling the government is only the beginning of an ultimate and epic race war. Extremist Christian Identity, which Beam followed, teaches that white people are the true descendants of the lost tribes of Israel. Its followers also believe God wants them to help rid the world of the damned—that is, non-whites, including Jews—before Jesus returns. A variety of Christian white separatist groups all ascribe to similar beliefs, including also Aryan Nations; the Covenant, the Sword, and the Arm of the Lord; and the cult at Elohim City. Through ten years of reporting, resulting in the masterpiece *Bring the War Home: The White Power Movement and Paramilitary America*, Kathleen Belew traces connections between groups, Christian or otherwise, that were previously assumed distinct. She proves that smaller cells across the country were indeed collaborating despite hiding their communications with one another in an effort to thwart an organization-wide takedown. The goal was to make each act of violence appear as if conducted by a lone wolf. She also draws a line directly from Louis Beam to Oklahoma City bomber Timothy McVeigh.

In the early nineties, Beam's efforts escalated. The United States had proved itself an aggressive superstate, he believed, with its outsized uses of force against separatist compounds, including that of the Waco, Texas, Branch Davidians in 1993. When we think of Waco, we think of David Koresh, the cult leader who arrived at the compound ten years prior, methodically took over, proclaimed he was the Messiah, changed his name, took a bunch of underaged wives, had a slew of babies, collected an unholy arsenal for an end-times battle, and then died during a government siege in 1993. Looking backward today, though, it's clear the story continued. The underground but well-connected white-power militia movement co-opted the Waco story—despite the cult's harmonious, multiracial demographics—and used it as a broad-based rallying cry to fight the American government.

To be fair, the Branch Davidians did share some ideology with the militias. Koresh had been preaching that the U.S. government—which he called the forces of Babylon—would soon wage war against the Davidians, God's chosen people. He'd trained his flock to use their arsenal in an imminent attack. They were not only ready but eager to die in this battle, believing they would immediately resurrect and lead God's army.

Koresh manifested what he preached. A botched raid by the Bureau of Alcohol, Tobacco, and Firearms on February 28 left dead six Branch Davidians, and four ATF agents. The fire that devoured the compound fifty-one days later on April 19 killed most of the seventy-five people who died, including twenty-five children. In the Netflix documentary series *Waco: American Apocalypse*, Chris Whitcomb, a sniper with the Hostage Rescue Team, describes the scene after the fire, where burning paper was floating above the ground in the thermal heat patterns. "It was raining Bible pages," he says. "In the embers were 1.6 million rounds of rifle ammo cooking off. So it's ammo popping off everywhere you go. And skulls everywhere. And half-burned bodies. It was apocalyptic carnage."[41]

Independent investigators determined that members of the cult started the fire.[42] Even so, most now agree that the ATF and FBI had far overstepped a boundary, using outsized force in the raid and siege. Following the disaster, when the public pointed its finger at the government, Beam and his conspirators were able to say, *We told you so*. This is also what they'd done a year prior, following the Ruby Ridge disaster, when the government came out full force against a single family.

Randy Weaver, Vietnam veteran, white separatist, and Aryan Nations member, lived with his family in a remote area of Idaho sympathetic to white separatists, called Ruby Ridge. At an Aryan Nations World Congress in 1989, an undercover ATF informant convinced Weaver to sell him two sawed-off shotguns. Weaver was indicted on illegal weapons charges. But then he failed to reappear in court, in part because he didn't know the date had changed. One escalation after another resulted in a shoot-out on his property, where Weaver had holed up with his wife and five children, one of whom was an infant. It left two dead: a deputy U.S. marshal and Weaver's fourteen-year-old son, who was shot in the back.

The government began a siege. Hundreds of federal agents appeared outside the remote Idaho home with military-grade equipment and set up a command post. Randy wrote a public letter explaining his family had met a "ZOG/ New World Order ambush."[43] His wife, Vicki, eventually took a gunshot to the head—while holding the couple's baby. The trope of the vulnerable white woman, long used by white supremacists to stoke fears, was called forth again: clearly, they claimed, white women were not only under attack by men of color but by the state itself.

White-power militia members argued the government was acting as a violent superstate, using excessive and tyrannical force against its citizens, at the behest of an evil ring. They believed the United Nations was coming soon to put white people into concentration camps. McVeigh was one of many who presumed the camps were already built and waiting to be filled. *Extermination and enslavement.*

McVeigh was directly influenced by Waco and Ruby Ridge and was inspired to fight back. Belew connects him to a variety of white-power cells and compounds, all on a neat timeline, leading up to their payback: the explosion outside the Alfred P. Murrah Federal Building in Oklahoma City that killed 168 people in 1995. He intentionally attacked on the same date as the Waco fire; he also made that date the birthday on his fake ID. He determined the civilian deaths were justified because, since they worked for the government, they were complicit in the New World Order. After Waco, the U.S. government had become more judicious with its use of force—a prudent move that nevertheless swung the pendulum too far. The reticence of law enforcement to move against the white-power movement likely contributed to its failure to ascertain and thwart McVeigh's plans.

The Oklahoma City bombing was followed by a dizzying number of violent acts committed by militia members and other white-power activists, including shootings, bombings, and attempted bombings at government buildings, abortion clinics, gay bars, and a Jewish community center. A year later, the number of extreme anti-government groups had risen sharply to 858, according to the Southern Poverty Law Center. By 2008, the number was down to 149, largely due to crackdowns from the federal government. But after the election of Barack Obama, it soared again to 1,360. The number has dipped since, but is once again on the rise. Members of militias including the Oath Keepers and the Texas Freedom Force, as well as extremist groups including the Three Percenters and the far right Proud Boys, were all present on January 6, 2021.

The Oath Keepers have been described by the FBI as a "large but loose, organized collection of militias who believe that the federal government has been coopted by a shadowy conspiracy that is trying to strip American citizens of their rights." Robert Gieswein, who met up with Proud Boys before storming the Capitol, where he sprayed multiple officers with an aerosol and tried to gain access to Nancy Pelosi's office, told reporters that "corrupt" politicians—including, he said, Joe Biden and Kamala Harris—were conspiring with the "Rothschilds and Rockefellers." (These two families are commonly believed by conspiracists to be part of a secret group controlling global currency.)[44]

But militia members were not the majority of those who stormed the Capitol on January 6, 2021. Most were not even conspiracy theorists—or at least hadn't been before they were indoctrinated into a kind of cult, the one that exists at the intersection of QAnon and Donald Trump.

Anti-elitism, rebellion, and fears of global collusion have come together spectacularly in the QAnon phenomenon. What began in October 2017 with a few random message-board posts and eventually gathered an estimated hundreds of thousands of followers is not a cult per se. It's a LARP (live action role play) by someone claiming to be a collection of high-ranking civilian and military personnel who work closely with Trump. This poster claims Trump has instructed them to leak information anonymously to the public—via 4chan and eventually 8kun, lightly trafficked message boards of highly questionable repute—about Trump's shadow war against pedophile Satan worshipers in government and media. It's a conspiracy theory. But when you combine QAnon with Trumpism—and almost every subscriber to this belief system does—you have what I and others argue is indeed a destructive cult.

Exhibit A: the group exercises undue influence. The anonymous con artist posing as Q uses psychological tricks, thought-stopping clichés, and isolation techniques to woo users and convince them of outlandish claims. Exhibit B: actual harm is done either to members or the public. In addition to a collection of outré crimes committed by adherents in the name of the movement, QAnon has wrecked countless families, as it encourages believers to separate themselves from loved ones. And, of course, the January 6 insurrection resulted in seven deaths (including the suicides of four officers, shortly thereafter), and left 150 officers injured.[45]

Exhibit C: a leader is worshiped. QAnon followers see Trump as a savior, ridding America of traitorous liberals and the deep state, of Satan-worshiping pedophiles and sex traffickers. This they believe will happen via secret military tribunals and, eventually, imprisonment or execution. In the beginning, Q promised it would happen soon. In "drop" (message posting) #34, in November 2017, right after the LARP began and was especially focused on Hillary Clinton, Q wrote, "Over the course of the next several days you will undoubtedly realize that we are taking back our great country (the land of the free) from the evil tyrants that wish to do us harm and destroy the last remaining refuge of shining light."[46] In that one post are all the hallmarks of the classic American conspiracy theory: the supposed collusion, the anti-elitism, the rebelliousness. As with Mankind United, there was something good simple folk could do: in this case, proselytize. YouTube pages, Facebook pages, and Twitter (now X) profiles kudzued the internet to interpret drops, spread the word, and #savethechildren. The internet has not only shattered traditional communities, but enabled ideological communities to sprout, wherein following and leading are explicit and groupthink stiffens.

Times of turmoil, transition, and uncertainty—for example, a global pandemic hitting at a time of extreme income inequality and a rapidly warming planet—are often accompanied by increases in apocalyptic movements. "People lose their sense of bearing in the world, and then the apocalyptic scenario provides a clean, simple answer," says Lorne Dawson, professor of sociology and religious studies at the University of Waterloo. Such clean, simple answers include the ideas that God has a plan; that a clear demarcation exists between who's good and evil; that a specific set of behaviors will ensure that good triumphs; and since it's God's plan, that extreme actions are justified. This is exactly how a bunch of otherwise law-abiding family people found themselves pushing through Capitol crowd-control gates, smashing windows, and assaulting officers on January 6, 2021.

What's happening in the center of the QAnon-Trump Venn diagram shares disturbing similarities with doomsday groups that have preceded it. "The same language is there. 'Trust the plan.' 'Enjoy the show,'" Dawson says, quoting a couple of common QAnon slogans. "The idea that it's all about to wrap up and the bad guys will be punished. Trump is a messiah figure here to 'drain the swamp.'"

Under the banner of Trump, the QAnon conspiracy theory went mainstream. The president of the United States retweeted hundreds of believers and often shared QAnon memes. Almost a hundred Q followers ran for political office on Republican tickets between 2018 and 2020.[47] A September 2020 poll discovered that 56 percent of Republican voters believed QAnon theories were either mostly or partly true.[48] In late 2023, 23 percent of Republicans said they "subscribe to the theory that the centers of power are controlled by Satan-worshiping pedophiles atop a child sex-trafficking operation."[49]

As a phenomenon, it seemed to have come out of nowhere. But of course, that wasn't the case—and not only because the New World Order conspiracy theory had been brewing for four hundred years under one name or another, but, more specifically, because in the 1950s, the basic ideas fueling classic American conspiracist thought were adopted and further legitimized by a handful of strategists who developed them into what has since become a powerful branch of the Republican Party.

———

Scholar Kevin Mattson calls the movement Post World War II Conservatism. In his book *Rebels All!: A Short History of the Conservative Mind in Postwar*

America, Mattson argues that in spite of the Republican Party's incredible twenty-first-century successes—not only in elections, but also Supreme Court nominees and infotainment media domination—a certain branch of conservativism still sees itself "as embattled populists ready to combat a monstrously powerful liberal elite." The movement was born during the apocalyptic battle of the Cold War. The "mindset of catastrophe," "framed by the necessity of war," never left it. Still today, "its sense of apocalypse and righteousness lends itself to the use of whatever means necessary."[50]

Post World War II Conservatism has been rebellious and anti-intellectual from the jump. It was pioneered by William F Buckley Jr., an intellectual himself who was nevertheless able to malign intellectualism and then equate it with liberalism. His book *God and Man at Yale* railed against university professors and exploded him onto the scene.[51] A few years later, he copublished a book defending Joseph McCarthy, and then, in 1955, founded the magazine *National Review*, which quickly became and remains a hallmark of American conservative thought. To Buckley, "The liberal bureaucrat, the staid university administrator, the left-wing journalist, the egghead intellectual—all of these figures constituted something bigger, a massive conspiracy against conservative authenticity and anger."[52]

Ironically, many in the first generation of this movement had previously been on the other end of extremism—as Communists, Trotskyists, or new radicals—before or during the sixties. Mattson argues that, although one ideology had been swapped for another among these hard leftists turned far rightists, the style of engagement remained the same: extremism, with which they were infatuated "because it ordered the world they observed." Mattson writes, "The conservative has become a ruckus hell raiser, tearing down structures."[53]

Siding with rebels over the years, the movement has rallied behind resistance: notably, against the push for civil rights in the South as well as against traditional education by supporting the homeschool movement and intelligent design. Mattson's book was published in 2008. During an interview, he told me, "I don't think much has changed, to be quite honest." Carrying the torch after Buckley, George W. Bush, and Ann Coulter, he says, have been Steve Bannon, Roger Stone, Marjorie Taylor Greene, and, of course, Trump. The far right's ousting of former speaker of the house Kevin McCarthy in 2023 proved the Republican Party so fractious and rebellious as to be outright ungovernable.

Another self-proclaimed and assured "warrior" of this movement is Ginni Thomas, wife of Supreme Court justice Clarence Thomas. In 2019, she secured $600,000 in anonymous donations for Crowdsourcers, an activist group intended to "focus on the Left's escalating war across American culture." At a Council for National Policy gathering in October 2018—a time when conservatives controlled the House, the Senate, and the presidency, a trifecta that hadn't occurred since 2005—Thomas nevertheless claimed that the "hard left" was "controlling the media and corporations and Hollywood and education. And we're in the minority in our country."[54] The similarities between her rhetoric and that of New World Order conspiracists is staggering. Only the enemy is different.

And how is it possible for a group with power to continually maintain it has none? Identity. By the time Reagan was in office, Mattson argues that the postmodern conservative had "embraced the status of permanent rebel against a liberal establishment, even though that liberal establishment was rather rickety by that point." Clinging to such a status provides one, no matter the movement, with certain privileges. For example, because rebels lack authority, they need not be held accountable; their persecuted status inherently legitimizes their needs and desires; and if they're fighting a tyrant, all tactics are justified. In order to achieve their goals, they *must* be the minority under attack. It's less an identity than a means to an end.

Look, I didn't set out to write a political book. (And I haven't.) I'm just trying to objectively locate the modern world's echoes of doomsday thought. Sure, there are examples of doomsday thought on the far left. For example, when Democrats refused to discuss Biden's age, that was us-versus-them thinking. And there have been far-left cults, the Sullivanians and Jonestown being two of the most well known. Nevertheless, in 2020s America, these ideologies are stationed with the alt-right. It's not my fault that most of the train lines I'm following terminate at the alt-right depot. Maybe I was naïve not to see it coming—perhaps there's a Mankind United textbook you want to sell me—but if you want to get on someone's case about it, talk to Marjorie Taylor Greene.

———

In March 2023, Trump held his first 2024 presidential campaign rally in Waco, the site of the catalyst of the anti-government movement—the one that gave millions of Americans an enemy and eventually swept Donald Trump into office. After railing against the government and Justice Department for the indictments brought against him, he ominously warned the crowd, "They're not coming after me, they're coming after you."[55] How might the Branch Davidians who perished in Waco feel about Trump co-opting their demise? We at least know what the group's current pastor, Charles Pace, believes: "Donald Trump is the anointed of God. He is the battering ram that God is using to bring down the Deep State of Babylon." If Trump's choice of locale was coincidence or cleverness, he won't say. But Pace believes it was "a statement—that he was sieged by the F.B.I. at Mar-a-Lago and that they were accusing him of different things that aren't really true, just like David Koresh was accused by the F.B.I. when they sieged him."[56]

Cult followers and conspiracists are treated like resources to be extracted. Trump, Q, and the various mouthpieces who spread the Big Lie for their own self-promotion, planted seeds of fury that were harvested on January 6, 2021. Former Oath Keeper and Capitol stormer Jason Dolan told the jury during his trial for seditious conspiracy in October 2022, "I wanted them to hear and feel the anger, the frustration, the rage that I felt."[57]

———

The Mankind United architect Arthur Bell is just one in a long line of conspiracy theorists who've mined rage and fear for their own benefit. When the government tried to stop him, the Voice of the Right Idea simply incorporated his organization into a church and funneled his money where it couldn't be taxed. Then he began recruiting. Eight hundred and fifty signed up to be student ministers in the newly founded Christ's Church of the Golden Rule, at which point they were "freed from the bondage of ownership" of their property and resources—that is, they had to give them to the church—and required to cut off connection with the rest of world.[58]

Bell put $3 million into more than a hundred real estate properties in California and Oregon—in 1945, California newspapers estimated church assets at $5 million ($83.6 million today)—and used his acolytes' free labor to run them all.[59] Student ministers worked a minimum of twelve hours a day, six days a week, a far cry from the white-hat Sponsors' promise of four hours a day, four days a week.[60] In 1945, the California attorney general came after the church, filing a complaint in state bankruptcy courts. The resulting battle played out for more than six years in federal court. Bell was forced to pay all claims, which he did by 1951.[61]

Then, after taking his followers' money, time, vitality, and connection to the outside world, he also stole their dream: he announced the Sponsors had changed their minds. Because "the overwhelming percentage of lazy, and almost wholly selfish, human beings now occupying this planet" were not worth saving, the Sponsors would let the Rulers destroy the world. Fortunately for his remaining followers, Bell explained that the Sponsors would at least spare a chosen few by sending them to a separate planetary system, a translation that would occur "during the brief instant immediately preceding one's so-called death."[62] Then Bell disappeared.

This is almost exactly what the Heaven's Gate followers of Marshall Applewhite believed, when thirty-nine of them together ingested fatal doses of phenobarbital inside a mansion in Rancho Santa Fe, California, in 1997. The only significant difference I see is that Applewhite seems to have believed what he preached. For Bell it was a grift. One wonders how many of his followers, as members of Heaven's Gate did, swallowed something in order to lose themselves in translation.

CHAPTER 4

LIAR FOR HIRE

ON CONSUMPTION AND SALVATION

In the fall of 1978, Peter McWilliams jumped up and down in a conference room in Philadelphia, shouting, "I want freedom! I want freedom!" His partner screamed, "How much do you want it?" and "Louder! I can't hear you!" They were among more than two hundred participants in a personal-growth seminar called Insight. The exercise had started calmly but developed into a cacophony of desire hollered at a conference-center ceiling. Then, McWilliams passed out.

Seminar assistants helped him into a chair. When the trainer announced a break, several of the helpers surrounded McWilliams in wonder. They had "never seen the Spirit hit anyone so powerfully." They said it had been as if "a lightning bolt came down from the highest heavens," and, cryptically, that "the Traveler must love you an awful lot to give you a gift like that."

This Traveler character, McWilliams later learned, was a guy who called himself John-Roger, leader of a group called the Movement of Spiritual Inner Awareness, or M.S.I.A. Insiders pronounced the acronym "Messiah." Turns out, this Insight class was not merely a personal-growth seminar—one of many in the heady "Me Decade" of the seventies and early eighties, when self-investigation was de rigueur—but also a pipeline leading unsuspecting New Age and self-help seekers into a destructive cult. Many inside that Philadelphia conference room were already members. They told McWilliams they could feel incredible energy radiating from him and that it was a blessing just to stand near him. He didn't look back. During his time in the group, he would give its leader, John-Roger, a total of a million dollars. It would be sixteen years before McWilliams left and finally got that freedom he so exuberantly desired.

McWilliams had learned about Insight during a low point. While seeking solace in self-help, he saw an advertisement in a New Age magazine that promised techniques for personal growth, and drove from New York to Philadelphia for a seminar that night. Since M.S.I.A. was headquartered on the West Coast, his next step in the pipeline was a series of prerecorded seminars. His new friends explained that once he'd been introduced to the guru's teachings, John-Roger, a powerful being who only comes around every twenty-five thousand years and has a direct line to God, would visit McWilliams in his dreams and initiate him into "the astral level of consciousness."[1] But such initiations came with a threat. During visitations, the guru also purportedly toured people through their terrible past lives, and previewed how horrific future lives would be if they didn't accept his teachings. It's like if the Ghosts of Christmas Past and Future were mafiosi.

McWilliams admits finding much of the doctrine silly. But he kept attending seminars. He liked the other people. He found in J-R's teachings at least some practical advice. And he was looking for guidance. Eventually, he moved to Los Angeles to be closer to the guru with a bad perm. It shouldn't be important that John-Roger permed his hair from, photographs suggest, around 1978 until he died in 2014, but I can't resist telling you. At no point during those thirty-six years was it a good look. But who could have told him? Surely no one criticized Jesus's strappy sandals or Buddha's belly fat; John-Roger claimed a higher divinity than both.

Specifically, he claimed three simultaneous spiritual identities. First, he was John-Roger, which itself contains two sub-identities: that of Roger Delano Hinkins, the man he was before a kidney-stone operation in 1963 sent him into a nine-day coma; and that of John the apostle, a being he claims entered him during that coma. After the operation, Hinkins began calling himself John-Roger and a guru con artist was born. A high school teacher at the time, he started instructing his students in self-hypnosis techniques, ran afoul with school administration, and left. He founded M.S.I.A. in 1971, pumped out pamphlets and audiocassettes, and quickly grew a following.[2]

His second supposed identity, as we move in order up the hierarchy, was the Mystical Traveler, sometimes known simply as the Traveler. This title referred to a mantle of sorts that was passed through history from one awakened guru to the next. It's kind of like this mug at my college that was willed down each year from a graduating senior to a junior, except that in the case of M.S.I.A., the mug gave its owner a direct link to God, and "complete, conscious awareness." My college friend could only have achieved that if her mug contained psilocybin tea. I'm sure at some point it did. So maybe she was also a Mystical Traveler and I was closest to God while sitting in Astronomy 201.

Except I'm sure she wasn't, not only because John-Roger invented the mantle but also because previous Mystical Travelers were almost exclusively men. Among the dozens John-Roger listed were Noah, Hammurabi, Ramses II, Confucius, Pythagoras, Merlin, Mohammed, Michelangelo, and Walt Whitman. Only one woman made the cut, Joan of Arc. John-Roger disliked women.[3] He arguably disliked gay men more, which was possibly a direct result of being one himself, a truth he hid fiercely.[4] To be clear, though, he seems to have preferred to coerce/rape *heterosexual* male disciples. But I'm getting ahead of myself. For now I'll just add that John-Roger probably didn't know Walt Whitman was queer.

His third claimed identity was called the Preceptor Consciousness. This paragraph will be short because the guy barely explained it, except to say this position was also a sort of mug-of-history, but one that sits in a cabinet for twenty-five thousand years between each physical incarnation. The position— and whoever happens to catch it—outranks every divinity in history, except God, but is also BFFs with God.[5] This time frame, of course, created a sense of urgency among John-Roger's followers. Exit the cage of reincarnation now or wait another twenty-five thousand years. That's a lot more lives to struggle through, an especially scary proposition in the eighties, when images of the future included aliens bursting from bellies.

If you're confused by John-Roger's ideology, you're paying attention. And Peter McWilliams was an intelligent man. And an accomplished one. He wrote best-selling books—that were *self-published*. A rare phenomenon. Even his self-published books of *poetry* sold well, an achievement so unlikely, it may as well happen every twenty-five thousand years.[6] His work was covered in *Time* magazine and the *Wall Street Journal*.[7]

And yet, when John-Roger casually said in 1988 that McWilliams had AIDS and about nine months to live, but that he, the Mystical Traveler, would keep McWilliams alive as long as the stricken agreed to make said Traveler the coauthor of any future books—an agreement that ultimately netted John-Roger an estimated $550,000, tax-free—McWilliams honestly believed this self-hating man with a bad perm. He fell for a ludicrous scam. He did so even though he was initially skeptical, particularly after the first taped John-Roger seminar he attended, the one where he was told this guy would terrify him in his dreams like some woo-woo Freddy Krueger.

Of that seminar, he writes that after the video of John-Roger "in his Hawaiian shirt, explaining how essential he was to the functioning of the planet earth" and "how cozy he was with God," "I was appalled. What arrogance. What megalomania. What a lousy shirt."[8] McWilliams was also a riot. His memoir, *Life 102: What to Do When Your Guru Sues You*, is the funniest cult book I've read. He wrote it in less than two months. Respect.

Even so, McWilliams was no match for undue influence and thought-control techniques, which eventually silenced his initial trepidations along with many of his critical-thinking skills. Even after allegations of sexual abuse surfaced, McWilliams remained unwaveringly loyal. You can find a clip of him in a *Geraldo* segment, blocking the camera of a reporter trying to ambush a book signing.[9] While reading *Life 102*, I couldn't help but fantasize about him bailing before they could hook him. But he had a vested interest. He desperately wanted enlightenment. He believed that somewhere the keys to the doors of perception waited to be found. At the time, much of America agreed.

"It was the zeitgeist," David Lane, a philosophy professor at Mt. San Antonio College, told me during an interview. "Back in the sixties and seventies, it was 'Hey man, let's get enlightened. Let's find some spiritual liberation.'" To dangerously reduce decades of cultural phenomena and movements into one handy list, some of the forces that led an entire generation to seek consciousness expansion include: the creation of and reports about LSD, the Cuban Missile

Crisis and fears of nuclear holocaust, the realities of Jim Crow being aired by
the Civil Rights Movement, and a string of assassinations.

Laying the groundwork for this national search for enlightenment was what
became known as the Human Potential Movement.[10] Proponents argued that
humans are capable of much more than previously explored; if we can tap into
unused potential, we can achieve fulfillment for ourselves while also spreading
enlightenment to others and toward the improvement of society at large. Soon,
the desire to achieve this kind of New Jerusalem through self-exploration would
rush the nation. In 1976, Tom Wolfe dubbed the seventies the "'Me' Decade"
in *New York* magazine, where he argued the movement constituted America's
Third Great Awakening.[11]

Fueling but also complicating the enlightenment rush was the 1965 Immigration and Nationality Act. When Lyndon Johnson abolished national-origins
quotas, Indians immigrated in droves, particularly to the West Coast. "They
brought spiritual ideas a lot of Americans were not yet exposed to," Lane
explains. This influx met a generation of young adults who desired the order,
comfort, and safety of spiritual salvation, but were too disillusioned by the
previous generation's actions to remain brand loyal to religions of their youth.
Eastern philosophies surrounding reincarnation, meditation, and consciousness, though not new to the country, suddenly went viral. Enter scam artists
looking to ride the guru wave, to exploit a new camouflage, in order to make a
buck and, at worst, secure the kind of absolute power only divinity provides.
For example, John-Roger. McWilliams wasn't the only intelligent person he
snagged.

Arianna Huffington followed too. She joined M.S.I.A. in the organization's
early years, long before Insight seminars were introduced as a pipeline. She was
baptized into the group in the River Jordan with other devotees. In 1978 she
became a minister.[12] Then, during her former husband Michael Huffington's
1994 Senate campaign, she distanced herself from John-Roger, and claimed
he was merely a friend.[13] According to McWilliams, the marriage had been
arranged in part by John-Roger, who was always eager to lure money into the
fold. (After Huffington's father sold his natural-gas business in 1990, Forbes
magazine estimated the magnate's wealth at $310 million.)[14]

These high-profile followers fell for what wasn't even a novel movement. M.S.I.A. rather blatantly ripped off the ideologies—and often the texts, word for word—of a movement called Eckankar. Lane noticed this because he was intimately familiar with the teachings of Eckankar on account of having exposed that group's leader for stealing most of its ideas from Radhasoami, a nineteenth-century Indian movement born of surat shabd yoga. And he knew Radhasoami because he was a devotee. Lane, at the time a young, floppy-haired college student and surfer, was also a seeker—but one with a low threshold for BS. His exposé prompted a substantial exodus from Eckankar.

Lane encountered one of John-Roger's books in a New Age bookstore, noticed the plagiarism, called to request an interview, and met with the self-styled guru at his mansion in Los Angeles's Mandeville Canyon. "I should've known something was weird when you see six really good-looking guys in short-shorts washing his Lincoln car," Lane explains. He had been told by an assistant that he'd have ten minutes with the master. When John-Roger saw him, he generously spent six hours. The guru appeared curious and helpful, and gave the handsome undergrad his personal phone number. After that, they met several more times. J-R, as his disciples called him, even sent Lane Christmas cards. "He always wanted to know my latest research," he says. At one point, he even offered $5,000 to help with it, which Lane declined.

Although Lane sensed M.S.I.A. was a scam, he was busy with other pursuits and had little interest in exposing it. But then in 1983, a handful of high-ranking staffers defected. They needed someone they could trust to tell their story, who already understood the organization. They called Lane, now in graduate school. After recording the defectors' testimony during a five-hour meeting, Lane recalls, "I called John-Roger at his personal bat number, and he goes absolutely apeshit. I thought, 'Oh yeah, they're telling the truth.'"

One of those Lincoln car-washing hunks may have been Victor Toso, who was invited to move into John-Roger's Mandeville Canyon home in the summer of 1977. Toso eventually became one of Insight's top "facilitators" (teachers). He was tall and handsome, serious but kind. A friend had introduced him to the movement in 1976. "I felt that I was on holy ground," he told me during an interview. "The first words out of [John-Roger's] mouth were 'Everything I'm going to tell you is a lie. You've got to find out what the truth is.'" As someone who'd grown up a missionary kid in the Lutheran Church, hearing thousands of sermons that claimed to be *the* truth, Toso was captivated. "Instead of making me suspicious, it took away all resistance." After only one night, he canceled his plans to attend Lutheran seminary school, and instead joined M.S.I.A.

Toso began meditating eight hours a day. The practice was to envisage the guru's face until you finally connected, at which point he'd appear. During Toso's first week of efforts, it worked. The Traveler appeared to him, he recalls, "but something was desperately wrong—his penis was hanging out." In retrospect, he thinks spirits were providing him with data of what his future held. At the time, he believed he was himself unclean and deviant, so much so that he had introduced a filthy image into something holy.

A year later, the Traveler asked the handsome devotee to move into Mandeville Canyon. There was no bedroom for him but, surprise, surprise, he could share John-Roger's king bed. "Late into the nights, he would talk. There was nothing sexual about it. I was just blissed out in paradise," Toso explains. But even in bliss, there were threats. "[J-R] said, 'There's no way to even describe how lucky you are to have found this place. But you've gotta be careful because if you slide off the path, you'll wish you'd never lived.'"

Here are some allegations of John-Roger's criminal activity: embezzlement, insurance fraud, and loads of petty crimes, such as illegal phone lines, exchanging foreign currency on the black market, and zoning violations. When one neighbor, who had vocally fought John-Roger's continued use of a residential home for commercial purposes, died of a heart attack, the Traveler took credit. "I had to remove him," he claimed. "He never should have struck against me."

And there was sexual coercion. Whatever one of J-R's targets wanted, whether spiritually or materially, the Traveler promised it in exchange for acquiescence. He even said sexual acts with him could cure illnesses. It was neither subtle nor poetic, when he told one staffer, "If you give me a blow job, that will get rid of your cold."

The guru sometimes told those he seduced that his sperm was a kind of intergalactic homing device, that if they had the "seed of the Traveler" in them, then the Traveler could never lose them in time and space. On other occasions, he explained to disciples that they needed "rectal innerphases" in order to burn off karma. And if these affairs resulted in any physical or emotional pain, that was just evidence that the sex was leading them to work off karma faster. He even claimed that the line "thy rod and thy staff, they comfort me" from Psalms was a specific reference to his erect penis. Imagine the amount of grooming and influence required for a person to hear that and not assume it's a joke.

The Traveler built a harem of heterosexual men, and cycled through its members at his whim, while keeping each from knowing he also enjoyed intercourse with the others. This harem was colloquially known as "the Guys." J-R said it was necessary they live in his home because the Traveler's physical body needed protection from negative forces that came at night while his spirit journeyed to other universes to do whatever Mystical Travelers do. Each evening, John-Roger announced to one of the Guys, "You'll be watching the body tonight."[15] Meanwhile, J-R claimed he was celibate.

The next step in John-Roger's eventual seduction of Victor Toso was to ice him out. He made a habit of mocking Victor while the latter was onstage before a thousand Insight trainees. Then J-R took all of his staff to Australia for Christmas—except Toso. Alone in Mandeville Canyon for the holiday, he did his best to eliminate negativity and doubt, to find his way back before the group returned.

"When I picked them up at the airport, there was this sinking feeling that I had not achieved it, and he was going to ask me to leave," Toso told me. Sure enough, the guru explained his plans to relocate Toso to one of the movement's centers in West Los Angeles. "My twenty-five-thousand-year chance was gone," he recalls thinking. "The doors were shut. I begged. I was on my knees. He was sitting in his chair." At this point in my conversation with him, Toso pauses for a few moments before continuing. "Even to this day, I can't picture how it was that I ended up with his penis in my mouth." Following that encounter, Toso was welcomed back without explanation. "The next day, the doors were open, and I could do no wrong. Anything I wanted, I could've had. There was a part of me that thought, 'If only I'd known it was this easy.'"

After many years and a lot of processing, Toso understands he was coerced and manipulated. At the time, he chastised himself for not figuring out the contract earlier, asking himself, he recalls, "Why did I not love him enough to be able to give him what he wanted?" The guru told him they had a unique relationship, that this didn't happen with anyone else. Toso believed that until, years later, he heard the unmistakable sounds of oral sex coming from an adjacent room at an Insight training. After that, he ended his sexual relationship with the Traveler. But he'd grown too valuable to banish.

Toso was one of the best and most beloved trainers in Insight. The program supposedly aimed to improve attendees' lives through awareness. (Its website today promises to "support you in looking at what's working and not working in your life and how you can make changes that will support you in creating and living a life you love.")[16] Insight was not only a pipeline for M.S.I.A. recruits but a huge moneymaker. By 1979, after less than two years in operation, it had brought in almost $2 million. The Traveler called it his "little money machine."[17] Toso estimates that during his last year alone, he personally delivered $750,000 to John-Roger through Insight.

During our interview, Toso took me through a few exercises. His joy for teaching them is palpable. One exercise—introduced while a loudspeaker played the Beatles' "Do You Want to Know a Secret?"—encouraged trainees to share the one secret they'd never told anyone, about which they felt the most shame. (Toso and McWilliams both recall hearing people admit to murders.) The experience for trainees was one of unburdening, freedom. "It was profound, the turnaround these people were having just by unloading those things," Toso recalls. He didn't know that John-Roger recorded many of the trainings as part of his power-hungry agenda.

This brings me back to the list of John-Rogers's alleged illegal activities. He bugged the rooms in his homes and centers to gather blackmailing fodder as well as information he could use to appear clairvoyant. (This is a common cult tactic.) He was also practicing medicine without a license (an ironic phrase, since there was no medicine involved). Tragically, when one M.S.I.A. follower discovered a lump in her breast, but received a good prognosis from her doctor, who wanted to surgically remove it, she first went to her guru for advice. John-Roger said simply, "I wouldn't let them cut into me." Instead, she saw a variety of healers he recommended. Much later, she relented to traditional treatment, but it was too late. McWilliams reports that when J-R heard she'd died, the Traveler responded, "I told her not to let them cut into her."[18]

In 1984, when about five thousand people were in the movement, Lane published a paper based in part on the accusations of the five defectors who'd approached him. "The J-R Controversy: A Critical Analysis of John-Roger Hinkins and M.S.I.A." barely cracked the surface—many of the allegations mentioned above only became public later—but even so, J-R went on the offensive. The defectors had acid thrown on their cars and their tires slashed. They and Lane all received death threats and endless harassing phone calls. Some of the defectors went into hiding. Later that year, one of them met with John-Roger and then shared the conversation with *People* magazine: "He informed me that some people wanted to kill [defectors] Wendell and Wesley. He spent 10 minutes telling me how they were going to make it look like a car accident. He said that no one would be able to trace it back to him."[19]

Toso was knee-deep in the drama too, but in the role of damage control. He reached his own breaking point a year later, in 1985. While at the Sea of Galilee, about to lead an advanced Insight seminar, a fellow staffer gave him a telegram bearing the news that his father was dying—the telegram was five days old. The guru said if he left, he would not be allowed to return. Toso left anyway. When he reached Minneapolis, his father had already slipped into a coma.

Not long thereafter, John-Roger came to Minneapolis to conduct trainings. Toso met him at a Marriott. The guru asked him to return. Toso declined. He says J-R took his jewelry, watch, and wallet. "I had to borrow money to get my mother's car out of the Marriott garage to get home."

Meanwhile Peter McWilliams missed the drama completely. When a book he wrote on computer literacy took off in 1982, he'd paused his participation. By the time he returned, the turmoil from the Lane paper had mostly subsided and Victor Toso had been painted a traitor. But scandal flared again in 1988 with the publication of two *Los Angeles Times* articles (which Lane says would've been far more scathing had a couple of reporters not backed out after John-Roger hired private investigators to find dirt on their sex lives). By then, though,

McWilliams was blindly devoted. In fact, it was that same year he entered into his verbal contract with his guru: if he kept writing and publishing books, listed John-Roger as a coauthor, and gave him half of all profits, J-R would, as he put it, "handle the health issue." By health issue, he meant the one he had just invented, which included AIDS *and* tuberculosis.[20]

The Traveler instituted this style of contract with all of his disciples, whether overtly or not. The teachings and practices of M.S.I.A. were designed to help followers exit the cycle of reincarnation faster. They did so, supposedly, by burning off negative karma (more or less what Christians would call sin) picked up during current and former lives, and by accelerating followers' ascension through a variety of levels until their souls could be released. J-R claimed to be able to remove existing bad karma from followers (sex with him was one way) and hold back additional negative karma headed their way. The guru also trapped them with more immediate material concerns, in that he promised to extend their lives in the here and now . . . if they would give him their devotion, time, labor, money, bodies. Since healthy people had no need for this particular bargain, he simply invented diseases, citing the absence of their symptoms as evidence of his work. Ironically, people with actual illnesses were harder to manipulate—they rarely improved while under his care. He claimed it was their bodies detoxifying the negative energies he excised. Or that they'd somehow failed to keep their agreement.

McWilliams certainly upheld his half of the bargain. He wrote three bestsellers in a row. Even though John-Roger had basically done nothing, his name appeared on the covers. McWilliams alleged, and Toso agrees, that these books single-handedly brought John-Roger back to prominence and popularity, following the media exposés of the late eighties.

But the subsequent publication, *Wealth 101*, didn't sell well, even after an appearance by McWilliams and John-Roger on *Larry King Live*. (Incidentally, King had a close relationship with and eventual engagement to a woman named Rama Fox, a minister in M.S.I.A. and one of John-Roger's earliest devotees.)[21] The Traveler pressured the author into investing $150,000 on PR for *Wealth 101*, which didn't increase sales. McWilliams claims the guru began threatening him for more money, explaining that if he stopped holding back the AIDS and tuberculosis now, after so many years, they would snap back like rubber bands and annihilate McWilliams instantly into a "crispy critter."[22]

Insight was one of many sensationally popular seminar trainings in the seventies and eighties that are now known as large group awareness trainings (LGATs) and are still popular. They're part of a family tree with roots including Christian Science, Freudian psychology, the power of positive thinking, Dale Carnegie, and Scientology. Among the tree's later branches are Tony Robbins, *The Secret*, the Prosperity Gospel, and NXIVM. This is the tree of self-investigation.

LGATs excel at navel-gazing. They promise that when you look inside you'll find you already have whatever you need to fulfill your desires. Whether you want happiness, love, financial success, enlightenment, or the perfect barre class, you have the power to manifest it—except that you'll need a guru/trainer/coach/motivational speaker to help you find that inner power. Then, as you're focusing on yourself, you're a sitting duck for bad actors, who, while claiming to help, can influence you to do whatever they want. Usually, that's to take more classes and buy more products, since they don't actually want to solve your problems or lead you to find answers—because then you'd stop purchasing their solutions. And if you don't have a problem, these secular false gurus will create one for you and then, wow, they have *that* solution too—but always for a price. No matter, we'll pay it. When salvation is for sale, we're buying.

Three major influences coalesced into what has become the feeding frenzy of the modern coaching and self-help industry: the mind-cure movement, psychotherapy, and a uniquely American obsession with success. It all starts with this guy Phineas P. Quimby, and no, I didn't make up that name.

In early 1800s Maine, a young Quimby contracted consumption (tuberculosis) and experimented with various states of mind in an effort to alleviate the pain. Doctors had been unable to help him. Later, he would claim to have cured himself. In the 1840s, he became interested in the potential healing power of hypnosis. After meeting a local teenager particularly susceptible to hypnosis, Quimby devised a kind of traveling road show. People paid in part to spectate and in part to ask the teen questions. Over time, those questions pertained more and more to illness. (Although contemporary doctors no longer used leeches, they still had a low batting average.)

Amazingly, the teen's advice often worked. People got better. Who knows whether this was due to coincidence, the placebo effect, or some other cause, but Quimby eventually decided it certainly couldn't be due to the kid; there was no way he actually saw inside people's bodies. Therefore, if patients improved following the diagnoses and prescriptions, Quimby reasoned that diseases must actually originate *inside patients' minds*. Disease was simply the result of erroneous thought. If Quimby could correct patients' thoughts, they would heal themselves. He ditched the kid and struck out on his own with a new kind of medicine.

The erstwhile doctor reasoned that the human body contained some portion that never got sick—and also never sinned. This was a little bit of Christ, he said, in all of us. God didn't actually want us to suffer from disease. Rather, our minds were the sources of our suffering, as "every phenomenon was first conceived in the mind."[23] The material world was actually created by the mental world. In 1863, he began using the name Christian Science.

Medicine and healing are often at the center of cults and cultlike movements in which people seek salvation, since life-threatening illness is one of the most pressing evils from which we desire rescue. Quimby doesn't appear to have been a scam artist. He was dedicated to his work, saw around five hundred patients a year, and kept prices affordable. The same cannot be said for Mary Baker Patterson, who met Quimby in 1859, became his patient, and, when he died, allegedly claimed his ideas as her own. In 1879, now going by the name of her third marriage, Mary Baker Eddy, she founded in Boston what would be known as the First Church of Christ, Scientist. Over time, she built a hugely successful organization. In 1880, there were 27 Christian Scientists, and by 1936 they numbered 269,000. She became a worshiped celebrity and allegedly bilked followers to fill her own pockets.

Regardless of how much she did or didn't pilfer Quimby's ideas, she certainly added flair. For example, if Quimby believed the material world was created by the mental world, Eddy argued the material world didn't exist at all. She straight-up denied its reality, including disease. "Tumors, ulcers, tubercles, inflammation, pain, deformed joints, are waking dream-shadows, dark images of mortal thought, which flee before the light of Truth."[24] She was a late nineteenth-century Neo, hell-bent on saving everyone from this Matrix, except she charged $300 tuition to do it (somewhere around $4,000 today).[25]

From 1906 to 1908, Willa Cather and Georgine Milmine authored a series of scathing magazine exposés of the cult leader.[26] Among its most explosive claims: she had declared herself a supernatural messiah figure whose scriptures ranked above Jesus's. She claimed even death itself was a fiction. When one reached true harmony with God, through the power of the mind, one became divine and immortal—no need to wait for doomsday. After Eddy died, some of her followers told the press she was not actually dead, and would soon return as the Son-Daughter of God. She didn't, but her ideas won't die.

She and Quimby contributed substantially to a popular metaphysical movement known rather generically as New Thought. In its early days, it was also called the Mind Cure movement, a moniker given by William James (brother of author Henry). James discussed healthy mindedness in his writing, arguing that certain ways of thinking, including optimism and hope, seemed to help people battle melancholy and depression. Although he didn't believe in many of his time period's unconventional healing methods, he did admit they often worked.[27] Largely influenced also by Ralph Waldo Emerson's theories on self-reliance and inner divinity, New Thought spread wide and branched in a variety of secular ways. Still, almost everything on its tree shared a few basic tenets.

First, all the branches rejected luck as a force in the world. Our species is so incredible that it must have a purpose, they reasoned. We are a chosen people, and God wants us to be happy and divine. Second, almost all of these beliefs stemmed from the assumption of a grace-nature divide, asserting that the human spirit is divine, while the world and everything in it is evil at worst, wrong at best, and imaginary at looniest. Third, when we achieve communion with God through mental connection, followers believed, we will be perfect, no longer corrupt. The promise of New Jerusalem has now moved *inside the mind*. Although many New Thought adherents still believed in the second coming of Christ, they assumed it would be "an inward presence in the souls of his followers."[28] And when that occurred, they claimed, we would *become* God.

Hopefully, those three ideas—we are chosen, nature is evil, and we can become perfectly godlike—by now sound familiar. If not, I know, I know: we've covered a lot. But there's also something new here, and particularly juicy: the intentional use of psychological influence techniques to achieve a certain goal. Quimby and Eddy both practiced overt programming, aka thought reform, aka undue influence, aka mind control, fka (formerly known as) brainwashing. Of course, they would argue otherwise. When Quimby swapped out sideshow performer for healer on his résumé, he dropped hypnotism from the special-skills section. And Eddy insisted her healing was no form of hypnotism, psychotherapy, or autosuggestion, but rather "the power of the divine mind and human consciousness."[29]

Regardless, it was thought reform. Quimby explained, "I tell the patient his troubles, and what he thinks is his disease; and my explanation is the cure. If I succeed in correcting his errors, I change the fluids of the system and establish the truth, or health. The truth is the cure."[30] He gave people what *he* considered truth . . . in order to change how they thought . . . which had a larger goal of literally affecting their physiology. That's influence, full stop. Sure, you could argue that any preacher in a pulpit is also influencing parishioners to behave morally by instilling a fear of God's wrath or a sense of duty to fellow humans. But New Thought introduced a more overt form of influence, bespoke in nature, and specifically sought by the public in order to solve distinct problems.

Around the time Quimby was out sideshowing with a teenager, two other streams of thought were developing: the success cult and Freudian psychotherapy. Before long, all three would cross streams and create one of the biggest economic drivers in modern America—all by getting people to pay for the privilege of being programmed.

———

Sigmund Freud didn't create psychology and neither did he take it mainstream. But the latter accomplishment does belong to his nephew Edward Bernays, the father of public relations. (The sister of the famed psychoanalyst was Bernays's mom, *and* Freud had married Bernays's father's sister, making the number of familial romantic relationships in this sentence Freudian in itself.)

After graduating college in 1912, Bernays worked in New York as a press agent in the theater world. Then he visited his uncle in Europe and came home full of beans about a way to incorporate his theories into his own work: he would manipulate people's unconscious drives in order to influence the way they behaved, that is, spent money. He had become "convinced that understanding the instincts and symbols that motivate an individual could help him shape the behavior of the masses."[31] He was right.

Previously, advertising had mostly provided people with information regarding products they might *need*. Sure, there was pressure to purchase, but it appealed to a buyer's rational brain. Bernays instead created emotional connections between consumers and products. This was particularly useful to the post–World War I market economy, as new systems of mass production pumped out a surplus of goods. Overproduction could imperil the economy, but so could backtracking the new engine of mass production. What if, instead, there were a way to move the extra goods? This conundrum led Paul Mazur, a banker at Lehman Brothers, to write, "We must shift America from a needs, to a desires culture. People must be trained to desire, to want new things even before the old had been entirely consumed."[32] This is exactly what Eddie Bernays had been developing.

You may have heard of his Lucky Strike campaign. By 1929, only 12 percent of cigarette consumers were female.[33] The American Tobacco Company wanted him to convince more women to smoke. Bernays consulted a psychoanalyst, a disciple of Freud's, who told the PR man that cigarettes were equated with men, the penis, and male power. Now that women were becoming emancipated, joining the workforce, and bearing fewer children, they might view smoking as a way to further challenge the patriarchy. Bernays aimed to equate smoking with feminist rebellion by manufacturing a seemingly authentic "Torches of Freedom" rally and ensuring pictures of it appeared in newspapers across the country.

First, he asked a friend at *Vogue* for a list of local debutantes and then sent them a telegraph that read, "In the interests of equality of the sexes and to fight another sex taboo, I and other young women will light another torch of freedom by smoking cigarettes while strolling on Fifth Avenue Easter Sunday . . . between

Eleven-Thirty and One O'Clock." He had his secretary sign the telegram, as if news were being spread by a woman behind the cause. A revealing event memo from his office explains that media stories "will take care of themselves, as legitimate news, if the staging is rightly done."[34]

The stunt was a smash success. One newspaper wrote, "Just as Miss Federica Freylinghusen, conspicuous in a tailored outfit of dark grey, pushed her way through the jam in front of St. Patrick's, Miss Bertha Hunt"—who was Bernays's secretary in disguise—"and six colleagues struck another blow on behalf of the liberty of women. Down Fifth Avenue they strolled, puffing at cigarettes. Miss Hunt issued the following communiqué from the smoke-clouded battlefield: 'I hope that we have started something and that these torches of freedom, with no particular brand favored, will smash the discriminatory taboo on cigarettes for women and that our sex will go on breaking down all discriminations.'"[35]

The event was so fruitful that over the next few days, in a handful of cities across the country, women took to the streets with lit cigarettes. Bernays had proved himself a semi-evil genius.

He was a master at creating a problem in order to sell a solution. In an earlier campaign for Lucky Strike, he was advised to recommend women smoke cigarettes to satisfy hunger, so he convinced photographer friends to write about how beautiful slender women are, and then launched a campaign recommending women reach for a cigarette instead of dessert. For Dixie Cups, he created a supposedly disinterested party, called by the hilariously specific name Committee for the Study and Promotion of the Sanitary Dispensing of Food and Drink. This committee deemed publicly shared drinking glasses unsanitary—but don't worry, individual, disposable Dixie Cups are coming to the rescue (sure, this one has some merit, though single-use cups have also been a disaster for the planet; regardless, the means and ends are skewed). But perhaps his most insidious campaign was to instill in Americans the belief that we should buy products not because we need them, but as a way to express our inner sense of self.

This not only created an engine that would continually compel people to purchase more—self-expression is ceaseless—but lead buyers to believe their consumption was their choice, and a positive and fulfilling choice at that. He "could change not only the way people bought, but the way they thought."[36] Honestly, the more I learn about him, the more he sounds like a cult leader.

He literally altered people's behavior. He often used pretty young women as bait. His campaigns usually attached his clients' wishes to a higher cause so customers believed they were making the world a better place. He was charismatic. He was somewhat controlling, was known to flirt with women at parties and work, "while at the same time worrying, to the point of calling the police, if his wife Doris stayed out late at a movie without telling him."[37] He had a bottomless need for esteem, respect, and adulation. And he's been called a narcissist.[38]

To be fair, from what I can tell, he did *not* spew his libido all over Manhattan (although his daughters did at times suspect infidelity). But other than that, I discern only one major difference between Bernays and cult leaders: he didn't need followers (at least not beyond the admiration of peers and clients). Granted, he did play God in Guatemala when he fomented an American government–backed coup in order to support his client United Fruit Company.[39] Still, he didn't fashion himself a messiah. So I guess he's a Cyrano cult leader, a cult leader on retainer.

Need to convince masses of people to give you money when they otherwise wouldn't and anyway shouldn't? You *could* start a cult . . . but if that's too much work, just call Eddie Bernays. While a psychoanalyst used "psychology to free his patients from emotional crutches, Bernays used it to rob consumers of their free will."[40] He was like a magician pirate. He could make money appear out of nowhere for his clients by conning it out of people. He was a messiah-for-hire.

A journalism professor who interviewed the PR man wrote that Bernays "saw what he called in our interview 'a world without God' rapidly descending into social chaos. Therefore, he contended that social manipulation by public relations counselors was justified by the end of creating man-made gods who could assert subtle social control and prevent disaster. . . . Pulling strings behind the scenes was necessary not only for personal advantage but for social salvation.'"[41] Whatever his self-understanding, his influence on others was clear. And when someone can control the masses, commercial brands are not the only ones to knock, knock.

At the time, some politicians and government leaders feared democracy. Waning were the strict moral edicts of organized religion, and the hierarchy and order of Victorian culture. If the people weren't controlled, these leaders reasoned, chaos would ensue. They turned to PR as another form of propaganda. Bernays had discovered how to sate desires—or stir them, depending on his goals—with consumption. He called this the "engineering of consent." The result of this irrational-desire sating was a happy and docile public. His daughter Anne Bernays says he viewed it as a kind of "enlightened despotism."[42]

Plus, it fueled a booming economy. In 1928, newly elected president Herbert Hoover told a group of PR men they had "transformed people into constantly moving happiness machines, machines which have become the key to economic progress." When people are fat and happy—and that's not just a metaphor, considering that our current obesity epidemic is due in part to the kind of rampant consumption born of Bernays's tactics—"then leadership can go on doing what it wants to do," explains one PR historian.[43] This is perhaps why Nazi propaganda minister Joseph Goebbels had a copy of Bernays's 1923 book, *Crystallizing Public Opinion*, in his library. In 1933, a Hearst foreign correspondent reported that Goebbels was using the book to spread Nazi ideology and intensify antisemitism.[44] It's impossible to know exactly how much influence the work had on Goebbels, but any analysis of his techniques reveals striking similarities with Bernays's.

———

Eddie Bernays seems to have understood preternaturally how to succeed. Most of us, though, could use advice. To an entrepreneur, that need constitutes a market. Following the Industrial Revolution, publishers, authors, and speakers created a booming business out of "success" pamphlets and seminars. It was a development so messed up it appears in two parts of this book. The content ultimately served as propaganda justifying the wealth of robber barons while convincing others to blame themselves for failure. However, before we get into that, I want to explore the success genre as one of the first forms of self-help books and the mother to all sales and motivational trainings, from Dale Carnegie to Tony Robbins and beyond.

Following the Civil War, Americans were hungry for help approaching the explosion of new opportunities created by the Industrial Revolution. Success manuals, pamphlets, lectures, and seminars eagerly filled the niche. Ostensibly, these publications provided insight and practical advice for the modern American upstart go-getter. In reality, they dwelled almost exclusively on character and morals, and promised that if you visualize your dream and travail righteously toward it, you'll receive what you desire. People were so eager to consume them, publishers rehashed each other's work in a rush to market. One historian argues, "Only a people mad with success could have endured the length and repetitiousness of these manuals."[45] Anyone who's wandered the self-help aisle in a bookstore today can relate.

The whole movement was heavily influenced by New Thought and prescribed a strict regimen of "right thinking" and thought control. Just as disease resulted from wrong thinking, these manuals reasoned, so did poverty. By the first decade of the twentieth century, James Allen, a pioneer of motivational thinking, exemplified the marriage of New Thought and the success cult when he wrote, "A man does not come to the almshouse or the jail by the tyranny of fate or circumstance but by the pathway of groveling thoughts and base desires."[46] Even before then, the germs of positive thinking existed in these manuals. "Will it, and it is thine," argued one from 1856. *Will it. Manifest it. Believe and it will be yours. Speak your desire and the universe will deliver.* It would take you thirty seconds to find those directives on Instagram, but they are nothing new.

In the early twentieth century, medical science began advancing dramatically and diminished the public's need for mental cures of physical ailments. New Thought advocates shifted their focus from health to prosperity. They went capitalist in a major way. Honestly, it was only a matter of time. *I can use my mind to get whatever I want? Great, I want money.*

New Thought and the success cult became linked irreducibly with the publication in 1937 of *Think and Grow Rich* by Napoleon Hill.[47] In this and his earlier books, Hill outlined what ultimately came to be known as the Law of Attraction, the practice of manipulating the material world simply by thinking about what you want and visualizing it until it arrives—which will sound familiar to those who lived through the Oprah-fueled mania following the

2006 release of the juggernaut bestseller *The Secret*. *Think and Grow Rich* was as successful and still sells well today. There's even a Napoleon Hill Foundation, which shares some of the legendary Napoleon Hill stories, such as the one claiming steel magnate Andrew Carnegie took him under his wing, and another that Hill advised President Wilson on a variety of matters of the state, and yet another that it was Hill who gave President Roosevelt the line "The only thing we have to fear is fear itself."[48]

None of it is true. Among a slew of biographers and researchers, none has found evidence he even met Carnegie, Wilson, or Roosevelt. Hill was a fraud— and a serial scam artist. His official biographers paint a picture of a naïve man, who was repeatedly duped by business partners. But as journalist Matt Novak points out, "There are only so many times that a man can be arrested for the sale of unlicensed stock, altering checks, and outright theft, before you have to question the official history."[49]

But Napoleon Hill did have one stunning, everlasting success: *Think and Grow Rich* . . . well, kind of. Turns out the first draft was a mess until his fourth wife, Rosa Lee Beeland, rewrote it. None of this is to say that Hill's (and, ahem, Beeland's) magnum opus should be discarded outright. Like all self-help and motivational texts, it offers some good advice. In addition to urging readers to visualize their desires, Hill and Beeland also preach self-confidence and tenacity. No one gets ahead in life without those, not even white men failing up. Regardless, Hill's career exemplifies something else true about the self-help industry: in your time of need, many authors, seminar leaders, and Instagram influencers only intend to take your money.

Even the phrase *Instagram influencer* owes some debt to the merging of psychology and New Thought into mid-century self-help. In 1936, Dale Carnegie published the juggernaut *How to Win Friends and Influence People*, which encouraged readers to apply commercial sales techniques toward their social lives and standings. The Los Angeles Public Library still can't keep copies of this book in its collection. Every time it replaces them, they disappear again. Among Carnegie's many students was William S. Casselberry, who ripped off Carnegie's ideas for his 1938 book *How to Use Psychology in Everyday Living* (and who invented multilevel marketing). And no survey of this genre would be complete without mentioning the 1952 publication of Norman Vincent Peale's *The Power of Positive Thinking*. He borrowed heavily from Napoleon Hill, whom he followed and admired. And who followed and admired Peale? Donald Trump, who grew up as a member of his congregation. Peale officiated Trump's marriage to Ivana.

These success seekers would later collide with the enlightenment seekers we discussed earlier, those "Me Decade" spiritual adherents of the Human Potential Movement. First, we have a generation suckled on *Think and Grow Rich* and *How to Win Friends*—on sales techniques, the application of psychology to sales techniques, and the application of sales techniques to life. Immediately after them, we have a generation looking for the modern, hippie, secular version of salvation via psychological techniques. The older generation, like good salespeople and entrepreneurs, saw a niche in the younger generation.

To feed the public's new appetite for consciousness, there appeared a slew of self-styled gurus—John-Roger among them—who more often than not were salesmen in disguise. The product they sold was inner New Jerusalem. The public paid handsomely. Sure, sixties culture had also rebelled against the kind of rampant consumerism wrought by Bernays-like tactics. But it was too late: it didn't matter if we rejected the consumerism of manufactured goods because we had long ago digested the consumerism of salvation.

What is a cult leader if not a salesman? Pay me with money, labor, adoration, and consent of bodily control, and in exchange I will give you . . . a bed in the fallout shelter (Church Universal and Triumphant) . . . perfection and immortality (Oneida) . . . protection from the Hidden Rulers (Mankind United) . . . release from reincarnation (M.S.I.A.) . . . a cure for disease (Christian Science) . . . the removal from your body of alien detritus (Scientology) . . . or a seat on the spaceship escaping this doomed world for the Evolutionary Kingdom Level Above Human (Heaven's Gate). It's a quid pro quo: believe to receive. And when a charlatan cult leader decides he really is God, he's merely bought his own product. He's found a customer in himself.

The Puritans signed a similar believe-to-receive contract. They gave their money, labor, and physical bodies to the building of a reformed church in a colony in a new world, believing that, in exchange, when doomsday arrived, they would receive eternal life. We've been signing that contract for four hundred years—we do it every day in new little ways. People who believe strongly in apocalyptic ideas are already looking for someone to deliver them salvation.[50] People unconsciously indoctrinated into a secular version of apocalyptic ideas crave the same. We are an eager and open market.

This particular exchange of goods is most common and overt in the consumer marketplace. Commercials promise products will solve our problems in exchange for proof of purchase. If a new product is developed, its promoters simply invent a new problem, program us to believe we suffer it, and sell us the cure. How? By connecting the product to a pathway to salvation. Buy this face cream and receive flawless skin (perfection). Buy this razor and receive a woman who will mate with you (immortality). Buy this self-help book and receive financial success (deliverance from hardship).

But you'll notice salvation is always just out of reach. They assure you it's around the bend if you pay a little more. How many internet ads offer the secret to [insert stigma here] but then won't reveal that secret until you've watched a ten-minute video/relinquished your data/agreed to a trial subscription. This is straight out of the cult playbook: for example, the Freemasons and, most notoriously, the Scientologists always kept or keep the highest levels of knowledge just out of reach, demanding more and more commitment before giving you the ultimate wisdom/answer/path.

We are a nation of customers. And we are a nation of salespeople. There's an old saying in sales circles that the most vulnerable marks are salespeople themselves. Perhaps the success cult ultimately began simply because a bunch of salesmen realized that if they created a nation of themselves, they'd always have leads.

Granted, the human instinct to sell salvation is not uniquely American. Still, even if we didn't design the ball, we excel at getting it to the end zone. Americans have engaged in this contract in some truly unique and spectacular ways.

On a Monday morning in September 1979, Evangeline Bojorquez began crying uncontrollably in her office, talking in a childlike voice, and hallucinating about drowning. Her friend found her in the middle of the night crawling on the floor like an infant, collecting bruises as she bumped into walls. By morning, she was somersaulting in the living room, shouting, "Let's play, let's play!"[51] An ambulance took her to Good Samaritan Hospital in San Jose, where one of the psychiatrists on call witnessed her shouting, "What the hell is wrong with you? I don't know. Yes, you do. Come on out, let it out. No, I don't. You're full of shit!" The doctor, Lloyd Moglen, immediately recognized that Bojorquez was carrying on two sides of a conversation—specifically, between a facilitator and a participant in a program called est.

Moglen was very familiar with est—an awakenings-oriented seminar series and one of the first LGATs—because he had experienced the training himself, having taken a special VIP course at the invitation of the seminar's founder, Werner Erhard. More recently, though, he had treated others who'd suffered psychological breaks following participation in the program. Later that day, Bojorquez crawled under the bed in her hospital ward and yelled, "Come watch her commit suicide," and "Look into my eyes so I can stare through your body as I die." Moglen diagnosed Bojorquez with "acute psychotic reaction secondary to est training."[52] The seminar name was *in the diagnosis*, which frankly is a move I wish more physicians were brave enough to make: *obesity as a secondary reaction to the Frito-Lay marketing department*; *hypertension as a secondary reaction to working for Jeff Bezos*.

Erhard seminar trainings (est) launched in 1972 with its creator, Werner Erhard, at the podium, presiding over four days of self-development workshops that occurred on two consecutive weekends. Before long, a staff of trainers led the sessions, typically for 200 to 250 people a pop, in cities across the country and globe. One reporter estimates that Erhard's courses, est and others that grew out of it, have been taught to more than a million people.[53] If you haven't heard of est, I can almost guarantee your parents have. Erhard became a celebrity—and, following a scathing *60 Minutes* exposé in 1991, a pariah.

The purpose of est, as often explained by Erhard, facilitators, and participants, was "to transform your ability to experience living so that the situations you have been trying to change or have been putting up with clear up just in the process of life itself."[54] Most people found it helpful, many transformative. Plenty thought it was bunk. And some were grievously damaged. Facilitators ripped people apart. It was four days of intense criticism and self-reflection, culminating in an outrageous love and hug fest. Erhard sold breakthroughs—emphasis on the *break*.

"What est did was to break down Mrs. Bojorquez's defenses and concept of reality," a court document quotes Dr. Moglen explaining. "Then they left her. They left her to put herself back together again. This she was unable to do."[55]

America has enjoyed a true smorgasbord of LGATs and personal development workshops over the years, including Lifespring, PSI Seminars, Insight, Actualizations, the Harmony Institute, Impact Trainings, Access Consciousness, Source Point Training, Choices, the Avatar Course, People Unlimited, Silva Mind Control (now the Silva Method), Direct Centering, Dimensional Mind Approach (now Integration of Consciousness), Context Associated, Rapport Leadership . . . and countless others.

Many LGATs owe the majority of their DNA to est . . . and to Lifespring . . . which also kind of copied est. John-Roger's Insight, by the way, ripped off Lifespring almost as a facsimile. But this is splitting hairs, since they all basically stole from Scientology. "It's three degrees to Scientology," explains Lane, the professor who studied M.S.I.A. and has also written extensively about the consciousness-seeking movements of the seventies and eighties. "Almost everybody had some contact with it. They were either in it for a year or a few months." Erhard was involved with Scientology from 1968 to 1970, during which he completed its communications course and underwent regular E-meter auditing sessions (the group's signature assessment of spiritual trauma/alleged tool to extract delicate information for potential blackmail).

In addition to Scientology, the group Erhard (and Lifespring, for that matter) most mimicked was Mind Dynamics, the brainchild of Alexander Everett . . . who himself ripped off a variety of existing New Thought and mind-cure programs. Mind Dynamics offered courses to help people tap into their potential, achieve their goals, and even improve their IQs and cure insomnia and cancer. Erhard eventually became a trainer. Then, in 1971, he had his staff copy the names and contact information for anyone who had taken or showed up at one of Erhard's Mind Dynamics courses or lectures. Shortly thereafter, he launched est and poached multiple Mind Dynamics staffers.

This wasn't difficult for him to do: Erhard was charming and, currently in his late eighties, presumably still is. Peter McWilliams (whom John-Roger diagnosed with AIDS) wrote of Erhard, "He's one of the few people I've met who genuinely had charisma: something around him crackled with electricity, the sort of presence people say John Kennedy had."[56] Erhard was also a master salesman, literally and in a variety of fields in his earlier career. Reportedly, he never took no for an answer.

The goal of est training was to attain what Erhard called "aliveness." John Denver was a devotee. When the singer-songwriter guest-hosted *The Tonight Show* in 1973, Erhard guested and explained that est helps people who've realized there's more in life and want "that extra eighth of an inch."[57] TV journalist Charlie Rose once asked the secular guru, "How true are they that it is just common sense, neatly packaged by a super salesman with a kind of capacity to galvanize an audience?" Erhard basically replied, Yes it is common sense, but most people don't remember/acknowledge/use common sense, and he helps them rediscover it in practical ways that allow them to be more effective in whatever they do.[58]

The two weekend sessions included several lectures, often about the need to take responsibility for life without excuses or self-victimization. The idea here is that we create our own realities. Participants gushed that the training was a wake-up call; improved their relationships, work productivity, and communication skills; and enabled them to face challenges more effectively. Celebrities flocked, including Denver, Valerie Harper, Carly Simon, Yoko Ono, Joanne Woodward, and Diana Ross. Raul Julia spent a month with Erhard in India. Ted Danson said the training helped him understand that, as he said, "I could affect the way I wanted my life to go. It's a cliché by now, but you do 'create your own reality.'"[59]

A participant and ex-con teamed up with a former prison therapist to bring est courses into prisons. According to the program's cofounder, "Incidents of misconduct among the prisoners who participated dropped 44% and participation in other rehabilitation programs and voluntary work assignments increased dramatically—78%."[60] A similar program offered to troubled youth boasted decreases in recidivism, drug use, and truancy.

By all accounts, est legitimately helped a number of participants. Honestly, though, it sounds like people were simply doing therapy for the first time. This isn't a knock against the program; perhaps Erhard's genius was in translating such techniques and ideas to the masses. Psychoanalysis had been around for decades but still carried a taboo. In the seventies, it grew popular, thanks in part to Erhard and his contemporaries. "The packaging was new," Lane explains. "It was accessible. He had a new way of presenting it in a much shorter period of time, and instead of going to therapy, you go to a group. It's much more appealing that way."

Even so, this wasn't Americans' first rodeo with self-examination. Looking inward was one of the Puritans' favorite pastimes. They would engage in it until they literally made themselves sick. Residents of the Massachusetts Bay Colony were desperate to pronounce themselves among the elect, as having received grace, as predestined by God to be saved on Judgment Day. They desired such proof for two all-consuming reasons: to gain status in the community and admission into the church. Anyone could attend sermons, but only those possessing grace could *join* the church.

To determine if they were in God's posse, community members turned within. At first, this was as simple as trying to feel Christ's presence in your heart. Over time, though, church leaders demanded more rigorous self-examination. As trials increased in intensity, so increased nervous breakdowns, melancholia, insanity, and even suicide. Mary Baker Eddy herself came from a strict Calvinist household—Calvinism being a branch of early Protestantism that largely influenced the Puritans—and wrote about the ill effects of constant rumination. "I was unwilling to be saved, if my brothers and sisters were to be numbered among those who were doomed to perpetual banishment from God," she recalls. "So perturbed was I by the thoughts aroused by this erroneous doctrine, that the family doctor was summoned, and pronounced me stricken with fever."[61]

In the second half of the nineteenth century, a curious new illness commanded national attention. People complained of headaches, exhaustion, back problems, melancholy, feebleness, and insomnia. It often resulted in invalidism. The neurologist George M. Beard dubbed this novel disease *neurasthenia*.[62] As the name suggests, he associated its cause with the nervous system as opposed to an outside agent. The diagnosis became somewhat of a catchall and was especially popular between 1869 and 1930.

As Barbara Ehrenreich points out in her book *Bright-Sided: How the Relentless Promotion of Positive Thinking Has Undermined America*, those diagnosed most often with neurasthenia were "precisely the groups most excluded from the frenzy of 19th century competitiveness." For example, clergymen, who were largely isolated and contemplative, and middle-class women, who were mostly excluded from the workplace and higher education but also didn't have many home tasks thanks to industrialization. "For many women, invalidism became a kind of alternative career."[63]

As was the case with MBC Puritans trying to get into the church, we also see here an exclusion (whether by choice or not) from society along with excess time to self-reflect. These circumstances amount to a kind of idleness: the devil's playground, which can only be cured with hard labor . . . unless you couldn't engage in such work on account of being a middle-class woman or in the clergy. Beard became interested in the "disease" in part because he suffered similar symptoms as a young adult, at a time of career indecision—when he was idle. This was also the general time when America was shifting from an economy of production to an economy of consumption, a kind of national idleness. To be clear, the theory here is not that idleness makes people ill but that sickness results from a certain self-loathing, which derives from the deep-seated Puritan tendency to see idleness as evil.

Phineas P. Quimby treated this amorphous disease with New Thought. He even intuited Calvinism as a cause, as a moral constriction on sufferers' lives, burdening them with guilt to the point of debilitation and depression.[64] His treatments worked. Some of the symptoms of neurasthenia and similar contemporary diagnoses *were* largely psychological or psychosomatic, of course. I argue that the actual cure was agency. People who felt powerless—whether having no control over their salvation, or no access to education or employment—and therefore left out or cast aside, were suddenly given agency. They could control their health through thoughts alone. Americans love agency, whether it's a can-do attitude from a motivational seminar or believing we can affect when and where Jesus will return for Judgment Day. Agency is an American panacea.

Werner Erhard made a fortune off of the American desire to examine ourselves. What did participants ultimately learn? Erhard and his trainers sometimes argued that the deepest understanding to be gained from his program was that there was actually nothing to understand—the grand meaningless of life, and all that. In one account, a trainer asked everyone who had "gotten it" to raise a hand. When someone responded, "I don't get it," the trainer replied, "Good. There's nothing to get so you got it."

"I get it," the participant responded. "So getting it is whatever you get."

To which the trainer cryptically said, "If that's what you got."[65]

I suppose there's some consciousness to be achieved in this Who's on First charade. But I'm convinced the larger point was to make money by indoctrinating people into a cultlike organization. That, I "get."

At the end of LGAT sessions, now that the trainees are high on . . . themselves, really . . . they are told the ultimate goal of the program is to advance consciousness (to, ahem, spread the good word). *Bring us your friends, your family, your countrymen. Convince them to open their hearts and bank accounts. We are enlightened. We are improving the world. Huzzah!* Cue the blink of a fluorescent light panel.

Onetime Lifespring vice president James Moore told a *Washington Post* reporter, "The more intense the experience that [participants] had, the more they marketed." Of course, trainees are also encouraged to commit to the next level of classes themselves. At one Lifespring session, attendees were told in advance this would happen, and to "allow yourself to make that choice. And that means bringing a credit card or checkbook or whatever you need to make that choice."[66]

LGATs eventually broke into a new market by disguising their seminars as corporate training programs, and scoring lucrative deals with businesses whose employees had no choice but to attend, and then were typically recruited afterward into additional levels. The Insight Consulting Group, born of that earlier pipeline to John-Roger, claims among its clients Beth Israel hospital, Lockheed, Campbell Soup, the UCLA Graduate School of Management, NBC, and the

U.S. Navy.[67] Lifespring worked with American Express, AT&T, Time/Life, the U.S. Air Force, and the San Jose Police Department.[68] Even Scientology found its way into work-training programs and the workplace itself via the organizations Sterling Management Systems, Applied Materials, and Stryker Systems, all of which utilized Scientology ideology, and sometimes made overt references to and pitches for the church and Hubbard.[69]

Werner Erhard became very wealthy. From 1982 to 1984, his programs brought in almost $113 million gross. Allegedly $1.2 million was paid out to the guru, who also took in $2 million from other est-related ventures. One can make even more money when not paying much out: in 1987, he had about three hundred people on the payroll and an additional thirty thousand who volunteered free labor.[70]

In the late aughts, my cousin Donnell Carr attended a two-weekend Landmark Education course (a personal-development program that derived from est). He had recently experienced a transformation during a sales training sponsored by his employer, wherein he realized he was getting in his own way—and saw how to stop doing it. "I felt like I had had a breakthrough and that maybe if I kept at it, I would have more breakthroughs," he explains. But eventually, the course "was less about me and more about Landmark." There was pressure to bring significant others to the final program. His wife, Hale, pushed back. She had been suspicious of Landmark from the start. But the more the group pressured Donnell, the more he pressured her, and she relented.

When she arrived, the facilitator separated the trainees from their significant others, who were taken to a separate room. A presentation ensued, and when a young woman sitting next to Hale said, "Wow, this is interesting," Hale immediately saw the scam.

"She was trying to be subtle," Hale recalls. "But it was bad acting, pretending like she's so interested, like she's never heard it before. And I thought, 'She's focusing a little too much on me.' You could just feel it in the room: half of those people were plants."

She called out the young woman directly; "I said, 'You're with this group—you are one of the people trying to convert me and my husband, aren't you?' And she was like, 'Yeah.'"

This is my favorite part of the story, that the poor kid immediately confessed. What a terrible cult recruiter. Shortly thereafter, the session paused for a scheduled break, and the Carrs left. "It was a relief that Hale helped me cut it off," Donnell shares. "I kept thinking there was more I could get out of it."

"Because salespeople are hopeful?" I asked.

"Yes," he says. Donnell was the one who'd told me about the adage in his industry that the easiest mark is a salesperson. I asked him if among the trainees were others in his line of work. "I assumed *everyone* was in sales," he replied. "I can't imagine who else would go to something like this." In that case, I asked, is it hope itself that makes these people easy marks?

"Absolutely."

Earlier, I argued we are a nation of two types: salespeople and consumers. Now I see no difference.

———

Sociologists have identified and outlined a variety of specific ways destructive cults and totalistic organizations exercise undue influence in order to control followers and participants. Almost all of the techniques categorized by scholars are present in LGATs. There are the carefully controlled environments: Lifespring covered any mirrors; est disallowed watches and bathroom visits outside of scheduled breaks. There's the kind of false spontaneity that leads participants to believe magic is happening: as discussed, "breakthroughs" are often manufactured; these groups are known to use volunteers and staffers as audience plants.

There's a culture of confession (I can't stop thinking about the *multiple people* who admitted murder in Insight trainings) and adjacent demands for a kind of purity (in est, arriving even just a few minutes late revealed one was not a person of their word). There's the claim to have developed a science that understands and can improve upon all of human behavior (LGAT trainers claim answers to life's biggest questions exist, and they have them and you don't). Any questioning of the system is disallowed (rebel trainees were often yelled at and sometimes removed). And there's the classic othering of outsiders: "Anyone who wasn't a part of Landmark was basically to be looked down upon like an enemy," a former Landmark volunteer told *New York* magazine. "I really didn't have any friends outside of Landmark. And other people really didn't like me after a while."[71]

Beyond spreading aliveness, Erhard was programming people. One of the first critical articles on est, a 1975 piece in the *San Francisco Bay Guardian*, wrote, "What the training is more than anything else—and far more than any wide-eyed description that est graduates or staff give—is a brave new application of classic techniques in indoctrination and mental conditioning worthy of Pavlov himself."[72]

He influenced participants to be more effective in life, sure (maybe), but also to deliver him money and all but openly worship him. How? Just as the *Bachelor* franchise on ABC manufactures romantic connection among its contestants by sending them on high-octane, adrenaline-fueled "dates" (twenty-somethings trying to kiss during a zero-gravity flight is a highlight), so do LGATs manufacture breakthroughs and revelations. Participants are torn down before being told they're perfect and their lives will greatly improve immediately after the seminar concludes with a full-body, crotch-to-crotch hug line.

Peter McWilliams explained the programming he experienced in Insight seminars (and M.S.I.A., for that matter) as a result of pressure-and-release patterns. The first half of each seminar, he writes, was dedicated to exploring trainees' "guilts, fears, angers, disappointments, hurts, inadequacies, unworthinesses, and all the other aspects we consider negative about ourselves." The result was intense negativity, and even depression. In tandem, these tactics engendered dependence on the trainer. "People do more and more of what the trainer asks, with less and less resistance."

Then everything changes. The trainer is positive and uplifting. The workshops build "esteem, cohesion, and eventually love within the individual and within the group." Just before the course ends, there's one more down-and-up, this time with an even more precipitous grade: trainees are taken to the depths of despair, and then "BOING! U-u-u-p you go." At that highest peak, they're pitched future seminars. McWilliams says a seminar high can last from anywhere between a few days to a few weeks. "It feels so good when the pressure stops—the greater the pressure, the better the release."[73] At some point, a session was added toward the end of the Insight seminar, called "Gift of Giving," in which some euphoric attendees donated checks for as much as $10,000.[74]

Offering a professional take on more or less the same idea is South African researcher John Hunter. Inspired by his own experience in an LGAT, he endeavored to crack their psychological code. First, he told me, LGATs "put people in a state, where they're very unlikely to think for themselves." Specifically, he argues LGATs hamstring our *motivation* and *ability* to work through evidence, both of which are necessary for critical thinking. When we lack these paths, we turn to shortcuts. One such shortcut is an elevated affective state—or, in layperson's terms, feeling good—which LGATs intentionally manufacture. Hunter calls his theory the dopaminergic-defense hypothesis. In short, when we lack critical thinking, we'll follow our feelings to belief.

In 2024, Hunter appeared as an expert witness in a US federal court case regarding LGATs. In that way, he follows in the footsteps of clinical psychologist and anti-cult expert Margaret Thaler Singer, who was consulted on roughly sixty legal cases brought against LGATs. She describes an intentional campaign to break people down psychologically and then build them back up in a different way. (This classic cult tactic is also foundational to advertising: that's what's happening when it creates a problem, convinces you of having it, and offers a solution for a price.) When facilitators tell participants their biggest hurdle is their "beliefs," it's a sign they ultimately intend to destroy those beliefs and indoctrinate the crowd with "a new belief system."[75] They literally tell us what they're doing.

But there are participants who shatter so thoroughly, they sruggle to reconstruct. Singer explains that some of her sources were still in the hospital as many as ten years after their LGAT-related mental breakdowns.[76] The *American Journal of Psychiatry* published a duo of articles in 1977 and 1978 regarding five est participants who thereafter experienced psychotic symptoms, including delusions, uncontrollable mood swings, and paranoia. The authors argue "that an authoritarian, confrontational, aggressive leadership style coupled with physiologic deprivation fosters an identification with the aggressor. The inability of this defense mechanism to contain overwhelming anxiety aroused by the process may lead to fusion with the leader, ego fragmentation and psychotic decompensation."[77] In 1978, the executive director at New York City's Lincoln Institute for Psychotherapy shared that "substantial numbers" of people entered his clinic following est trainings, all exhibiting similar patterns of "elation, depression, feelings of omnipotence, followed by feelings of helplessness."[78] In the 1980s, four out of eleven Lifespring offices closed, following publicity of psychotic episodes occurring during and after trainings, including deaths.[79]

As for Evangeline Bojorquez, the est trainee who was diagnosed with "acute psychotic reaction secondary to est training," she spent twenty-five days in the hospital and the next four months at home, heavily sedated. It would be another year before she was able to take on full-time work. Meanwhile, she sued Erhard and est. The day before the trial was set to begin, Erhard's lawyers settled.

———

Werner Erhard was no Jim Jones . . . or even John-Roger. I've read accounts of thoughtful letters he wrote to former employees in an effort to reconcile and of strong efforts made in support of friends. Nevertheless, no one is immune to power. Numerous allegations paint the guru as a boor. As his celebrity and collection of acolytes grew, he became known as the Source. There was even talk of surrendering to the Source.

He introduced a Scientology-style consulting practice into the organization. While holding E-meter-like contraptions, staffers reportedly were encouraged to divulge personal information and confessions, and were pressed about their loyalty to Werner, whether or not they accepted him as the Source. Any who had a "bad thought about Werner," reportedly faced additional consulting until the thought disappeared, after which they were instructed to write Erhard requesting forgiveness for "living in disloyalty."[80] Plus, there's all the allegations you'd expect: yelling at assistants, forcing volunteers to clean his home, and demanding a human snooze button . . . you know, a trainee who woke Erhard in the morning by entering his bedroom and massaging his feet while announcing the time every five minutes until the Source arose.

He enjoyed the spoils of his kingdom. He admitted to engaging in sexual affairs with young staffers and acolytes. He sought forgiveness from his second wife, Ellen. When he suspected Ellen of adultery, however, he verbally attacked her in a town hall–style meeting known as a "fishbowl," which devolved into physical violence.

The details of this event are hotly contested. In October 1977, according to some sources present, a group of people, including all seven of Erhard's children, and both his first and current wife, gathered on the third floor of his San Francisco house, where Erhard demanded that Ellen admit her infidelity. In the book *Outrageous Betrayal: The Dark Journey of Werner Erhard from est to Exile*, Steven Pressman writes that someone—accounts differ—stood and lightly kicked her. Then Erhard allegedly slapped her, knocked her to the floor, and started kicking her, until his brother and an assistant pulled him away. Erhard later admitted that he shook her and "may" have slapped her, but denied the kicks.[81]

A week later, he held another fishbowl focused on Ellen. Following more demands that she confess her alleged affair, one of his key staffers, Bob Larzelere, approached Ellen and began to strangle her. Larzelere claims, as do others, that Erhard had asked someone to come forward and "handle" her. Some present, however, deny that Erhard invited the attack. Larzelere claims he believed this was his chance to prove his loyalty to Erhard. He strangled her until she lost color in her face and drooled. Ellen's daughter Celeste yelled for Larzelere to stop. *Allegedly*, Erhard yelled back, "Sit down! Or you're going to get the same treatment."[82]

This story was recounted on that infamous *60 Minutes* episode I mentioned. It aired on March 3, 1991. It was shocking. In addition to the fishbowl anecdote and interviews about the nightmare of working for the guru, the story alleged Erhard had beaten his children and featured an interview with Erhard's daughter Deborah, from his first marriage, who accused her father of molesting her and raping her sister. "I believe my sister when she says that my father raped her . . . forcibly had sexual intercourse with her," she told Ed Bradley. She claimed that when she asked her father about it, he admitted the intercourse, but claimed it wasn't rape, because "it had been a nurturing experience" for her.[83]

Erhard had known these accusations were coming. He sold his company barely a month prior, to some of his most trusted staffers (for $3 million plus an eighteen-year licensing fee of up to $15 million; now called Landmark World-wide LLC, it has been attended by millions of Americans). Then, two days before the show aired, he left the country on a ticket with an open-ended return.

There was a major problem with the episode, though. Some of its sources *might* have been participating in a long, documented, well-orchestrated, under-cover attack executed by the Church of Scientology. Ten months after the episode aired, a private detective named Ted Heisig came forward, explaining he had been hired by Scientology in 1989 to investigate Erhard. The PI told reporters Scientology had five file cabinets of information on Erhard and his organizations, was planning a media blitz, and wanted him to collect and spread information without disclosing his involvement with the church. L. Ron Hub-bard believed, according to the *LA Times*, that Erhard had "incorporated some of its teachings into est, making a fortune in the process," and was infuriated by it.[84]

On the job, Heisig made contact with disgruntled former employees and participants, persuading some to file sworn affidavits. He and his sources anony-mously disseminated allegations and affidavits to journalists across the country. Two who collaborated with him, Paul Gutfreund and Dawn Damas, were also integral to the *60 Minutes* reporting. Heisig, Damas, and Gutfreund all claim the latter two were unaware of Scientology's involvement.[85] After the *60 Min-utes* episode aired, Erhard and some of his allies recruited Jane Self, a reporter from the *Macon Telegraph*, who had written about Erhard's courses in 1989. Based on a collection of interviews, sworn affidavits, and other reporting, she published the 1992 book *60 Minutes and the Assassination of Werner Erhard*.

Hubbard died five years before the *60 Minutes* expose aired, but his decades' long grudge outlived him. Although Erhard doesn't seem to have known about Heisig's operation, he had long been aware of Hubbard's anger. One of the most inflammatory assertions in Self's book regards an internal memo from 1983 suggesting Erhard was alerted by his lawyer, who had been informed by a former Church of Scientology attorney, that at one point a contract had been put out on the est leader's life.[86] In addition to recounting Heisig's claims about his work for Scientology, Self suggests another potential agenda: that Dawn Damas, who was BFFs with Ellen, the second wife, may have sought revenge on her behalf, since Ellen had signed an agreement barring her from speaking out.

Self also asserts, based on interviews with witnesses and loyalists, that Damas and others fabricated or exaggerated accusations of child beatings, and that they and reporters pressured some of Erhard's children to participate in the takedown. We may never know the truth. Same goes for the charges of sexual abuse. Erhard's first wife claims Deborah told her about the alleged molestation after it happened, but said it was an accident: she and Erhard were sleeping in a hotel bed together, when he rolled over in his sleep, and his arm landed on her breast. Perhaps she didn't realize at the time what was actually happening or perhaps she later decided something different had happened. She eventually recanted the story.[87] The unnamed sister, whom Deborah claimed was raped, has never spoken about the accusation publicly.

A year after the *60 Minutes* episode aired, Erhard sued CBS for "false, misleading and defamatory" statements (that suit alleges Damas was having an affair with *60 Minutes* producer David Gelber).[88] But a few months later, he dropped the lawsuit. CBS later made the transcript unavailable, sharing this disclaimer: "This segment has been deleted at the request of CBS News for legal or copyright reasons."[89]

At least one aspect of the *60 Minutes* story I don't doubt: Erhard had somewhat of a god complex. At a retreat for seminar leaders in 1977, a discussion ensued about Erhard's spot in the hierarchy of human transformation. Purportedly, someone in the room asked him point-blank if he was the Messiah, to which he replied, "No, I am who sent him." OK, possibly he was kidding? But another anecdote has him wondering out loud to a friend, "How do I know I'm not the reincarnation of Jesus Christ?" Still, I suppose this too could have been a joke.[90]

Regardless of whether or not he wanted to be a god, he certainly behaved like one. In 1978, when two trainers were promoted to his inner circle of elite staff, he made clear a certain contract. "Let's be clear between you and me that you have no rights," he said, "that if you accept the job of trainer that you give up your rights . . . and that you've got nothing to lose." By the mid-eighties, all staff members were expected to make such vows—and in perpetuity. At centers across the country, staff were pressured to stand and publicly pledge to do "Werner's work" *forever*.[91]

Here we go again with these contracts. Erhard promised his staff a kind of salvation, one even more magnificent than that afforded to the participants in his courses, a level of consciousness only available through closer contact with him. In exchange, they gave a lifetime of loyalty, fealty, and service. In effect, they gave themselves.

This is what cult leaders always eventually demand. This is where the desire for power, when consistently fed, leads: ultimate control over personhoods and lives. The destination is indeed ultimate, for desire of power is insatiable, can only terminate when it's ingested everything there is, consuming even people. This is what happened in Jonestown. This was behind the Heaven's Gate group suicide. I'm definitely not saying Werner Erhard aimed to kill his staff. Even in true destructive cults, only a handful ever reach this terminus. Regardless, the pathway is the same: what power ultimately wants, whether it's dressed up as sex, money, labor, status, or a human snooze button, is control. And there is no greater control than power over life and death. It's literally what gods do.

LGATs and personal-growth seminars—including est, Lifespring, Insight— offer a commodified version of that cult contract. Americans wanted consciousness, self-expression, and an understanding of their place in the universe. The entrepreneurs developed a way to fill that niche in the market by selling salvation at scale.

In that famous *New York* magazine article "The 'Me' Decade," Tom Wolfe writes of the ecstatic fervor of the Human Potential Movement, in addition to its spiritual undertones, which support his argument that it constitutes a Third Great Awakening. I see something additional in the analogy. The First and Second Great Awakenings were each responsible for a proliferation of charismatic preachers. Suddenly, anyone could lead a cult. In their own unique ways, the awakenings flattened church hierarchies. Anyone with enough charm could sell their ideas in a free and ever-opening marketplace of faith: everyone a salesperson. The Third Great Awakening—if we believe the personal-growth movement is worthy of that moniker, and I do—unleashed a powerful salesforce on the latent indoctrination that leads us to desire an inner New Jerusalem, an apotheosis of identity.

When Puritans looked inward for proof of salvation, they either felt sure they'd found it or fretted themselves sick with uncertainty. Such uncertainty is the real niche filled by the enlightenment salesforce of the 1970s. With confident smiles, they seemed to ask, *Hey, unsure that you're saved? It's OK, we all are. And today is your lucky day. I happen to* sell *salvation. If you act now, I'll throw in this spatula.* The contract guarantees you'll be rescued at the destination. The fine print says you'll get closer and closer but not reach it.

We are a nation of salespeople/customers. We are a nation of suckers.

Just as the effects of the first two Great Awakenings reverberated through the decades following, so are we still experiencing the effects of the third. Today, the preacherpreneurs it begat stand on a leviathan self-help industry of wellness brands, social-media influencers, life coaches, nutrition gurus, and a never-ending Imperial Army of Tony Robbins clones. From their pulpits, they thunder, "But are you *really* well?"

We pay more to be programmed and influenced today than ever before, through books and seminars, sure, but also weight-loss apps, tarot readings, memory-repression therapy, past-life regressions, future-life regressions, get-a-life regressions, and improv class. We pay to be plucked from our suffering, from our corrupt and evil unactualized existence, and then perfected on some ethereal plane. What is the latest manifestation of salvation? Based on my Instagram feed, I'm guessing mushroom skin serums.

Success pamphlets, New Thought, the development of psychological influence techniques, and the Human Potential Movement all conspired to bring us here. They're still out there delivering sermons on personal responsibility, positive thinking, and mind control, and promising awakenings and rescue. Market data expects the self-improvement industry to be worth $14 billion in 2025, a number that doesn't even include the woo-woo stuff.[92]

But is it working? Nah. Measurements of happiness in America peaked in the 1990s and have slowly declined since 2000. Between 1990 and 2018, the number of people who say they're *un*happy has risen by 50 percent. This, even as the self-help movement has ballooned. Or possibly this is why the self-help movement has ballooned. We're turning toward it as stress and anxiety reach crisis levels. But it's not clear we are aided by it. One theory posits that the more we focus on or value—or are *encouraged* to value—happiness, the less able we are to achieve it. A study out of Berkeley tested people after they viewed a happy movie. Before the film, half read an article about how important happiness is, while the second half did not. Following the screening, those who had read the article reported feeling *less* happy than the other group did.[93]

Scientists aren't alone in figuring this out. As early as the mid-aughts, self-help publisher Rodale learned from market research that "the most likely customer for a book on any given topic was someone who had bought a similar book within the preceding eighteen months."[94] The industry makes its money on repeat customers. Surely some of these people simply want more help, perhaps as a reminder lest they backslide into bad habits. But it's also a market truth that a customer without needs is not a customer at all. Like automobiles and smartphones, self-help exhibits a certain amount of planned obsolescence. The industry makes more money when it appears to help but in reality doesn't. Is it possible that some bad actors among this industry's purveyors intentionally work toward our continued imprisonment, so they can keep taking advantage of us, which I guess is one of the plot lines in the movie *Shawshank Redemption*? Rhetorical question. Obviously, we are being shawshanked.

An egregious example is skin-care products that not only fail to achieve their bombastic claims, but also inhibit the skin's natural ability to achieve those same goals. Your skin gets worse. You buy more products. What they actually sell is addiction.

Beware especially of products and coaches who accuse every other product and coach of being ineffective or lying to you. They paint you the victim so they can swoop in and save you. (Shout-out to the sweaty creep who once approached me in an East Village bar, pointed at a random man in the room, and said, "That guy told me he wants to hurt you. You'll be safe with me.") It's a dynamic we've already discussed in the context of thieves, but now with a new spin. *When someone says no one else is telling you the truth, the liar is the one talking.* (Unless the person talking is a friend warning that your motivational coach is swindling you. Do listen to her.)

What happens if you try their product or program and it doesn't help? They claim you clearly need more of the product or program. And if that still doesn't help? The problem must be you. *You're not positive enough, you're not trying hard enough.* A classic tool of the oppressor is to keep those beneath them in battle with one another. It was an ingenious development to next convince people to *internalize* such a battle. Now every person is fighting themself.

Advice to remove negativity is also a dire warning that negative people can themselves be removed. Barbara Ehrenreich believes an aversion to negativity (what New Thought might call "wrong thinking") led us into the subprime mortgage crisis by encouraging people to ignore nagging doubts within themselves or from others. She cites Adam Michaelson, former senior vice president of Countrywide Financial, one of the main purveyors of the questionable loans that triggered the global financial crisis, who has written of the company's "marginally cultish behavior," of the cheerleading, and motivational speeches and platitudes. He claims that when he questioned the assumption that housing prices would never fall, in 2004, he was told, "You worry too much." He writes that the person "with a negative comment or a cautious appraisal might be the first to be ostracized."[95]

American culture teaches that success comes from endless striving, tireless work, and the motivated positive belief system that allows for those. That formula simply isn't accurate. Most impoverished and marginalized citizens in our country will never achieve financial success. In such an impossible scenario, continued striving can literally kill them. Curious to understand why Black men experience higher rates of disease and shorter lifespans than other Americans, social epidemiologist Sherman James developed a theory known as John Henryism. Also known as high-effort coping, John Henryism is "a thinking pattern regarding one's ability to meet the overwhelming demands of their environment (psychosocial stressors) through hard work and determination, which can result in cardiovascular risk."[96] The continued stress of inequality paired with the psychological coping method of Herculean perseverance in the face of that stress can lead to burnout, hypertension, and a variety of other adverse psychological and physiological outcomes.

James's theory has two namesakes. In 1978, he met John Henry Martin, a former sharecropper in North Carolina, who had been able to free himself and his family from that system through hard work. By his fifties, he had already developed serious health problems. Coincidentally, poetically, and heartbreakingly, the man had been named for railroad-steel-driving folk hero John Henry. In the mid-1800s, when machines came to replace the largely Black railroad labor, Henry, according to legend, challenged a machine to a contest, beat it, and then died on the spot. James argues the poor health outcomes of John Henryism result not only from societal stressors, but also specifically from the can-do hard-work attitude that leads us to believe we can overcome any obstacle.

An outsized focus on mindset is another modern manifestation of the grace-nature divide. It's *mind over matter*, and "matter" is the rest of your body. This kind of hierarchy is possible only in the wake of a division. Which is why bad actors engender such a split. If the mind is put above the body, they can silence your instincts with their rhetoric. This was a textbook tactic in the self-help therapy cult NXIVM, according to former member Jessica Joan.

"In the curriculum, you focused more on the mental and intellectual aspects of understanding," Joan told me. "If you had a physical reaction, like a gut feeling, they would say, 'Oh, that's just a bodily expression.'" Joan had discerned Keith Raniere's general scheme relatively quickly, and she then helped the FBI take him down. When I met her, I had one burning question: "Why didn't his influence and thought reform work on you?"

"What they were doing was cutting people off from their intuition," she explained, "which I would *never* do." Joan had a tough childhood. Her mother disappeared into addiction, her father ran a meth lab in the home and went to prison, and she was sexually abused. She overcame her trauma specifically by listening to and trusting herself. So, when NXIVM tried to convince students to ignore their intuition, her Spidey sense flared.

Joan was eventually recruited into a secret sorority-like women-only group. Not long after, she received a special assignment from Allison Mack, Raniere's handmaiden, who served two years in prison. Mack told her to seduce Keith and have him take a naked picture of her to prove she did it. After receiving this directive, Joan writes in her memoir, *The Untouchable Jessica Joan: The Downfall of NXIVM*, "the room started spinning and the walls felt like they were melting," as she realized, "Oh shit, I accidentally joined a cult, and the leader wants to have sex with me."[97] She started taking screenshots. Her testimony helped nab Raniere on attempted sex trafficking. She never conducted her special assignment.

The self-help industry and purveyors of happiness are in many ways causing us to be helpless and unhappy. Worse, some people in power may intentionally fill our minds with these belief systems as a way to distract us from working toward what could actually make us happy: more stable jobs with benefits, shorter workweeks, more paid vacation and family leave, improved or universal healthcare, bodily autonomy, and racial, ethnic, and religious equality. Those outcomes don't make money for the people in power; in fact, they *take* money.

For example, positive thinking, which encourages us to focus only on our thoughts and actions, has been used expertly by corporations that bring in motivational speakers before or after layoffs. Such coaching convinces employees that their successes or failures are the result of their own mindsets, not the whims of corporate restructuring—making former and current employees unlikely to band together in response. It's far more lucrative to convince have-nots that they can think their way out of problems by buying into certain mindset-driven belief systems. This is the twenty-first-century version of "let them eat cake"—the cake being the wealth and happiness promised by the American dream.

It's no surprise that we fall for this ideology and its associated manipulative tactics, considering our responses are not rational. Bad actors parrot our culturally indoctrinated beliefs, and we become lost in the ecstasy, trying to tongue each other on zero-gravity flights. In response to our manipulation, I do not argue in favor of personal responsibility. Whether our illnesses are real or fictive, only when we acknowledge exploitation can we turn judge and jury against the perpetrators, against those who wish to take our money, attention, and labor before collecting our spent husks, grinding them into a supplement, and selling them back to us.

———

Which brings me to an age-old question: Is enlightenment even achievable? Former M.S.I.A. member and Insight trainer Victor Toso still believes. He's a fan of fin de siècle "spiritual scientist" Rudolf Steiner, whom Toso paraphrases, saying, "Every day you live, a miracle happens. If you don't see it, you're not paying attention." He chooses to look for miracles. "Amazing things go under our radar," he says, "freaking amazing things. Enlightenment is just a matter of how awake and how open we are to the grace that's there all the time." I know. A bird shat on my ex-husband's car this week. Miracles are everywhere.

But it was something else Toso shared during our interview that sticks in my mind the way Steiner sticks in his: his description of that crotch-to-crotch hug line. At the end of an Insight training, participants lined up in a row, facing each other, and with each new partner signaled varying degrees of consent by how many fingers they held up: from one (no contact at all) to four (full body hug). "'May the fours be with you' was our joke," he recalls. "By the end, everybody was embracing. There was this sense that a street person could be met by a high-powered attorney, and the attorney would look at and focus on that guy and see his humanity for the first time." In so doing, Toso seems to argue, the attorney would also see himself. "In a time when intellects govern everything, we've lost any idea of soul and spirit. We need connection, and we need some way to find this invisible part of ourselves that we can't recover."

We need other people. Maybe the thing we feel is missing in our lives—the thing we keep trying to purchase from those preacherpreneurs, whether in pill bottles or conference rooms—is really just simple human connection. By encouraging us to turn ever inward, the personal-growth and self-help movements isolate us from one another. Consumerism also separates us, of course, escalating the assault into a one-two punch.

Today's messianic marketplace is commodified, atomized, and scaled. In her expertly researched book *The Gospel of Wellness*, Rina Raphael describes the modern spiritual consumer as creating individualized, bespoke practices and belief systems by "purchasing and picking only what you want from different faiths, like some sort of spiritual Sizzler buffet."[98] You might light candles bearing images of saints while you toss a few tarot cards after your hatha yoga class, hoping to gain more insight into the sound bath you attended last weekend, fearful that the vision board you made in preparation has led you to manifest Justin Bieber instead of Harry Styles.

But when we pick and choose, Raphael argues, "very few seem to pick the more communal aspects, like service, charity, and responsibility," in other words, those aspects of faith-based organizations that create and nurture community.[99] Worse, when we each choose our own adventure, each goes solo. There is no community, or at least not of people sharing in our journey. I was initially amused by the crotch-to-crotch hug line, but now I grieve it.

A 2018 study identified among its participants two basic strategies for seeking happiness: one social and one individual. The study determined that people with goals of "seeing friends and family more, joining a nonprofit, or helping people in need" reported increased life satisfaction a year later. Those who focused on goals such as "staying healthy, finding a better job, or quitting smoking" reported no increase in life satisfaction. In fact, "the self-focused road to happiness was even less effective than having no plans for action at all."[100] Research consistently finds that social connection leads to happiness and physical health, while isolation results in loneliness and death.

M.S.I.A. made Peter McWilliams lonely. And miserable and broke. In the end, self-help didn't help him. In 1993, he finally saw a proper, credentialed, mental-health professional and received a diagnosis of depression. He started taking Prozac and almost immediately felt "the floor of the dungeon" rise and "began feeling spiritual for the first time."[101]

With his newly cleared eyes, McWilliams saw depression everywhere among the ranks of M.S.I.A. members. He came to believe people suffering from depression are more vulnerable to programming and that John-Roger "was a heat-seeking missile" in search of such vulnerability. If someone *wasn't* depressed, criticisms, disapproval, and attack therapies could create the depressed state necessary for J-R to trap and ensnare. As McWilliams's mental health and livelihood improved, John-Roger took notice—and advised that the Prozac would impede Peter's ability to work off karma and thereby doom him to return to earth in his next life. But by then, the acolyte realized, "I didn't need John-Roger anymore. I never had."[102]

This story ends in heartbreaking irony: Peter McWilliams actually did have

AIDS. Three years later, he would be diagnosed with non-Hodgkin's lymphoma, as a result. Certainly J-R could not have known this all those years prior. I'm just as certain that, whenever he heard, he claimed the onset of the condition resulted from the removal of his protection.

McWilliams managed his pain and nausea with cannabis. He grew it. It was legal in California following the passage of Prop 215 in 1996. He also became a vocal member of the cannabis community and a civil-liberties advocate, along the way befriending William F. Buckley, strange bedfellows though they were. Before he died, McWilliams and Victor Toso connected and made peace. The activist dedicated *Life 102* to his old friend.

Toso also told me that years earlier, after that day he'd borrowed money to get his mom's car out of the Marriott garage, he actually drove back to see John-Roger off at the airport. He still had questions. Toso had received every initiation except the final, the soul initiation, when the guru supposedly released one's spirit from the cycle once and for all. When he mentioned this, J-R offered to perform it on the spot. "It was like he had a Cracker Jacks box, and was all, 'Here, I'll give you a little prize now,'" Toso explains. "It was so offhand. It was shocking." Toso declined and walked away. He eventually became an entrepreneur and built a family. John-Roger died in 2014 from pneumonia at the age of eighty, still very much adored by devotees.[103] M.S.I.A. lives.

Marshall Applewhite, the ultimate leader of Heaven's Gate, said, "This world is rotten and I would rather die in service to my interpretation of what God is than stay here."[104] His followers signed an invisible contract, trading their current lives for a spaceship ride to a perfect eternal life, for an apotheosis. On a smaller and more socially sanctioned scale, we Americans seek apotheosis every day in a million ways. We see ourselves as flowers growing toward the sun. We imagine our blooms will separate and float into some flower heaven in the sky, forgetting they can't live without leaves, roots, and far-reaching mycelium networks. Or maybe eighties glam-rock band Poison said it better, when they sang "every rose has its thorn." Applewhite despised the "rotten" earth because it represented the thorns he found and feared within himself.

CHAPTER 5

NANNY NANNY BOO BOO

ON EXTRACTION AND SUCCESS

"I do not recall at exactly what point we surrendered our entire life to The Business," writes Eric Scheibeler, at the time under a pseudonym.[1] Within a year of joining, in the late eighties, he and his family had almost no contact outside of the organization. He spent every free moment working, recruiting, or consuming instructional materials. These materials—tapes, books, and seminar talks—were collectively known as "tools." To achieve financial independence, all anyone needed was to follow the advice in the tools and recruit more people to do the same. Scheibeler was fastidious. He and his wife quickly ascended the ladder. Meanwhile, they continually lost money. There was income, but it hardly covered expenses for product investment, travel, and tools. The Business slowly sucked them dry, and simultaneously convinced them to pull in hundreds more.

This historical phenomenon is commonly known as the "tapes scandal" or the "tools cult." It wasn't the Business itself, but a side con that developed out of it. If I haven't told you yet that the Business was Amway, it's because Scheibeler was instructed not to mention it either. Americans had grown so exhausted by friends' sales pitches for soaps and cleaning products from the organization founded in 1959, that Amway's own sales force distanced itself from the company name. Scheibeler was trained to obfuscate when recruiting "distributors," as salespeople are called in the industry.

When I was growing up in the nineties, Amway was a punch line. If someone asked, "What do you want to do?" my handy reply was "I want to tell you about Amway." I wasn't alone in laughing. But the joke's on us because, amazingly,

Amway lives. The privately held company reported sales of $7.7 billion in 2023. Amway is a multilevel marketing organization (MLM), meaning a participant is not salaried but paid on commission. Some of those commissions result from direct sales, while some derive from wholesale purchases made by others the participant has recruited to join the organization (and still others those recruits have recruited). But almost all MLM distributors lose money every year. Many allege the company is more of a cult than a corporation, or else how could it continue to convince so many to lose so much? Scheibeler agrees, according to his book, *Merchants of Deception* (which is out of print but can still be found in PDF form online). The organization also lives thanks to staggering political corruption. And that has occurred in part because of the other reason for the organization's staying power: Americans, including politicians, have been indoctrinated to believe that work is holy, idleness is sin, and the number in a bank account represents the moral character of its holder.

Whether or not Amway itself is a high-control group, the adjacent "tapes" operation of the eighties and nineties looks to me like a fully realized, true-blue, and very destructive American cult. The gods worshiped were the Amway kingpins, the multimillionaires at the top of distributor chains, who spoke at countless seminars, whose voices were recorded and put on cassette tapes so their motivational speaking could fill the cars of thousands of hungry distributors on the road. These tapes and seminars, some of the aforementioned "tools," were one branch of a system of undue influence that programmed recruits to stick around. The tapes praised the Business's system for its ease ("even a blind dog with a tape in his mouth could go direct"), equated the Business with American ideals, explained it was better to owe money to a bank than to one's upline, and promised you don't need anyone in your life who tells you the Business is foolish. They suggested distributors would one day control the world economy, argued that "successful people will always do what losers refuse to do," and guaranteed "this business works and in a big, big, big, big, big, big, big, big way."[2] The kingpins were royalty. The monarch was Dexter R. Yager Sr.

In 1964, five years after Richard DeVos and Jay Van Andel founded Amway in Ada, Michigan, Yager began selling its cleaning products in Rome, New York. Twenty years later, he was the most successful distributor in Amway. It's said that Yager and his downline—the people he'd recruited, and those they'd recruited, etc.—were responsible for 90 percent of Amway's total revenue. Yager, who died in 2019, was stinking rich. Based on information from a 1997 lawsuit, he appears to have made almost $60 million gross income that year alone, which would be $117.6 million today.[3] "When Yager held a 'Free Enterprise Day' in Charlotte, NC, motels filled up months in advance," a journalist explains. "Buses of distributors trekked out to Yager's house to see the mansion, swimming pool, Rolls-Royces, and antique cars." In a 1982 *60 Minutes* piece, Mike Wallace says of Yager, "They treat him almost like a God."[4]

Joel McConnell—his father, another tools kingpin, worked under Yager—told me about seeing hundreds of distributors leave their seats to stand at the foot of the stage when Yager spoke. "They'd come down like they had just had an invitation to accept Christ," he said. Yager showed them the proof, the wealth he knew they wanted. But his proof was a mirage. Only a small fraction of his millions came from Amway. His whole spiel—his whole persona—was a lie.

———

Amway's top distributors at times painted the organization as Christian. Prayers occurred before seminars and training sessions. Scripture was utilized to support certain doctrines. They were taught it was biblical to remain positive at all times. "Diamonds would repeat the phrase 'what-so-ever ye sayeth shall come to pass,' a loose translation of Mark 11:23. To speak negatively was not only harmful, it was against God's word," Scheibeler writes.[5] I believe Amway conflated itself with the existing belief system of its marks, to manipulate them more easily. Whatever its doctrine, when Scheibeler joined, he exhibited a convert's enthusiasm. When I spoke with him in 2024, there was a lot he couldn't say; he'd signed a non-disparagement agreement years ago. But he did share thoughts about multilevel marketing in general, gleaned from his involvement with a nameless "global multilevel marketing business." You could probably guess which one.

Eric and his wife were recruited and sponsored in 1989 by a neighbor. They were often told they were special—a classic cult tactic of "love bombing" recruits.

People they barely knew said, "We love you." Before long, a successful millionaire distributor visited to share advice. Scheibeler calls him Zack Walters (internet sleuths allege it is Fred Harteis). When he "drove up in his Mercedes, people were rushing to hold the door open for him and to carry his briefcase."[6]

Seemingly unconcerned about the Renfield vibes, Scheibeler felt lucky to receive business advice from someone so wealthy. After calculating that in order to receive a bonus, he'd need to sell more than he'd initially been told, he raised his hand. Zack responded dismissively, "Most people do not find it confusing."[7] Burn! In fact, it's ludicrously (and, some allege, intentionally) confusing. But, no matter, since Scheibeler and other distributors in his chain were advised not to sell products anyway. The guidance was simply to purchase products for their *own* use and recruit new members to join beneath them.

This is the definition of a closed system, where an organization's salespeople are also its end users, buying products at inflated prices, while profits move to the top of the chain. In other words, it's a pyramid scheme, a wealth-redistribution system: those at the bottom pay in, but only receive money if they're able to continue building the pyramid's base beneath them, which becomes increasingly difficult as the pyramid grows. The more confusing the numbers and math, the harder it is to ascertain the grift.

Scheibeler kept positive and followed the plan. He was out almost every night of the week and on weekends, traveling to and from recruitment meetings or seminars, logging tens of thousands of miles in his car a year, all while listening to tapes. Before long, he and his wife worked their way up to "Pearl Direct." At a rally, after the *Rocky* theme played and the crowd of hundreds chanted, "Fired up! Fired up! Fired up!," the proud couple was paraded onstage. "The standing ovation and yelling seemed like it would never end," he writes. "People ran forward to take pictures of us. . . . Some of the women cried."

Zack made sure they understood they were now accountable not only to themselves but to God. Believing he shilled for God helped Scheibeler stomach that, although he had been promised $100,000 a year in income after reaching Pearl, he instead brought in closer to $20,000 (about $48,000 today). This, in exchange for a hundred hours a week between the two of them, all in addition to Eric's full-time job as an underwriter for a large insurance company, which he couldn't afford to quit.[8] Regular jobs were mocked derisively. Amway equated entrepreneurialism with masculinity; what kind of cuck would work to put money in someone else's pocket? Never mind that's exactly what every distributor did for their uplines; it's classic projection. The organization claimed its system gave people freedom, what America is all about, but of course, in reality, distributors were trapped.

What happened when they quit their jobs? All their eggs were in the Amway basket. Scheibeler experienced incredible pressure to quit. He did, in 1992, though he was still losing money in Amway. The Scheibelers blew through their savings. When they went to Zack, trying to fathom how they could simultaneously succeed fabulously and fail extravagantly, he advised them to get a second mortgage. They did. They also owed the government back taxes; owed $100,000 to friends, family, and credit card companies; and had sold everything they could—all in order to go Diamond.[9] They'd been told all Diamonds were millionaires raking in passive income, no longer out recruiting. Whenever he questioned the system or his motivation lagged, Scheibeler was prescribed more tapes.

Eric's wife had started to question the system, though she was initially afraid to speak up. (Spouses commonly discerned the truth before distributors did, which is allegedly why ample tape and stage time was dedicated to indoctrinating wives.) Scheibeler's breaking point arrived not long after. Spending more time with his family had been one of his original goals. Yet he never saw his children. They begged for him. He told them again and again that as soon as he made Diamond, they would be together all the time. Then he overheard a Diamond at a seminar bragging that he'd been out recruiting so much he'd only slept in his own bed eight nights that month. This latest revelation of deceit finally jolted Eric from his catatonic state. He saw that the promise of freedom was actually a cage. He decided to "'unplug' from the system"—to stop listening to tapes.

———

Only a few years after Dexter Yager signed up to sell Amway, he was applying for other jobs.[10] Not long after that, he instead cocreated his own side job: selling motivational recordings. Such content was already popular in America's early

MLMs for an obvious reason: it requires a lot of motivation to keep banging your head against the wall when all you receive is headaches.

In 1972, Yager cut out the middleman. He invested $50,000 (about $163,000 today) to launch his own manufacturing plant. He recorded seminars, duplicated them at scale for pennies, and sold the tapes for five or six dollars each.[11] It eventually brought him around $40 million a year (as reported in 1997, which today would be about $78 million).[12] But distributors were told the tapes yielded no profits. "If somebody asked you about it, it'd be like, 'Yeah, it costs money to put gas in the truck that brings you the tape, it costs money to pay the guy to make it,'" explains McConnell, whose father was high enough in Yager's chain to receive a cut of the profits. Yager and a handful of other top Amway distributors didn't share this stream of income with DeVos and Van Andel. The tapes were never officially part of Amway.[13]

The very existence of the tools cult proves Amway doesn't work. Yager only really made money after he began selling tools, which gave him enough income to pretend it had come from Amway, which fooled more people into joining. He had to lie because ultimately an MLM is just a money-transfer scheme, and "give me all your money" only works at gunpoint.

But you can't fool people forever. They tend to wise up. "The churn rate is amazing, just ridiculous," McConnell says. "You were always recruiting." Today, somewhere between 50 and 80 percent of people engaged in an MLM quit every year.[14] Herein lies the evil genius of the tools scheme: while the money generated from it provided false evidence strong enough to pull people in, the indoctrination and undue influence inherent in it silenced people's inner voices, so they stayed far longer than they otherwise would.

Whenever a distributor began to question why he was losing instead of generating, he was fed more tapes. Scheibeler writes of the vacant stares and "thousand-tape smiles" on distributors' faces at seminars, of the rabid hunger and the ecstasy of belief. Add a splash of worship in that distributors were forbidden to question their upline, forced always to "edify" (Amway talk) them, and encouraged to treat them as heroes and kings. The result is another closed system of sorts, wherein influence is self-perpetuating, victims willingly proffer their funds, and then the accosted thank and honor the thieves for robbing them. "I remember walking out on my deck when I had finally figured it all out," Scheibeler told me, "and actually admiring that it was really well done. It's franchised fraud. It's cultism perfected."

After comprehending that truth, Scheibeler ran some numbers and determined he had personally "collected somewhere in the range of $3 million to $4 million in book, tapes, videos, and seminar money from my dearest friends and family."[15] He had been unduly influenced to the degree that he not only agreed to be extracted from but also to engage in additional extraction himself. He was the field *and* the farmhand . . . and the overseer . . . and the farm itself.

———

The kingpins weren't the first to sell us a rags-to-riches story. It's one of America's foremost creeds, that one can start with nothing and end with everything, thanks only to hard work. When the poor kid makes good, it's a beautiful thing. But that's not what was happening in Amway. That's not why the tools cult succeeded.

Rather, it did so by perverting our deeply held, Puritan-bred beliefs about hard work: that God rewards it, therefore wealth is a sign of being chosen. In reality, no amount of effort could have brought success to Scheibeler and other distributors, because the pyramid was already too big. To hide that fact, the kingpins made sure people believed their failures were their own fault, that they hadn't worked hard enough or didn't have the guts. On tapes, Diamonds mocked the "idiots" who complained, with lines such as "You can make excuses or money, but not both"; "A real man solves the money problem"; and the most effective, "If you don't like your income, look in the mirror."[16] So, Scheibeler blamed himself, believing some inner character flaw kept him from succeeding. He assumed he was the only one drowning.

Distributors weren't allowed to talk to one another about their businesses, effectively siloing them. The rule kept them from discerning the truth, and encouraged them to internalize shame and guilt about their "failures," while assuming everyone else was getting it right. *Failure* is in quotation marks because that's what they were designed to be. Therefore, you could say they were succeeding. Victim blaming is a hallmark of almost every abusive relationship because it leads to silence. It's especially pernicious in financial scams because those who see wealth as proof of salvation also claim poverty indicates sin. Writing of the mansions, fur coats, and Lamborghinis on parade, Scheibeler notes, "Speakers would teach us from stage that God made these sorts of things for His kids, not Satan's."[17]

Seminar speakers lambasted evil liberals, who wanted to take from "hardworking, honest producers" and give to "lazy, nonproductive members of society," Scheibeler writes. "They tried to explain that logically there ought to be a tax on the poor. After all, it was the lazy poor who drained the system supported by the hardworking families in America." He explains that while he was in Amway, his compassion for the poor alchemized into contempt.[18] All of this fed directly into the kingpins' pockets, because if poverty is a choice, then you can choose not to fail by working harder, signing up more recruits, and paying for more seminars and tapes. "It's a choice!" Yager said in a seminar. "I get so sick and tired of hearing people talk about luck luck luck. That's a loser's excuse. . . . It's a cop-out." On the recording, the crowd goes wild.[19]

But what if you labored harder and harder, and still didn't succeed? In that case, according to tools-cult doctrine, the problem was inside you. Your best option was to leave quietly and hope no one notices what a filthy turd you are. "The guilt and shame was unbelievable," Scheibeler told me over the phone. "I went to the altar after these weekend seminars with tears streaming down my face, just praying God would take whatever defects were within me. I didn't realize I was just a conduit to pump millions of dollars to my upline."

Still, in spite of all of this, he experienced withdrawal symptoms after quitting the tapes. (His wife had also given up on the program.) He kind of missed them, even as his brain slowly picked apart the indoctrination. This went on for more than a year. Meanwhile, he collected evidence. In the previous year, only about ten people out of the more than two thousand he had recruited had netted more than one dollar. "To me, that looked like just under a 100% failure rate."[20] Yet he still believed Amway was a legitimate company that just had a few bad kingpin apples. After all, Ronald Reagan, Mary Lou Retton, Gerald Ford, Dave Thomas, Jack Kemp, Jerry Falwell, Oliver North, and Newt Gingrich had spoken at seminars. Surely they wouldn't lend their support to a scam!

Then he discovered that the DeVos and Van Andel families had known about the tools cult since at least 1983 and done almost nothing because, as historian Sean Munger alleges, "the Amway corporation realized that a significant portion of their income came from the downlines of the tools kingpins—all those distributors, hooked on tapes and rallies, buying . . . soap."[21]

Scheibeler also found a 1991 *Forbes* article full of terrifying allegations. A former CFO, who resigned in 1979, claimed his family received threats for years afterward. "Everyone assumed that the phones were tapped, and that Amway had something on everybody," he told *Forbes*. A former administrative assistant, who helped the Canadian government's 1980s investigation into Amway, claims she was roughed up once in Chicago and told to "stay away from Amway." Philip Kerns, a former distributor, who published a tell-all book, says Amway sent detectives to follow him around and assault him.[22]

"I felt certain that I was going to be killed," Scheibeler writes, acknowledging that he had "told too many people" of his plans to expose everything and write a book. "There was too much money at stake. I became nearly insane with paranoia. When I walked alone, I walked in a stagger step, as I knew that kind of a gait made it more difficult for snipers."

He realized his double-agent cover was blown when, he writes, he received a thinly veiled death threat from Zack's most loyal lackey, who told Scheibeler "he was not afraid of prison, and would 'take me out' if I ever messed with Zack."[23] Scheibeler blew the whistle anyway. He prepared a packet "nearly a quarter inch thick," including information about court cases, transcripts of audio and video evidence, and other details revealing the fraud of the tools cult, and mailed it to his downline. Many of them were shocked. But it's hard to imagine how deeply that shock could have penetrated when Amway and even its illicit tools cult aren't that different from modern American capitalism itself.

O ur country's current capitalist system was kind of a mistake. A big whoopsie. The word *capitalism* came into use in the middle of the nineteenth century as a result of the Industrial Revolution, when critics started to investigate how some leapt into unimaginable wealth as others sank into destitution. At the time, capitalism represented everything the New England Puritan clergy had fought to avoid. For decades, they'd thwarted a certain kind of acquisitive spirit, that which serves the self without regard for others. A code of conduct was explained to Massachusetts Bay Colonists before they even arrived, in the famous city-upon-a-hill speech by newly appointed governor John Winthrop: "Thou must observe whether thy brother hath present or probable or possible means of repaying thee, if there be none of those, thou must give him according to his necessity . . . though there be danger of losing it."[24]

They instituted laws controlling wages and prices, and even how people could and couldn't spend their money. "Indeed, few states in the early modern world were less receptive to profit seeking for individualistic rather than communal purposes," writes Stephen Innes, author of *Creating the Commonwealth: The Economic Culture of Puritan New England*. "Those prospective immigrants hoping to come for worldly and self-regarding ends were told candidly to seek their fortune elsewhere."[25]

And yet, the kind of capitalism we participate in today in America, arguably more self-serving than ever, is a direct result of Puritanism. As previously mentioned, the Puritans saw hard work as a foundational way to glorify God. Since wealth is a natural outcome of hard work, striving for wealth itself became not only OK but expected. Plus if God rewarded his chosen with eternal life, wouldn't he also reward them in earthly endeavors? The richer you got, the more evidence he loved you back. These religious beliefs created an economic engine that propelled New England to dominate Atlantic trade.

But, as Cotton Mather put it in the 1690s, "religion begot prosperity, and the daughter devoured the mother."[26] In this way, in addition to being a mistake, American capitalism was also inevitable. Those driven by greed instead of piety began perverting these Puritan ideals to justify their own acquisitiveness, and that engine the Puritans had created became too powerful to control. *Whoops.*

In 1905, economist and sociologist Max Weber noticed that "for any country in which several religions coexist . . . people who own capital . . . tend to be, with striking frequency, overwhelmingly Protestant."[27] In New England, specifically, these Protestant ideas developed free of preexisting and mediating cultural and government forces *and* were baked into the very foundation of the country. In his classic book, *The Protestant Ethic and the Spirit of Capitalism*, Weber quotes at length the writings of America's most popular secular prophet of wealth creation, Benjamin Franklin—"time is money," "credit is money," "money can beget money," etc.—and notes that Americans held on to money rather than spend it. Making money, he argued, had become an end itself.

And so, the so-called self-made man was born. In the years following the Civil War, as the Industrial Revolution tore through New England cities, members of the business class broke traditional hierarchies to acquire incredible wealth and, with it, power. This #hustleculture began almost as an egalitarian movement of lowly merchants slingshotting aristocrats in the eye with nothing but their work ethic and strong moral character. But once they had power, they became Goliath.

The MO for maintaining superiority was the use of what historian Irvin G. Wyllie, in his 1954 book, *The Self-Made Man in America: The Myth of Rags to Riches*, calls the "success rationale."[28] Wealthy businessmen claimed their success was evidence of being chosen by God, while poor people had either failed or lost God's favor. In other words, if you didn't get rich, it was your own damn fault. You'll notice the Puritanism in this doctrine. However, other parts of the success rationale shook off their Puritan shackles.

Mostly gone was belief in predestination, and in utter human sin and depravity. Instead, clergy argued that God wanted us to be good—and happy. That's why he invented cat videos. Minister and onetime Brown University president, Francis Wayland argued, "The universe around us is composed of objects suited to gratify our desire, and thus minister to our happiness."[29] Even if we use those objects for reasons beyond our sustenance—for profit and trade, which bring us more comfort and convenience in exchange—that's still part of God's plan.[30] Also, far from abhorring social mobility as Puritans had, Industrial Revolution–era Americans were obsessed with it. Horatio Alger wrote more than a hundred rags-to-riches stories, young adult novels about poor boys who strike it rich as a result of hard work and strong moral character. By 1910, more than a million copies of his novels were selling a year. For the first time in history, any white male person had the chance to be filthy rich.

Clergymen preached this success rationale from the pulpit. Fawning media and publishers pumped out pamphlets and guides lionizing the self-made man and teaching youth how to mimic his path. Lecture series abounded, teaching the doctrine to hungry upstart hustlers (in ways that, as discussed, would eventually develop into our modern self-help economy). Unfortunately, by the time all of these acolytes began indoctrinating youth into the movement, the window was closing. Even after that truth became undeniable, by the early twentieth century, acolytes still preached the gospel. It was convenient for them to do so. If the masses remained focused on the dream, they'd be too busy hustling to fight for social services, government regulations, or collective power, any of which would have alleviated the poverty ravaging America, but specifically at the expense of the self-made men. This is the intersection of con artistry and cult.

So you can imagine my delight when I opened Wyllie's book, published in 1954, and saw he referred to this decades-long American phenomenon as the "success cult" and the "cult of the self-made man." How I wish he were alive so I could ask about that word choice. (I should also tell you I'm starting to have parasocial relationships with dead scholars.) Presumably, Wyllie mostly leaned on the traditional definition of the word *cult*, meaning a group of people who all venerate the same idea or person. But the religious undertones are no doubt intentional, as he also uses the words *prophet* and *doctrine*.

By the middle of the nineteenth century, "success," to most Americans, "had long since come to mean achievement in business, and in making money." But they didn't understand that much of the wealth they witnessed had simply been redistributed. Instead, there was a general assumption in America that riches were infinite, that we all had the opportunity to partake of an endless bounty. The beast that Puritan clergy had tried so hard to cage was rampaging. In 1842, the *New York Sun* published *Wealth and Pedigree of the Wealthy Citizens of New York City*, America's first directory of people "distinguished chiefly for their possession of money."[31]

In 1859, Abraham Lincoln said, "If any continue through life in the condition of the hired laborer," it was surely "because of either a dependent nature which prefers it, or improvidence, folly, or singular misfortune."[32] Messaging suggested there was plenty to go around, and only chumps didn't get theirs.

To be sure, in the wide-open days of the early industrial era, there were men who built incredible fortunes from the bottom up. For context, most on the *Sun*'s list had acquired wealth numbering in the low six figures.[33] Then there was John Jacob Astor, a German immigrant who was America's first multimillionaire and worth $20 million when he died.[34] And of course, Andrew Carnegie: also an immigrant, the Scottish-born steel magnate arrived in Pennsylvania in 1848 at the age of twelve with his recently impoverished parents. That same year he began working in a cotton factory as a bobbin boy.[35] At the turn of the twentieth century, Carnegie's share of the steel industry was $225 million, the biggest liquid fortune in the world.[36]

But these men were outliers. And anyway, as the Industrial Revolution wore on, it became harder and harder for poor boys even to catch a break. One study determined that among businessmen who reached elite status in 1870, 43 percent had come from the lower classes.[37] But by the first decade of the twentieth century, only 5 percent of leading corporate executives had risen from poverty.[38] The number would continue to shrink.

I wrote *so-called* before "self-made man," by the way, because no one does anything in a vacuum. What about their loans and investors, not to mention government rebates? As a noted nineteenth-century political scientist said to a friend, "*Self-made men*, indeed! Why don't you tell me of a self-laid egg?"[39]

For that matter, what about the wives who supported these men? As comedian and actor Ali Wong once joked, "Do you know how much more successful I would be if I had a wife?"[40]

And, perhaps most important, let's not forget that each of us is comprised of more microbial cells than human cells. We are mostly not ourselves. And these microbes literally influence our brains.[41] *Do you know how much more successful I would be if I had more Lactobacillus rhamnosus JB1?*

But, my apologies: how dare I puncture the myth of the self-made man before I've allowed you to fondle its dewy contours. Let's do that now. . . . You're getting verrrrrrry sleepy.

If you want to make more money, that must mean you've been called to do so by God. However, unlike the Puritans, we in the success cult embrace acquisitiveness by exploiting a logic loophole: What if the act of acquiring is your calling?

In that case, you must surely be a businessman! You will know that's your path as soon as you feel "the organ of acquisitiveness" inside you.[42] *At that point, all you'll need to succeed is a strong moral character. So go out there and get it! OK, nice talking to you, goodb— What's that, you have questions? Was I not clear?*

Few of the success-cult handbooks of that time provided practical business advice, for example, on accounting, advertising, production, or investment. More important was for you to be industrious, frugal, honest, sober, etc. Also, far from being a hindrance, your poverty was your ticket because it forced you to overcome adversity—overcome sin itself—which is how you developed the aforementioned moral character deemed so essential.

Such arguments are tautological. God rewards good moral character. Ergo, if you are rich, you are good. Therefore, money is good simply because you have it. John D. Rockefeller was fond of saying he received his money from God. On the other hand, "Those who were poor had no reason to reproach the Giver of Gifts, for they had been tested and found deficient in virtue."[43] God was thinking about making you rich, but then he saw your TikTok page.

Top of these deficits was idleness, naturally. One Connecticut schoolmaster referred to idle man as a lesser beast, saying, "he is half quadruped, and of the most stupid species."[44] (Strictly speaking, I think half a quadruped is a biped, but perhaps no one was editing this guy's insults.) Better to be friends with murderers because at least stabbing is hard labor. One British reporter who visited America found the work ethic boring: "There were no interesting men with whom to do nothing."[45]

The success cult endured in large part thanks to the imprimatur of prominent clergy. "You need not be ashamed to be rich," Henry Ward Beecher told his Brooklyn Heights congregation, and "you need not be ashamed to be thought to be seeking riches." Beecher saw America playing a special providential role in the pursuit of civilization by accumulation: "Nowhere else does wealth so directly point towards virtue in morality . . . as in America," he preached. "We have been put in the van among nations."[46]

Massachusetts-born Philadelphia minister and Temple University founder Russell Conwell argued in a sermon he delivered more than six thousand times, that out of every one hundred rich Americans, ninety-eight were honest, and "that is why they are rich."[47] If you think this is all headed toward the prosperity gospel, you're right (and clearly smart—but hopefully not a "genius"; how "wretched" is your poetry?).

However, they did reason that when God gave money, he expected it to be used in a godly manner—for libraries, schools, museums, hospitals, and orphanages—and not exclusively for the millionaire's own benefit. Andrew Carnegie agreed. He wrote in 1889, "the man who dies leaving behind him many millions of available wealth, which was his to administer during life, will pass away 'unwept, unhonored, and unsung.'"[48] Peter Cooper and John D. Rockefeller also distributed much of their estates. Carnegie went so far as to advocate for excessive inheritance taxes that would make it impossible for fortunes to pass through generations, since children born rich were considered incompetent and soft: "I should as soon leave to my son a curse as the almighty dollar."[49] Most stopped short of Carnegie's extreme take, arguing instead that spoiled kids needn't be barred from inheriting money since they would surely lose it to the next generation of poor upstarts anyway, and the cycle would start anew. This sounds like the plot of a great rom-com, not least because such a storyline is clearly fictional.

Carnegie and others saw an important distinction between philanthropy and charity, though. It's one thing to build a hospital. But giving directly to the poor would only "teach the hard-working, industrious man that there is an easier path." None of the $125 million he gave away between 1887 and 1907 went to direct relief because, Carnegie believed, "every drunken vagabond or lazy idler supported by alms bestowed by wealthy people is a source of moral infection to a neighborhood."[50]

Church leaders mostly agreed. Beecher said, "Looking comprehensively . . . no man in this land suffers from poverty unless it be more than his fault—unless it be his sin."[51] Wyllie's research turned up a handful of extreme views, including from one leader who wanted to abolish almshouses altogether and instead send missionaries to tell the needy that God had decreed only those who work get to eat. Another advocated systematic starvation of the impoverished since they had deliberately chosen poverty and therefore should be allowed to suffer its natural consequences.

The cult's logic required a near total negation of luck. When the occasional businessman attributed some degree of his achievement to luck, acolytes were quick to "reassert the merit principle . . . for if luck could be said to account for the successes of the few, there might be grounds for dispossessing them in the interests of the many."[52] More universal was the assumption that wealth couldn't result from serendipity because good things happen to good people and bad things happen to bad people. This was the new moral law. Luck wasn't really a thing anymore—the Reformation and the Enlightenment had killed it.

Cultures affected by the Protestant Reformation became "obsessed with the idea of defining right and wrong in an objective way that everyone can agree with," scholar Angus Fletcher told me. "Once you have that, that's the end of stories because they all become allegories." Fletcher is both a neuroscientist and a literature PhD. His book *Wonderworks: Literary Invention and the Science of Stories* explores, among other topics, the death of what he calls the Lucky Twist.[53] It was murdered by Charles Perrault, the French writer who "translated" ancient folktales into morality stories, aka fairy tales, in 1697. The Lucky Twist is bludgeoned anew almost annually by Disney. The refusal to acknowledge luck as a force in the world is central to cultlike thinking.

Throughout almost all of recorded human history and, probably, thousands and thousands of years of oral history, humans have told stories about lucky reversals of fortune. For example, the oldest known iteration of *Cinderella* is the tale of a woman with few prospects for love or money. Her name is Rhodopis. One day, while she bathed, a bird landed on her pile of clothes and flew away with one of her shoes. In flight, the bird dropped the shoe without intention, and it landed in the lap of a king. Understanding the sandal as heaven-sent, he ordered his men to find its owner, and when they did, he married her. Rhodopis gets the happily ever after not because she made the right choice or proved herself worthy, but due to random chance. You probably expect Rhodopis at least to represent the kind of moral character typically lauded by eighteenth- and nineteenth-century Western society, so thoroughly has your brain been trained by Perrault-style fairy tales. She was a sex worker.

Among traditional folktales are countless stories containing similarly random Lucky Twists of fate. People who behave badly are rewarded just as often if not more so than those who behave well. That was the whole point: sometimes bad things happen. Not because you deserve them but simply because life is hard. Perrault would have none of this. He changed the stories he translated, baking in poetic justice that rewarded societally condoned behavior and punished villains—so kids would behave accordingly. This was a grave mistake. As Perrault was not a neuroscientist, he didn't understand the reason for the Lucky Twist's endurance. It wires our brains for optimism.

The existence of true luck tells us that good things *can* happen, not that they will or won't based on certain criteria but simply that they might at any moment for no reason at all. "That creates durable optimism," Fletcher explains. "If something bad happens to you, you just say, 'Well, bad things can happen but that doesn't mean a good thing couldn't happen tomorrow.' That keeps alive your optimism."

In contrast, the fairy tales of Perrault and Disney can lead us to catastrophize by causing our brains to think, Fletcher writes, "Since my efforts have come to no good, then I must be no good. . . . I'll keep failing forever," and "Maybe I'm unhappy because I deserve to be unhappy."[54]

For millennia, stories have helped humans develop empathy, resilience, imagination, and an understanding of life as messy and complicated, all of which lead to better problem-solving. "These deeper emotional processes have been nuked by modern fairy tales," Fletcher explains. "As a result, kids are coming out with more anxiety and anger. They think of everything in terms of right or wrong. If something's wrong, it's either their fault or somebody else's." Shame or blame. Victim or righteous. Damned or saved. Ursula or Ariel.

When we blame others, we tend toward conspiracist thinking. When we blame ourselves, we are more easily victimized. Personal responsibility has a place in society. But when someone encourages us to take none or all of it, that person has something to gain from our consent.

Now, you may be asking yourself, didn't Horatio Alger's wildly popular, industrial-era, rags-to-riches young adult stories contain a healthy dose of luck? Yes and no. It is correct that the poor but morally upright boys almost always start along their path to success thanks to the kindness of an older, prosperous man who gives them a chance. Alger had a series that was literally titled "Luck and Pluck." But ultimately my response is no, because in those stories, good things only happen to good kids, as a rule, making the kids' morality a criteria. Also, I would describe Alger's trope of the fairy godfather less as a Lucky Twist and more as grooming. Alger appears to have been a pedophile. In 1866, before he had a writing career, he was accused of "the abominable and revolting crime of gross familiarity with boys," while working as a parson at a Congregationalist church. Stories surfaced of two victims, one fifteen and one thirteen. Alger's father, a minister, brokered a quiet dismissal for his son in exchange for his promise never to return to the ministry.[55]

Alger's later best-selling stories were somewhat autobiographical, as he was himself an older prosperous man who helped homeless boys living on the streets of New York City in the second half of the nineteenth century. He would gather them, give them money and candy, and invite them into his rooming house. He eventually adopted two off the street to live with him. Whatever happened between him and those boys in private is lost to history, but you can forgive me for doubting that the young boys found this "help" very lucky.

As the nineteenth century wore on, homeless children became harder for success-cult acolytes to ignore. Already by 1850 they were estimated to number between twelve and fifteen thousand in New York City alone.[56] The unprecedented wealth of some people was matched by poverty at a scale never before experienced in America, caused by a variety of factors: the end of westward expansion (and the "free," aka stolen, land it had delivered), diminishing farm jobs due to mechanization, the replacement of independently owned shops by large-scale manufacturing, and an influx of immigrants to already overcrowded cities. In urban areas, wage employment suffered unchecked exploitation: low pay, overly long workdays, unsafe conditions, child labor. Unemployment was rampant. Church leaders who'd previously beaten the success-gospel drum began to suspect the masses couldn't all be personally responsible for their destitution. The depression of the 1880s and '90s, and the riots and strikes therein, drew more attention to the incredible inequality in America. Jacob

Riis's shocking images of urban poverty, captured with the brand-new technology of mobile flashes, brought these realities into the mainstream's gaze.

The end of the century turned into the Progressive Era, and the gospel of the self-made man ebbed. But some held on to the dream—even as scrutiny revealed the monopolies and trusts had made it literally impossible for any young entrepreneur to compete and rise in the ranks; even as the public became aware that much of the barons' wealth had resulted from government initiatives. For example, in the 1860s and early '70s, $100 million in U.S. bonds and loans and 100 million acres of U.S. land were given to the railroads. Ida M. Tarbell's meticulous investigation into the Standard Oil Company revealed "that rebates, rather than righteousness, provided the foundation for the Rockefeller fortune."[57] Even Carnegie acknowledged his fortune had been made off of an undeveloped continent under conditions no longer existing, and also literally admitted, "The fact is that most of us can never hope to be rich."[58]

Journalists uncovered some of the more dubious methods engaged by titans when building their empires, "tactics that are today the hallmark of organized crime: intimidation, violence, corruption, conspiracies, and fraud."[59] One muckraker wrote, "Like the agents of a great lottery, they appeal to your gambling instinct; they tell you of the big winning. . . . Under even favored conditions . . . not one of you in ten thousand can reasonably hope for a prize."[60] The numerous success guides and pamphlets came into ridicule.

Ultimately, the cult of the self-made man was a house of cards. Nevertheless, we are all deeply indoctrinated into this belief system of financial success or failure as evidence of morality or sin. Our inherited Puritan beliefs—of work as holy and idleness as evil—have been perverted by those wishing to plunder, to justify having already done so, and to ensure their ability to continue on. These beliefs have metastasized to the degree that today, what's often being plundered are people themselves. It's classic extraction economics.

Before anyone called it New England, the area was populated by a people and culture that didn't understand itself as separate from the rest of the earth.

In the Ojibwe language, many words that in English are nouns or adjectives are instead verbs. For example, one wouldn't just say *mountain* or *river* but, rather, *to be a mountain* or *to be a river*. "To be a hill, to be a sandy beach, to be a Saturday, all are possible verbs in a world where everything is alive," writes Robin Wall Kimmerer, botanist, mother, and member of the Citizen Potawatomi Nation, in her book *Braiding Sweetgrass*. She describes such a language as "a mirror for seeing the animacy of the world, the life that pulses through all things, through pines and nuthatches and mushrooms."[61]

She writes that "in Native ways of knowing, human people are often referred to as 'the younger brothers of Creation,'" as opposed to being "the pinnacle of evolution, the darling of Creation."[62] Viewing the world as animated, she argues, allows us to develop a more fulsome relationship with it, which could grow into a sacred bond.

American culture has since been dominated by a different relationship between people and natural resources, one driven by the Puritan grace-nature divide, which holds that God's chosen are completely separate from plants and animals. (Even some of our movements to fight the indiscriminate extraction of natural resources are built upon the same ideology: "Save the Earth!," as if it's something separate upon which we can act.) This is because, as the theory goes, God's favorites are of the spiritual realm, while the natural world is corrupt. Or maybe because one time John Cotton got a tapeworm. It also holds that God has commanded his chosen to charitably improve the natural world by using its resources to sweeten the lives of the chosen. Empty a mountain of ore, abandon its scarred carcass, and move to the next mountain. Of course, I could list some of the innumerable Protestants past and present who do not support extraction economics. No matter; this Puritan ethic is now part of secular American culture writ large. And some of us have leaned in further.

Over the last four centuries, many have come to believe sinful "nature" also includes certain groups of people and have accordingly exploited them as resources, the most glaring examples being the transatlantic slave trade and the massacre or resettlement of Native Americans. Then, as this bit of ideology ransacked its way through American history, it met and merged with the work-is-holy-and-idleness-is-sin doctrine. They are natural collaborators because the belief that poverty results from sin diminishes the humanity of the impoverished in the same way the grace-nature divide diminishes nature. Together, these two bits of Puritan doomsday ideology have collaborated to uncover a new and abundant natural resource: the lower classes. Together, they have justified the ability of the supposedly chosen and deserving wealthy to plunder the allegedly undeserving lower classes. This has been incredibly good for business because, unlike ore in a mountain, the American poor are a renewable resource.

Certainly, MLMs are a glaring example: each bankrupted recruit is replaced with a new one, and each time an organization saturates a geographic area with distributors, it moves down the road. But it is merely a symptom of a larger problem. Over the last four decades, America's richest have amassed colossal wealth by plundering funds otherwise earmarked for the middle and lower classes. For example, company profits: since 1980, average worker paychecks have only increased by 12 percent, while CEO pay has risen by 940 percent. When adjusted for inflation, earnings of the bottom 90 percent have barely risen at all. In the 1960s, typical American workers earned about 20 times less than their CEOs did; now they earn 300 times less.[63]

For example, tax cuts. In 2017, Trump dropped the corporate tax rate from 35 percent of income to 21 percent—which ultimately increased the federal debt by $1.9 trillion. "Which meant less federal money for schools, healthcare, education, and other public services," writes scholar and former secretary of labor Robert B. Reich, in *The System*. Boards used the majority of their saved cash to buy back their own stock, which increased their profits and paychecks even more. That same year of the tax cut, Walmart put thousands of Americans out of work. That same year, Whole Foods announced the end of medical benefits for all part-time workers, a move that annually saves the company the same amount that its overlord, Jeff Bezos, makes in two hours.[64]

Profits move to the top of the chain. This is wealth redistribution. It's more or less a pyramid scheme. The result is staggering inequality. The 1 percent of Americans at the top own the same amount of wealth as the bottom 90 percent. During the COVID-19 pandemic alone, they increased their fortunes by a third.[65] And if you instead look only at the bottom 50 percent of Americans, you see that they collectively own only 1.3 percent of the total wealth in our nation. In 2020, heirs to the Walmart empire alone had more wealth than 42 percent of Americans—almost 140 million people combined—and their fortune was growing by $70,000 a minute, $100 million a day.[66]

Everyone else in the nation and our government—and by extension we—have let them do it. Through lobbying, influence, and ever-ballooning campaign donations, the wealthiest members of our nation have, since Reagan's administration, wooed the government to cut taxes for the wealthy and for corporations, roll back regulations protecting the public from risky corporate behavior, neuter unions empowering workers to thwart exploitation, and allow corporations to move overseas and leave American workers in the dust. Between 1975 and 2020, *fifty trillion dollars* moved from the bottom 90 percent of Americans to the top 1 percent.[67]

Future workers, meanwhile, are hobbled not only by their parents' ever-shrinking bank accounts, but also by "deteriorating schools, unaffordable college tuition, decaying infrastructure, soaring healthcare costs, and diminishing basic research" because the wealthiest Americans have plundered our nation's collective coffers in a race to top each other on the list of largest penises, sorry, I mean biggest douchebags, oops, I mean the *Forbes* World's Billionaires List.[68] For the last decade, seven or eight out of the top ten on this list have consistently been Americans.[69] The fact that the wealthy aren't competing to *fall off* this list demonstrates how irreducibly our culture associates acquisitiveness with moral character.

We live in an oligarchy, wherein only a small number of Americans control the country. More specifically, it's a plutocracy: a small number of *rich people* run the show. Robert Johnson, president of the Institute for New Economic Thinking, a think tank founded in the wake of the subprime mortgage crisis, told me his career has been a tour "of seeing the contradictions between a system that uses the economy to foster innovation and the well-being of people versus a system of plutocratic wealth extraction that has made the currency of money much more powerful politically than the currency of votes." After our conversation, I emailed him an early draft of this chapter. He responded, "The false spirituality of ego legitimation, of exploitation and wealth accumulation is a toxic disease and at the core of the deterioration of governance."

But we're all so indoctrinated into believing the wealthy earned their just deserts through hard work—and that the same can rescue anyone who struggles—that few saw the coup occur. Even some of the politicians being bought didn't see a connection between the redistribution of wealth and the lower classes' increasing need to take extra jobs, spend their savings, and take on debt. In 2005, George W. Bush responded to a town-hall question from a divorced mother of three in Nebraska, who shared that she was working three jobs to make ends meet. "You work three jobs?" he said with inspired awe. "Uniquely American, isn't it? I mean, that is fantastic that you're doing that."[70]

Our collective indoctrination into the belief that work is holy and idleness a sin not only robs the poor but entraps them. Once you fall below the poverty line, there's no escape because, at that point, we've unconsciously decided you're choosing to be poor by not working, that you have the ability to pull yourself out if you actually want to. If that's not a foundational belief, then why do welfare programs typically require recipients of government assistance to be employed in order to receive benefits?

In 1996, President Bill Clinton signed one of the biggest overhauls of the government-aid system in American history, the Personal Responsibility and Work Opportunity Reconciliation Act.[71] He warned of impoverished people developing dependency, as if government aid were heroin. The takeaway: people were *choosing* poverty. Reformers instituted welfare-to-work programs to ensure beneficiaries would look for jobs and take them. But the percentage of people living below the poverty line barely budged.

At the time, James Jennings, retired Tufts University political scientist and author of *Welfare Reform and the Revitalization of Inner City Neighborhoods*, was involved with a nonprofit program. "Some of the women I worked with were in community college to learn a skill," he recalls. "All of a sudden that was no longer a possibility because they had to work jobs—ones their local training assistance center told them to, or for twenty hours a week, or whatever the case. So their schooling went out the window." They were forced to trade opportunities to gain skills to secure higher paying jobs that would pull them out of poverty for unskilled dead-end jobs that kept them trapped. Clinton's administration literally created the dependency it feared.

Yet welfare-to-work programs continue to be pushed. During the 2023 debt-ceiling crisis, a compromise was finally struck in part by meeting Republican demands to enact stricter work requirements on food-stamp eligibility.[72] It all sounds sensible. It simply doesn't work. A 2016 study by the Center on Budget and Policy Priorities found that, among those subject to work requirements, employment increases "were modest and faded over time" and that stable employment "proved the exception, not the norm." It determined that the most successful programs were those boosting "the education and skills of those subject to work requirements, rather than simply requiring them to search for work or find a job," and that "such requirements do little to reduce poverty, and in some cases, push families deeper into it."[73] Even with this research available, politicians continuously place blame for the system's failures elsewhere. I'll give you one guess who gets the finger.

Ronald Reagan pointed to the welfare queen, a villain of his staff's invention used to stoke fear. As the story went, the rising number of pregnancies to unwed women resulted from government aid to single mothers, who, allegedly, would rather raise a child on welfare than with a partner. This claim has never been supported by credible social science. Nevertheless, Reagan's campaign advisors found a real life "queen"(Linda Taylor, also an alleged kidnapper and murderer), suggested she indicated a pattern, and referenced her at rallies.

Jennings argues that welfare reform traditionally functions more like punishment. Perhaps this is because, if one believes a surfeit or dearth of wealth reflects inner character, then one also believes there's nothing we even can do about poverty. If you believe certain people are simply destined to be poor, you might look at that barely changing percentage of people beneath the poverty line as evidence of your belief. So why help? Sin should be punished. In 2024, the Supreme Court made it illegal to sleep on the streets. Losing access to a home—often a result of runaway housing and rent prices, as there are now between 1.5 and 5.5 million fewer housing units than people who need them—can now land one in our labyrinthine incarceration system out of which there is often no escape.[74]

The propagation of the ideology claiming work is holy and idleness a sin continues because it is convenient to those who profit off of it—who profit by seeing the chronically poor as a resource they can extract. For example, the $11 billion charged in overdraft fees in 2021 by the biggest banks. Those most likely to overdraw their accounts are, of course, those with the least amount of money in the accounts. (The alternative is for funds not to be available.) The 9 percent of customers who carried average balances of less than $350 were responsible for 84 percent of that $11 billion gross profit. Sometimes people were charged overdraft fees on the same account multiple times a day. "The poor were made to pay for their poverty," writes Matthew Desmond, a sociologist at Princeton University and author of *Poverty, by America*.[75] The American dream is a Ponzi scheme. This kind of exploitation is exactly what the robber barons did in the Gilded Age, is exactly what Amway and other MLMs continue to do today.

In truth, alleviating poverty in America is a pretty straightforward endeavor. The problem is an invested opposition with powerful lobbies that encourages a focus on individuals—say, welfare queens—instead of the system. We are so quick to accept blame for problems created by powerful interests. Manufacturers of plastics have literally convinced consumers to clean up the mess they made. It's called plastic recycling. And it doesn't even work—except it does "work," in that part of its intention is to remove blame from the corporations that created the problem and also burden the public with solving the problem, which distracts us from the continual proliferation of the problem. Absolute insanity. I'm starting to lose my cool. At a recent playdate, I overheard my child's best friend say, "Your mom bought stale taco shells again," at which point I spun around, wild-eyed, and said, "You meant to say, 'Trader Joe's *sold* your mom stale taco shells again.'" She turned to my daughter and asked, "Do you like my hair clip?" so I had clearly made an impression.

Yes, people must have personal choice: whether that is to smoke cigarettes, eat Doritos, or buy plastic bottles. I agree. But it's extreme that we've decided as a community that one can make a buck absolutely any way at all, as long as they can find a market, even if they have to lie to a market to get its money. And that brings us back to the rash of multilevel marketing "companies" literally consuming our country.

Here's the thing, though: we can just as easily decide this system is *not* OK.

To stop MLMs, we'll have to, because our government won't help us. It's in on it. The sales call is coming from inside the house.

Do you like tricking people? Do you want to invite your friends over only to try to sell them products that have no market value because no one wants them? What if I told you the products are also overpriced and may contain carcinogens? Do you want to post sales pitches on social media until all of your connections block you? Stop getting asked to dinner parties? Embarrass your children by pitching other parents at playdates? Believe that people who disagree with you are demonic? Get divorced, become estranged from your kids, and lose thousands of dollars to credit card companies? . . . Wait, you do? I wasn't expecting that.

Ninety-nine percent of all participants in any kind of MLM lose money, a statistic so well documented, I don't even know what to cite. In spite of these staggering losses, people keep signing up. According to MLM representatives, 18 million American households are under contract with one of these companies each year, and spend $20 to $30 billion in fees and purchases.[76] That's one in six Americans, the same number who get food poisoning annually (kind of a similar feeling), the same number who report depression (coincidence?). Each year, more than half of those 18 million are new recruits—replacing the same number who tired of losing money and dropped out.

MLM is *not* direct sales. To make money in direct sales, you would need a much higher profit margin, never turn your customers into salespeople with whom you compete, and sell something people can't find in a store. The products—pretty much anything you can imagine—in MLM are not the point. Very few people even move them beyond their own closets, after purchasing a certain amount in order to remain active. The real focus is on recruiting others, who also buy starter packs and meet quotas, a cut of which moves up the line. Only at tax time do participants realize they spent more than earned.

OK, if it's not sales, what is it? Noted religious-studies scholar David G. Bromley researched Amway in the nineties. In his paper, he called it a "quasi-religious corporation." Bromley deciphered that the relatively new business endeavor and others like it function more like religions than companies. He notes these organizations' mission to transform the social order, the importance of belief and commitment over skills and experience, the tight-knit communal networks of participants, and the appeal to a transcendent purpose. He describes recruitment as "evangelizing," and membership as "the product of a conversion experience." And, of course, he explores the charismatic authority of these groups' founders and leaders.[77] In addition to Amway, he labels six other organizations as quasi-religious corporations, including Herbalife, Nu Skin, and Mary Kay—all MLMs.

More recently, MLMs have been described by journalist and activist Robert FitzPatrick in his book *Ponzinomics: The Untold Story of Multi-Level Marketing* as "a cultic, delusional and fraudulent belief system, using the inherently deceptive pyramid scheme or 'endless chain' as a mechanism for swindle." Only those at the very top (less than 1 percent) make money, and do so specifically as a result of everyone else's loss. "The [1%] had not out-performed the other 99%. They had plundered them," FitzPatrick writes.[78]

Or, as Roberta Blevins, a former sales rep for the MLM LuLaRoe, told me, "The dead weight is what propels this industry forward." It's literally impossible for these companies to function the way they claim to. For example, if participants could actually sell products to customers outside of the scheme, these products would immediately dominate a market, due to the sheer number of participants in any market, thereby consuming any need for what's sold—and the company would collapse. In the 2018 season of the podcast *The Dream*, host Jane Marie points out that lotion and soap MLM Rodan + Fields had 400,000 distributors across the country when, by her math, America has "fewer than 20,000 CVSes and Walgreens—aka lotion and soap stores—combined."[79]

Typically, "distributors" (in quotes because they rarely distribute anything) are underemployed or economically insecure, often as a result of recessions, job outsourcing, and corporate restructuring.[80] MLMs victimize those without other options, who are desperate enough to sign up. "People lose everything. They lose their homes, ruin their credit," Fitzpatrick told me. "I've been involved in numerous cases for families of people who committed suicide."

Almost all of the business's profits come directly from its recruits. Fitz-Patrick says, "the primary goal of MLM promoters is to capture minds. The money follows." So much money, in fact, that these scams, often heralded as the opportunity of a lifetime, have proliferated at an astonishing rate. The Direct Selling Association (DSA), estimates that eleven hundred MLMs operate in America today.[81]

———

Cultlike indoctrination isn't the whole story. Yes, it's how MLMs capture victims. But this doesn't ultimately explain why so many Americans still sign up for them today. Amway has flourished for more than seventy-five years in large part because, for the last fifty, the government has colluded.

In the early days of MLMs, the feds policed them as the scams they are. The very first company of this sort was Nutrilite, a supplement pusher that basically failed as a direct-sales organization and so rose from the ashes in 1948 as a multitiered, chain-structured organization that today would be called an MLM. Within only sixteen months, Nutrilite's sales revenue jumped from $2,000 a month to $60,000 a month. Neither the product nor the market had changed. The only novel aspect was the new structure and its blanket promise of infinite wealth. Eventually, two of Nutrilite's top recruiters left to start their own company. These were Rich DeVos and Jay Van Andel, who founded Amway in Michigan, in 1959.[82]

Unsurprisingly, other companies developed similar structures. The Federal Trade Commission (FTC) took note and investigated, winning one case and settling another two. Then the FTC went after Amway, the white whale, filing prosecution in 1975. By then, however, DeVos and Van Andel had friends in high places.

Soon-to-become president Gerald Ford, who was raised ten minutes away from where DeVos and Van Andel grew up, was already a friend and fund recipient of Amway. In 1979, the verdict came in: Amway was guilty of deceptive recruitment tactics, but innocent of the government's biggest allegation, that the organization was an "endless chain" (aka pyramid scheme).[83] The FTC had witness testimony and data supporting market saturation in five different states in America. It had used similar allegations and evidence against three other similarly tiered organizations. But the judge instead based his decision on witnesses put forth by Amway, none of whom lived in the allegedly saturated areas.

Without a finding of market saturation, the judge determined that Amway was not a pyramid scheme. DeVos and Van Andel paid a fine for the price-fixing charge and went about their business. The FTC, meanwhile, was baffled. But then, in 1984, a light bulb: the *Washington Post* reported, "In 1975, when Amway came under a Federal Trade Commission investigation as an alleged pyramid scheme . . . Van Andel and DeVos had a 43-minute Oval Office visit with [then president Gerald R.] Ford. A month later, Van Andel was quoted in a Michigan newspaper as saying that Ford was aware of Amway's troubles with the FTC.[84] You tell me what happened.

That's how the US government opened Pandora's product-sample case. Since 1979, pyramid schemes have proliferated in America at an astonishing rate, all of them claiming they're legitimate businesses because they're just like Amway, and the government said Amway isn't a pyramid scheme, so they aren't either. It's as if the judge in 1979 said the sky is green and we rewrote the laws of light refraction in response. It's government-level gaslighting. And for forty-six years, it's continued.

Here is a small sample of collusion, graft, and questionable relationships between MLMs and government officials, presented in no specific order because what would that even matter.

- In the early eighties, Alexander Haig, former chief of staff to President Ford, became a paid consultant for Amway.[85]

- In 1979 DeVos and Van Andel—then listed as two of the four richest people in America—reached the title of "eagle" for how much they donated to the Republican National Committee. In 1981, Richard DeVos became the finance chairman of the committee, but in 1982 he was removed after "referring to the recession as 'a cleansing process' and saying he never saw an unemployed person who wanted to work."[86]

- *Dateline* aired a damning Amway exposé in 2004. At least six tell-all books of fraud and deception in Amway were published during the eighties and nineties. England tried to shut down Amway in 2007 after learning that 71 percent of salespeople in the country earned zero commissions and two-thirds of the remaining people only made $27 a year. And Canada prosecuted Amway in 1982 for criminal tax evasion, to which Amway pled guilty. None of these events led the FTC or the U.S. government to investigate the company. In fact, while Canada was trying to extradite DeVos and Van Andel, the two men attended a Reagan White House event honoring a head of state.[87]

- In 1997, House speaker Newt Gingrich, who had close ties to Amway, intervened just before Congress passed its budget package, to insert a special tax break "worth $283 million to one corporation: Amway." Four months prior, the Amway Corporation had donated $1 million to the Republican Party, at the time one of the largest individual donations on record.[88]

- For years, Amway used a system it called Amvox, a network of sorts that allowed distributors to send voice messages to one another. In his book, Scheibeler writes, "Each election, Zack would pass along a list by Amvox from Dexter as to who he was voting for. We were all to vote similarly."[89]

- During questioning in 2017, Betsy DeVos, daughter-in-law of Rich, agreed it was possible the DeVos family had spent $200 million on Republicans over the years.[90]

- In 1996, President Clinton spoke on a video produced by the Direct Selling Association (DSA), which was by now comprised completely of MLM representatives. In his speech, he calls direct selling the "heart of the American dream."[91] And in 2013, he received a $700,000 speaking fee from Amway for a speech he gave at an event in Japan.[92]

- In 2015, a journalist asked an FTC spokesperson the difference between a legal MLM and a pyramid scheme. The spokesperson responded, "I have nothing for you. Lots of reporters have asked that question. Our final response is, We're not going to answer it."[93]

- Then, in March 2024, a bit of good news: the FTC informed the DSA that if compensation is primarily derived from recruitment, rather than sales, the entity would be considered a pyramid scheme.[94] That's a reversal of twenty years of opinion. It doesn't mean anything yet, since cases brought by the FTC will be decided by judges and juries, not the FTC. Further, new FTC members could reverse the stance at any time. But at least the organization's current membership is beginning to suggest the emperor might be nude.

People join MLMs because they're tricked. And they stay because they've already sunk costs, MLMs are usually high-control groups, and latent indoctrination into the cultural remnants of Puritan doomsday ideology has trained them to blame themselves for failing and believe they can still succeed if they work harder. Eventually, though, no longer able to ignore their mounting debt, they quietly leave. By my best guesstimate, about half of the members of any destructive cult eventually leave. (This is why recruitment is so important.) That's exactly the number of people who quit MLMs each year.

A few days after Eric Scheibeler mailed his whistleblowing packet to his downline, his phone started ringing. He and his wife spent nearly ten hours each day on the telephone with bewildered, concerned distributors. In response, he alleges the kingpins launched a campaign to isolate him. The Scheibelers learned that their friends and colleagues had been told Eric was an alcoholic and drug addict, and wanted no one to contact him. Additional rumors included that Eric had been gambling and cheating on his wife, that she had been cheating on him, and that they were getting a divorce. Eric learned from the pastor at his children's Christian school about an anonymous call warning that he "was involved in immoral activities" and "might be a danger to the children."

The couple also received nearly identical cease-and-desist notices in the mail from leaders and friends in their downline, threatening legal action if the Scheibelers reached out. Eric developed an ulcer and experienced frequent "false heart attacks." He cried frequently in public and started carrying a gun.[95] His low point came one Fourth of July around 10 p.m. when he heard something moving rapidly in the woods by his house and assumed the assassin had finally come. He dove behind a parked car with his dog and punched the animal to silence it. Then he bolted indoors, screaming for his family to get inside, grabbed his gun, and huddled in the bedroom while his children cried.

He claims Amway tried repeatedly to push him into binding arbitration, after which he was likely to receive a settlement, but with a gag order. Believing that pushing desperate, destitute whistleblowers into these kinds of agreements was how the business had been able to continue victimizing people, he refused. Eventually, Scheibeler found a lawyer willing to take his case on a contingency basis. In 2001, he filed a civil action against Amway, but eventually succumbed to arbitration anyway, which ruled against him. In May 2004, NBC's *Dateline* ran an exposé Scheibeler had helped put together.[96] At some point along the way, Scheibeler filed for bankruptcy. It went on and on until he broke and signed a non-disparagement agreement to make it go away.

———

Scheibeler is one of the few who've ascertained the scheme. Most are too distracted to see it. That's intentional. Gilded Age robber barons told poor people they could gain wealth partly to distract them from revolting against their exploitation. MLMs tell participants they can be rich to distract them from the experience of being robbed. Politicians suggest welfare recipients don't want to work partly to distract the public from demanding social reform. Political power players racialize poverty to distract poor whites from banding together with poor people of color. Giant corporations offer wellness services partly to distract employees from the real sources of burnout. Starbucks sells $5 bracelets to support investment in impoverished communities, which distracts from the fact that it keeps almost $2 billion offshore to avoid paying taxes that would support investment in impoverished communities.[97] Meanwhile, those being distracted are also taught to internalize blame for their own exploitation so that when the distraction wears off, they'll point the finger at themselves.

It's like grabbing someone's hand, smacking them in the face with it, and asking, "Why are you hitting yourself?"

The Puritans would hate the greed on display among Amway kingpins and leadership, and I do feel comfortable speaking for them posthumously. They believed in stewardship and social responsibility. Joel McConnell thinks the kingpins' lack of morality was a result of inflated egos and the corrupting nature of power. Increases in power correlate with, for example, avoiding taxes, cheating on taxes, skipping fare on public transport, applying for government benefits for which you don't qualify, accepting bribes, and shoplifting.[98] There's a pattern in those examples: *taking.*

Wealth, perhaps the most enduring indicator of power, justifies one to take even more. Cult leaders are able to *hold* their power because they hack a community's natural ability to police them. (Gossip, for example, developed in human communities as a way to check power.) They silence dissent and thwart insurrection with the priceless tools of undue influence. One of the most useful in any mind-control toolbox is ideology. I believe we have so far been unable to check the power of America's bad-actor billionaires because we are all to a certain degree indoctrinated into certain ideologies, which hold that wealth is a sign of grace and election, and poverty is a sign of sin.

We need that ideology because sometimes, even after all our efforts to buy salvation on the open market, we are still sick, balding, lacking Harry Styles, or otherwise unsure of our election into perfection. Fortunately, even if we can't feel our chosen-ness within, there's a way to prove it without: wealth. *Any way you can get it will be justified by its existence in your bank account. Any natural resources you extract along the way are fair game, including persons who lack wealth. They are less valuable than you are; they were put there for your benefit.* These ideas are as American as taking three-quarters of the apple pie.

Those numbers I shared earlier, detailing that the wealthiest 1 percent of Americans own about the same amount of money as the bottom 90 percent combined?[99] They are nauseatingly similar to a typical MLM payment structure, in which the top 1 percent makes the same as the bottom 94 percent.

FitzPatrick argues that MLMs are the quintessential manifestation of late-stage capitalism: "Slavery, colonialism, and then cannibalism. We finally just eat each other," he opines.

After his comment about late-stage capitalism, FitzPatrick wryly jokes, "But you know, it does make money."

I interject and say, "No, it *takes* money."

"That's right," he replies. "The difference between taking money and making money has kind of been obliterated."

FitzPatrick does not find MLM leaders unique. "Are they fundamentally different from traders on Wall Street or marketers on Madison Avenue? The CEO of Herbalife previously had been the CEO of Disney."

Conspiracy theorists are right that an elite group puppeteers the U.S. government—they're called plutocrats. The only reason this isn't a conspiracy theory is because it doesn't happen in secret. There are other differences, for example, plutocrats don't want to "exterminate" the rest of us (probably because they can't extract resources from corpses). Regardless, the plutocracy is the aristocratic takeover our founding fathers feared. It's already occurred. It happened under our noses.

It feels like we are on one of those Gravitron rides at the fair in which centrifugal force pins you helplessly against the wall, and just when you think it can't get worse, some kid barfs. It's enough to make you think we've let it go too far, that there's no way to take power back. Democrats and Republicans alike are under the plutocrats' thumbs. After all, now that they have most of the money, *only* they can afford campaign contributions. As of October 2024, Elon Musk had donated $118 million to Donald Trump's presidential campaign. Meanwhile, 80 percent of Americans live paycheck to paycheck.[100]

Fortunately, on his album *Perfectly Stupid*, comedian Kurt Braunohler pitches a solution:

> *Billionaires are not rational, they make no rational sense. They have more money than they could ever spend in their entire lives. . . . That seems insane to me. . . . I do know that in this country we have a show called* Hoarders *where if an old lady has like twenty-five thousand magazines,*

we kick her door down. We're like, "You can't have these magazines!"
She's like, "No, let me have my magazines!" We're like, "No, you can't
have these magazines—we're going to burn your house down!"Anyway,
I'm pitching Hoarders 2.[101]

Why not kick down billionaires' doors? There's no longer a difference
between making money and taking it.

CHAPTER 6

US VERSUS THEM
ON IDENTITY AND ISOLATION

D wight York entered the Eatonton, Georgia, courthouse in the summer of 1999 flexing on local reporters. Though they hadn't met, he called them by name, a way of saying he'd been watching them too. Outside, around seven hundred of his followers, all wearing black, circled the courthouse. They set up a military-style perimeter, with sentries and patrols in formation. An unknown number of additional men circled in a packed U-Haul, ready to deploy. This excessive protection and theater was in response to a zoning violation. But three years later, he'd face another court date, this time indicted by the state on close to 120 counts, including rape, the trafficking of minors, and child molestation.

Georgia was only the latest of York's group's homes. Even its identity shifted multiple times over the years. When members first began arriving in Eaton-ton in 1993—after York paid almost $1 million for 476 acres—they dressed as cowboys. Then, after hundreds more joined, York renamed himself Chief Black Eagle and claimed they were the Yamasee Native American Moors of the Creek Nation. *Then*, after he failed to secure a casino license, York dubbed them the United Nuwaubian Nation of Moors, adopted Egyptian mythology, built pyramids and a sphinx out of plywood and stucco, and announced he was an Egyptian god. Sometime around then, he also said he was a rabbi (and created a synagogue). He later claimed to be an alien savior, here from Planet Rizq to take 144,000 chosen ones back to his home galaxy.[1] But these were only the group's last masks. For most of its history it was Muslim . . . or Muslim adjacent. Ultimately, of course, the identity and beliefs didn't matter to York. In later years, he told one of his sons, "I don't believe any of this [expletive]. If I had to dress up like a nun, if I had to be a Jew, I'd do it for this kind of money."[2]

Jamiyla Chisholm's parents joined York in 1978, when he called his group the Ansaru Allah Community and himself Isa Abdullah. At the time, he preached a hodgepodge of Black nationalism and Islam he had co-opted from contemporary movements and tweaked to serve his needs. She writes in her memoir, *The Community*, that her father, "an unwavering believer in Malcolm X and Marcus Garvey's Back to Africa movement," bought into York's supposed philosophy because "it filled a historical void."[3] York preached separatism and Black self-sufficiency when the United States had delivered Black Americans countless broken promises.

A thimbleful of context: in 1964, about two weeks after President Johnson signed the Civil Rights Act, a white off-duty cop in Harlem killed Black fifteen-year-old James Powell, which eventually sparked a six-night uprising in both Harlem and Brooklyn's Bedford-Stuyvesant neighborhood. Malcolm X was assassinated in 1965, followed months later by the Watts unrest, after which the Student Nonviolent Coordinating Committee broke from the Civil Rights Movement, seeking a more militant approach to take power rather than ask for it. In 1966 Stokely Carmichael called for "Black power" and Bobby Seale and Huey P. Newton founded the Black Panther Party. Martin Luther King Jr. was assassinated in 1968, followed by widespread national revolts. In 1969, Black Panthers Fred Hampton and Mark Clark were assassinated by Chicago police officers. And two years prior, Dwight York founded a small organization that would eventually develop into the Ansaru Allah Community.

His group's growth resulted in part from his outreach efforts, which Chisholm describes as genius. He deployed young men all over New York to sell colorful glossy pamphlets, always featuring him on the cover and preaching "a way of thinking about Blackness that was completely different," she told me in an interview. "A lot of Brown and Black people in New York knew about him." But the larger impact on growth was thanks to that aforementioned historical void, the reason his message resonated.

By the late seventies, the Civil Rights Movement had basically ended. The Panthers and other Black-emancipation groups were waning in popularity.

And white people had moved on. "People were not as focused on social issues anymore," Chisholm said. "It was more about, How can we be free in the most happy way possible?" She went on, "But that wasn't an option for a lot of African-Americans, who felt they'd been left behind or just completely ignored." York saw that. He exploited it. He did provide a sense of purpose and self-sufficiency to his followers, but at a steep price. He made a fortune off of his acolytes. He lived like a king and indulged his most disinhibited and abusive sexual desires. He fathered an estimated three hundred children.

For years, only a handful listened to York. But by the late seventies, his community had purportedly grown to five hundred, most living together in a collection of buildings on Bushwick Avenue in Brooklyn. He built an empire there, eventually owning twenty apartment buildings, along with a school, a mosque, and stores. Most were painted the same way, tan with brown trim. According to an FBI intelligence report, York acquired real estate by bullying neighbors to sell and, if they refused his offered price, firebombing their buildings and scooping up what remained.[4] At the organization's height, he had additional chapters in eight other U.S. cities, as well as in London, Toronto, Jamaica, and Trinidad.

Jamiyla Chisholm was two when her family surrendered all its possessions and moved in. She was separated from her parents, as they were from each other, each placed in a different building. Jamiyla slept on mats in a room with forty toddlers stuffed into it. In her mother's cramped living quarters, most women slept on cots. She saw her mother only sporadically, and always under supervision. She saw her father almost never. Married couples needed permission for occasional conjugal visits, which happened in a designated space called the Green Room and could be forbidden as punishment for any number of transgressions. For example, men were sent out daily to fundraise by selling pamphlets and incense, or begging. (One former follower said he once took half a million to the bank in cash, adding, "There were so many coins that they closed the bank for two hours, so that they could count them.")[5] Failure to meet quotas, ranging from $25 to $100 a day, depending on York's desires, could result in loss of conjugal visits or beatings.

The women, except for York's wives—at the time, he had four, along with countless concubines—didn't leave the compound. They cooked, cleaned, and handled administrative duties. But they nevertheless secured income for the community through pressure to commit welfare fraud. Former members claimed they used urine samples from pregnant women in order to increase their checks. They also allege that York impregnated members specifically so they could claim more from the government.

Chisholm, who wrote her book after extensive interviews with her mother and tells both of their stories, explains that York kept his flock paranoid. He often warned they were under surveillance and that informants had surely infiltrated the community. He preached that Big Brother wanted to keep Black folks from thriving. Of course, he wasn't wrong about most of that. In the micro, it would turn out the FBI had indeed been watching the community. In the macro . . . I mean, where to begin? I'll choose just one example: Nixon's war on drugs. In 1994, John Ehrlichman, Nixon's domestic policy advisor and a Watergate co-conspirator, straight up admitted the scheme to a reporter. He explained that the biggest enemies of Nixon's campaign had been Black Americans and the antiwar left. "We knew we couldn't make it illegal to be either against the war or Black, but by getting the public to associate the hippies with marijuana and Blacks with heroin, and then criminalizing both heavily, we could disrupt those communities. We could arrest their leaders, raid their homes, break up their meetings, and vilify them night after night on the evening news. Did we know we were lying about the drugs? Of course we did."[6]

Chisholm told me, "We were this big beehive, trying to attain the thing everybody wanted more than anything: freedom. Freedom of mind, freedom of movement, freedom to be whomever they wanted to be," she said. "A lot of Black people felt they were up against the ropes. There was a bit of desperation. They were looking for something that said to them, 'You're great. You are divine. You're not an animal.'"

York offered an alliance against a common foe. *We're right, they're wrong. We're good, they're evil.* It was easy to do. Although he had close to twenty aliases over the years—including Malachi, Dr. Imam Isa Abd'allah Mohamed Al Mahdi, and the Imperial Grand Potentate—the Southern Poverty Law Center simply calls him a Black supremacist.

He taught that white people are devils, who descended from humans who had mated with jackals and dogs, and who lack true emotions. In a letter written in 2004, York explains that the white race could never live peacefully because they were specifically bred to be inferior, to be guard dogs to the Black race. "They were only created to fight other invading races, to protect the God race Negroids," he writes. "But they went insane, lost control when they were left unattended. They were never to taste blood. They did, and their true nature came out."[7]

And this was written in later years, *after* he'd begun toning down the hate (and focusing instead on doomsday, a classic choice when cult leaders need to shore up shaking loyalty—it's a desperate move). Again, based on the behavior of a significant number of white people in America at the time (at *any time*), it's not surprising York's preaching caught purchase. Of all the destructive groups explored in this book, the Nuwaubians had the right to be paranoid. In a 1962 *New Yorker* essay, James Baldwin discussed the Nation of Islam, another alleged Black-supremacist, Muslim-ish doomsday group (from which York may have borrowed heavily). Baldwin explains, "One did not need to prove to a Harlem audience that all white men were devils. They were merely glad to have, at last, divine corroboration of their experience, to hear . . . that their captivity was ending, for God was black."[8] Sadly, York's depiction of a debased oppressor was also projection.

Perhaps unsurprisingly, York was an entertainer. Before founding a cult, he worked in music. Over the years, he continued to record and release. In turn, his teachings affected other musicians, including Doug E. Fresh, Afrika Bambaataa, Posdnuos of De La Soul, Prodigy of Mobb Deep, and MF Doom. York built a studio on Bushwick Avenue. Between 1979 and 1984, he made three disco-ish albums. The track you'll find most easily is "It's Only a Dream." His handpicked concubines all worked for him inside his studio on Bushwick Ave. Often, four or five were pregnant at a time.

Jamiyla's mother eventually ascertained that community members lived in squalor not out of necessity but because York was taking all the money. She also discovered the women in charge of the toddler room had been beating Jamiyla regularly with a ruler, typically whenever the child begged or cried for her mother. After two years on Bushwick Avenue, the mother and daughter left, but only after a fierce physical altercation with another community member trying to stop them. Then they returned. Then they left again. Cults are hard to quit.

That same year, York announced he was the second coming of Christ, promised to Christians and Muslims alike. He printed posters and pamphlets bearing his image and "The savior has returned."[9] In 1983, he bought property in Sullivan County, New York, and spent a purported $5 million building a mansion, to and from which underage girls were bussed during his stays. His special forces security teams grew brasher over the years. The so-called "construction crew" were the alleged real estate arsonists. The Mujahad allegedly engaged in mafia-style protection rackets and narcotics. Community members were allegedly responsible for a series of bank robberies in Maryland between 1990 and 1991, one of which resulted in the shooting of a clerk. The FBI investigated all of this, including the 1979 murder of Horace Greene, a Brooklyn activist who spoke out against York and the community and was gunned down, informants claim, by one of York's henchmen.

By the early nineties, York had caught wind of the FBI investigation and upcoming report. Meanwhile, the movement experienced an exodus of members due to persistent rumors of molestation and rape. York had to make a drastic move. He began to talk more of "a real nation, our own nation. With our own passports, with our own tax system, where no one tells us what to do but us."[10] In Eatonton, Georgia, Chisholm believes York was banking on being ignored, was counting on white apathy to lead locals to think, she explains, "'If those Black people aren't eating, or don't have electricity and live on a dirt compound, who cares?'" Instead, he landed in an area that was mostly racially harmonious. Three years later, a new sheriff was elected who became eager to investigate a rash of counterfeit checks and underage Black girls giving birth in area hospitals.

Like a supernova, the cult swelled before it imploded: in addition to between two and four hundred living in the compound, an estimated one to two thousand followers fanned across neighboring counties. Al Sharpton and Jesse Jackson each traveled to speak to the community. Contemporary separatist leaders and organizers visited and allied with York. (They made strange bedfellows, as most sovereign-citizen movements were also white supremacist.) And York began conducting paramilitary drills, hoarding more weapons, and warning his followers to prepare for an imminent outside attack.

U s-versus-them thinking is so central to cult success that if you don't see it being manipulated, you're probably not looking at a cult (but a Utopian community or group of fanatics). Sometimes the enemy is overt, as it was for the Nuwaubians. The Puritans' "them" was Catholicism. Mankind United used the Hidden Rulers. And countless groups warn of a cabal . . . or lizard people, liberals, Jews. Enemies also always include those who question the leader or try to extract followers. The specter of "them" motivates us to piety and keeps us in need of protection.

A con artist's manipulation of us-versus-them thinking is especially effective on those legitimately wronged. But the tactic works on all of us because the human tendency to see the world as comprised of in groups and out groups— the most basic and foundational characteristic of all cultlike thinking—long predates the Protestant Reformation. Puritan and American culture have exaggerated these innate tendencies, but to fully understand them, we must return to the birth of our species.

We evolved to trust people within our communities and distrust people outside of them. This is because in-group cooperation has always been our evolutionary edge. We shot to the top of the food chain because we learned to cooperate with one another (not thanks to the size of our brains). But we didn't just *choose* to cooperate. We were forced to in self-defense against outside communities. Competition led to cooperation, which improved us as competitors, which required more cooperation. To be clear, competition among our forebearers was not of the NCAA variety. Usually, when an outsider showed up, it was to kill you. *Us* has been killing *them* for as long as *us* has existed. It's a defining aspect of our species. It's amazing we think we even deserve to go to heaven.

In the early 1970s, researchers noticed a surprising behavior in our closest relative, chimpanzees. Cohorts of males would gather, psych themselves up, and then wander the borders of the group's territory, pushing beyond those borders a little at a time, until they found chimpanzees from neighboring groups, whom they promptly beat, often to death. These marauding cohorts are called *raid teams*. In their groundbreaking book, *Demonic Males: Apes and the Origin of Human Violence*, Richard Wrangham and Dale Peterson write that out of the millions of species on our planet, this "system of intense, male-initiated territorial aggression, including lethal raiding into neighboring communities in search of vulnerable enemies to attack and kill," has only been documented in two: chimpanzees and humans.[11] We've been doing it for longer even than we've been human. The tendency for *us* to kill *them* is baked into our DNA.

OK, but why do we *want* to kill "outsiders"? Theories are still evolving, but the dominant one points to territory and resources. Over nine years in the aughts, primatologists recorded a group of chimpanzees executing 114 patrols that resulted in the killing of twenty-one members of other troops. As a result, the group leading the patrols expanded its territory by 22.3 percent.[12] In a similar study, primatologists found that when a community increased its territory, the animals ate better, bred faster, and generally were better able to survive.[13]

Communities throughout history and around the world have been so concerned about discerning outsiders from insiders that some have literally reformed their skulls into the same distinctive, recognizable shape. The practice, called cranial reformation, starts in infancy by, for example, strapping babies into wooden contraptions that gently push against their heads in the desired fashion.[14] Recall that the deceased Heaven's Gate members were found wearing matching Nike sneakers.

Cooperation is how we evolved so much faster than other species, and it resulted from the constant threat of violence; ergo, we evolved because we killed each other. The meek shall inherit the earth, my ass. (There is evidence, though, that the *friendly* will inherit the earth. More on that later.) An ability to pit *us* against *them* is how our ancestors survived, is why each of us is alive today. When cult leaders, con artists, grifters, demagogues, dictators, domestic abusers, or other selfish dillweeds wish to manipulate or exploit others, all they need do is raise the specter of an outside enemy. Any will do, it doesn't matter which.

Next they manufacture a crisis, which triggers an increase in our us-versus-them thinking, and our amygdalas start prepping for battle.

Cooperation was key to survival because it helped groups develop specialized behaviors everyone could agree on in advance, bits of culturally shared knowledge that researchers refer to as *social norms*. For example, using a certain rock to smash open nuts is a kind of social norm. Once we learn the best rock and the best way to smash, we share that information until we're all smashing faster and eating more. Social norms can also be more complicated, such as agreements not to steal other people's mates or to share food with certain relations, both of which also help communities succeed.[15] Think about it: if you're angry and hurt over your mate getting swiped, you're probably too distracted to smash many nuts, meaning someone's not going to eat. You're probably planning to smash instead whoever stole your mate, so then two people would be absent from nut smashing. Following norms makes groups stronger.

It helped us so much that we evolved to place a lot of value on norms. When someone doesn't follow one, we tattle. It remains part of our brain chemistry to police social norms in one another; even three-year-old children have been documented doing it. Neurologists have discovered that when people punish norm violators, their rewards circuits fire—the same areas that light up in the brain when we are given money or food.[16] Evolutionary biologists have yet to determine whether prehistory snitches got stitches, but we know they got a dopamine rush.

———

Cults are A+ students in the creation and enforcement of social norms. Warren Jeffs, convicted pedophile and former leader of the Fundamentalist Church of Jesus Christ of Latter-day Saints, trained adolescent boys to be part of his "Missionary Program," wherein they visited homes to ask if the families owned any prohibited gentile books or music and if everyone there believed in Uncle Warren. (Those are two great first-date questions, by the way.) Scientology members are allegedly encouraged to submit "knowledge reports" when another member exhibits behavior contrary to group norms, after which the subject of the knowledge report may have to discuss said behavior before an "Ethics" committee (according to the blog of the church's former top spokesman, Mike Rinder).[17]

India Oxenberg joined the sex-abuse pyramid scheme in NXIVM that was masquerading as a women's empowerment society. She writes in her memoir, *Still Learning*, "If I deviated from any of these rules, then Allison gave me a penance, which would be any kind of display of pain to show my loyalty and willingness to correct a transgression."[18] The notion of penance was explained as a shortcut—a hack—to self-improvement. From an evolutionary perspective, that's actually pretty accurate: punishments for transgressing norms are as central to group success as the norms themselves.

But if a social-norm violation is extreme enough—for example, speaking out against the group—rehabilitation is not available. The punishment in such cases is ostracism. When former NXIVM member Sarah Edmondson took her story to the press, remaining followers heard a variety of slanders about her, including, Oxenberg told me in an interview, "[She] was throwing a tantrum, she's a washed-up hack just trying to get attention." Sarah Edmondson came out all right, though—during prehistoric times, ostracism never resulted in a successful podcast and starring role in an HBO documentary. Punishments then were much harsher. Can't stop stealing mates? Good luck in the tundra. (Cancel culture is nothing new.)

Evolutionary biologist Joseph Henrich describes the ladder of punishments for social-norm violations when he writes, "If violators are not brought into line, matters may escalate to ostracism or physical violence . . . and occasionally culminate in coordinated group executions."[19] Being able to cooperate during times of attack—or when launching our own attack—was so important, we killed members of our own group who mitigated that effectiveness.

Research bears out an increase in the enforcement of social norms today whenever communities face violence or natural disasters (the ultimate hazards to territory and resources). Further, Henrich argues, "Under threat, increased sanctions in the form of ostracism, injury, and execution may have favored an automatic and unconscious innate response to cling more tightly to our social norms in groups, including their beliefs, values, and worldviews."[20] When your questioning of your aunt's loyalty to QAnon led her to double down on her beliefs, it was wrong of you to say she wasn't "evolved." In a way, that's exactly what she was.

The point is that we followed social norms in order to be strong and skilled enough to fight off outsiders when they came to kill us—and to go kill outsiders ourselves. To be real, there was a lot of killing. And enslaving. Conspiracy theorists' warnings of shadowy threats coming to exterminate and enslave are possibly a vestigial response to eons of supporting evidence. And, of course, humans are still excessively violent.

But, wait! Before you become so distraught you join a YouTube cult, know that we kill each other much less now, and the number has consistently decreased for millennia. All those extreme norm breakers over the last two hundred thousand years who weren't allowed to marry, or who behaved so uncooperatively or antisocially they were excommunicated or executed? Often, they were kicked out because of their extreme violence. Their genes ended with them. We have been domesticating our own species almost from the beginning. The trait we select for is friendliness. We can be certain about this because the removal of the most violent aspects of our species has resulted in actual physical changes. When anthropologists compare early remains of our species to our current physiognomy, the differences between them are very similar to the differences between wild foxes and domesticated foxes (which were bred specifically by selecting for the trait of friendliness).[21]

The second reason we kill less today is because our groups have become less isolated. Over time, we've preferred to grow our communities and connect them to others. And of course we have: in order to protect your group from the aggressions of a larger foe, you and other neighbors must join forces. In this way, as we populate the earth, there are by default fewer outsiders. Plus, we share all the knowledge accumulated by each group, and thereby become more successful.

We are social animals. We innately, nonconsciously make social choices. That is why the world has climate deniers and anti-vaxxers. It wouldn't matter how many studies you trotted out connecting human behavior to global warming or how many times that guy Andrew Wakefield admitted he was basically paid to fake the research connecting the measles vaccine to autism. Knowledge resistance has nothing to do with facts. When faced with two opposing pieces of information, we will almost always nonconsciously choose to adhere to whichever is believed by our group. We didn't evolve to seek truth; we evolved to be social.

In fact, as sociologist Mikael Klintman explores in his research, sometimes resisting certain pieces of knowledge can actually strengthen social bonds within a group. In this way, such dismissals or denials of truth are "socially rational."[22] We evolved to hew toward the center of the herd. We can't face excommunication in the tundra. Studies even suggest that the smarter one is, the *more* inclined to resist knowledge. Doing so proves loyalty to a group. "The more outrageous and unsubstantiated a knowledge claim is that members in a particular community hold, the more profound loyalty the members show the others in that community."[23] And it enables a group to distinguish itself from surrounding groups—to *brand* itself, if you will—which further strengthens bonds within it. On the flip side, we are also highly motivated to believe false information about other groups. All of this fuels us-versus-them thinking.

The more outrageous the belief and the more aberrant it is from the beliefs of surrounding cultures, the stronger the social bonds within the group and the stronger the loyalty of members to the group. We see this play out again and again in cults, which, when threatened by outsiders or concerned family members trying to spread quote-unquote truth, will adopt even wilder ideologies. And when a cult isolates itself, it once again becomes a solo act, bereft of cooperation from neighbors, surrounded by foes and fearful of attack.

While researching this book, I almost fell for a cult phishing scam. An old-school one. It didn't hook me online, but in the stacks of the Los Angeles Public Library. While I was perusing, a book caught my eye called *The Coming Kingdom: Essays in American Millennialism & Eschatology*. I started with the last essay, by Richard Rubenstein, listed as a distinguished professor of religion at Florida State University. It is exquisite.

He argues that monotheism has been engaged in a slow suicide since birth. "It has been the paradoxical destiny of biblical religion to negate itself."[24] If that's true, the accelerating unchurching of the West, which has religious leaders all in a tizzy, is not a failure of the church in its battle with secular society, but a direct result of the church doing what it was always fated to do. This kind of argument makes theology and religious-history nerds reach for popcorn.

The theory is not new, but Rubenstein then connects it to his ideas surrounding the phenomenon of surplus populations (when the number of people in a society suddenly exceeds the number of opportunities available). In particular, he focuses on a couple of historical patterns that typically arise when surplus populations do. First, overpopulation is usually accompanied by an increase in cults and doomsday thinking. The basic idea here is that when people feel shut out (of, for example, the job market or dating pool), they may grow defensive and think, "Y'all see me as worthless, but God says I'm on top."

I had elsewhere read an argument connecting the cult explosion of the late sixties and early seventies to the coming of age of baby boomers, a generation so big that many had nowhere to turn in the traditional labor market.[25] And then I remembered that England had been busting at its seams, with no economic prospects for rising youth, when the Puritan doomsday movement exploded and fled for the New World. (Remember that many on those early ships were simply looking for opportunity.) This brings me to Rubenstein's second point about surplus populations: that societies often solve such a problem via removal or slaughter. For centuries, America absorbed Europe's surplus populations. But in the 1930s, America's economy, reeling from the Great Depression, could take no more—circumstances Rubenstein connects to the rise of that time period's largest millennial movement, the Nazi Party, which of course found its own "solution" to overpopulation (after having mastered the art of us-versus-them and then scapegoating the *them*).[26]

Rubenstein recalls that Jim Jones built his People's Temple community mostly out of "unemployed, surplus people," and, what's more, their last stop before Guyana was California, which has often been the eventual destination of out-of-luck Americans in search of better prospects . . . and, he also wonders, hey, maybe that's partly why California has always been cult country.[27] By this point, my head was tweaking and armpits sweating because this stuff excites me more than Adderall.

But then, in this otherwise delicious essay, Rubenstein does something strange. He suggests that, as we face potential annihilation via technologically driven population redundancy, cultlike movements might actually be what saves us. *What?*

I started Googling. Turns out the religious scholar and rabbi received some amount of fame in the 1960s following the publication of *After Auschwitz*, in which he basically argues that God, as the Jews had traditionally understood him, either no longer existed or never had (because how could that God have let the Holocaust happen to his people?). This planted Rubenstein in league with the "Death of God" movement, a development among thinkers that went secular enough to wind up on the cover of *Time* magazine in 1966. Also, the novelist William Styron credits Rubenstein's work as a major influence on *Sophie's Choice*, and wrote the introduction to one of Rubenstein's books. OK, cool.

Then I searched for the publisher of the essay collection I'd been holding in my hands. *Not* cool. Both New Era Books and its parent publisher, the International Religious Foundation, Inc., appear on lists of organizations allegedly controlled by or associated with the Unification Church, aka the Moonies, one of the biggest and most powerful cults in American history.[28] It was led by Sun Myung Moon from 1950 until his death in 2012. One of its foundational tenets argued that God had sent a new messiah—Moon, of course—to finish Jesus's job.

I flipped through the rest of the book. Some essays are like Rubenstein's: actual scholarship on American doomsday thought. Others are straight-up propaganda about Moon, the anointed one, the world's savior, the Lord of the Second Advent. Why was Moon publishing books containing such wildly disparate content? Had my new scholar crush been a Moonie? And either way, how did he get from saying *God is dead* to saying *God might actually be this dude from Korea*?

Moon, who was worth almost a billion dollars, was an ace influencer. He buddied up to Presidents Nixon, Reagan, and H. W. Bush, and owned the *Washington Times*. He also sought legitimacy of thought. That's where academics came in. The ersatz messiah funded and produced conferences, invited prestigious scholars whom he believed would be sympathetic, promised they could write or say whatever they wanted (a pledge he appears to have kept), and offered hefty honorariums. Many took the bait.

"Look, [Rubenstein] was very smart. He had to know that they were using him for legitimacy," explains Michael Berenbaum, a lifelong friend and former grad student of the late scholar, who spoke with me. But, Berenbaum adds, "He was offered alternative opportunities that were not coming to him any other way." The sun had basically set on Rubenstein's academic career until along comes Moon, and suddenly the good professor is traveling the globe, speaking and publishing alongside world-class figures, and heading up a think tank. When Moon purchased an actual accredited university, Rubenstein became its president.

He is a classic example of the so-called cult apologist. In the eighties and nineties, he was in good company. This was the heyday of the cult wars, when controversial religions fought back against a growing anti-cult movement by courting and sometimes paying professors and scholars to publicly describe the groups as valid spiritual communities. (Several scholars allegedly received payment from Scientology.) The anti-cultists accused the academic apologists of accepting bribes. The apologists in turn accused the anti-cultists of making unfair accusations against groups, infringing on devotees' First Amendment right to the free exercise of religion, and charging parents exorbitant sums to kidnap their children out of such groups.

This bitter rivalry lasted from the late seventies all the way through the nineties. I've had sources in both camps admit getting into screaming matches at conferences. Professors in screaming matches! Ridiculous. Imagine the pit-stained tweed.

Both sides were a little right and a little wrong. First, not all of the academics who supported new religious movements were paid to do so, and not all of the movements were destructive. On the other hand, many of the "kidnappings"—known as deprogramming efforts by the anti-cultists—were effective as last-resort efforts to pull people from destructive groups. I'm not here to litigate their arguments, though, but to make my own: they all should've known better than to pick a side in the first place. Guess who benefited from all these otherwise sensible people distracting themselves by fighting with one another? The malignant megalomaniacs in charge of certain destructive groups, and the systems that enabled them to harm vulnerable people. They manipulated our latent indoctrination into us-versus-them thinking in order to distract the anti-cultists and academics from working together to discern exactly what abuse did or didn't occur.

From the late seventies through the end of the nineties, the cult wars continually escalated, as us-versus-them thinking always does. Same story; different book cover in the Los Angeles Public Library. It was in this powder keg that the theory of brainwashing caught fire—and that the cults pulled the magic trick of making the American court system believe brainwashing doesn't exist.

———

The term *brainwashing* was coined in 1950 by Edward Hunter, a CIA operative who wrote about a trend among American prisoners in the Korean War, who had been subjected to Chinese Communist thought reform and came out of prisoner camps praising Chairman Mao.[29] The word itself is a rough translation of *xi nao*—the pinyin version of two Mandarin characters, which literally translate to "wash" and "brain"—a colloquial phrase for the formal thought-reform process exercised under the Mao government. Parents of children who had disappeared into controversial religious movements, jumped at the explanation, eager to account for their children's seemingly aberrant behavior.

As fears escalated, parents turned to the judicial system. This required them to prove in court that their children had been mentally incapacitated via "mind control." In all of these cases, lawyers needed expert testimony—and called on apologists or anti-cultists, accordingly, all of which escalated disputes further. There's nothing like the legal system to obliterate nuance and make enemies. Courts also heard a number of suits filed by former members who had been successfully deprogrammed and now sought damages. Juries, sympathetic to families telling stories of, for example, Moonie kids sleeping in vans, barely eating, and disallowed from returning to the group until they had met flower-sales quotas, awarded multimillion-dollar settlements in multiple cases against alleged cults.

But then, in 1987, the American Psychological Association basically determined brainwashing isn't real.[30] The APA had created a task force in 1983 to investigate, as its title suggests, Deceptive and Indirect Methods of Persuasion and Control (DIMPAC). Then it flatly rejected the findings.[31] That was the end of expert brainwashing testimony in court, and is why, even today, some argue brainwashing isn't real because science says so. It would be hard to overstate how huge of a win the DIMPAC ruling was for cults. If no "brainwashing" had occurred, then former members had participated in groups by their own volition and at their own risk, therefore no multimillion-dollar payouts were necessary. The negation of the existence of brainwashing basically allowed these groups to say, *Nothing to see here.*

Without getting too much in the weeds, it seems that DIMPAC could have done a much more precise job. Or maybe, as its chair claimed, the apologists and the cults were behind a conspiracy to discredit her within the APA and the judicial system. On the one hand, that sounds paranoid and reactionary. On the other hand, I wouldn't be surprised.

Here's what I want to know: When the APA rejected DIMPAC, why was that conclusion weaponized instead of problem-solved in order to determine what degree of thought coercion *does* occur in high-control groups? It's true, as critics of the brainwashing theory argue, that plenty of people attend recruiting events but don't join and, among those who do join, many later leave—so many, in fact, that these groups must recruit aggressively in order to keep their numbers. But it's possible that brainwashing only works after a certain amount of time and only on certain people, due to their life circumstances, and only to a certain degree, depending on context. That's not a crazy suggestion. It also happens to be the truth, although now experts use the terms *thought control*, *coercive persuasion*, and *undue influence*. Granted, I have the benefit of an additional thirty years of research. But still.

Seems to me the two camps were more interested in squashing one another than finding truth. We evolved because competition led us to collaborate. When we stop collaborating, we devolve. Meanwhile, Sun Myung Moon and Scientology leader David Miscavige laughed all the way to the offshore bank.

Ultimately, both camps missed blind spots. For example, surprise surprise, turns out most of the groups targeted by the anti-cult movement were indeed engaging in systematic financial exploitation, and sexual and personal assault. (However, as David G. Bromley—sociologist and alleged apologist—pointed out to me, "If you look at sexual assault, there's no group that's going to trump the Catholics. And I would guess megachurches are places where the most wealth has been captured and misappropriated." Touché.) As for the other camp, surprise surprise, when guards were hired to physically restrain humans during deprogrammings, abuse and sexual harassment sometimes occurred. I guess the real lesson here is one we already knew: corruption exists everywhere. To that point, I'd argue that plenty of people in both camps were simply out to make a buck.

By the end of the nineties, everyone was dialing back the extremism, engaging in more dialogue, and acknowledging the validity of some of the other side's arguments. In 2000, a representative from each faction cohosted what one journalist called the "Camp David of the cult wars."[32] Within a few more years, as one religious-studies scholar told me off the record, both camps had basically met in the middle. But at least two things stand from their descent into us-versus-them thinking: people can still legally argue brainwashing isn't real, and Moon's academic propaganda is still in the LA Public Library.

Members of the King James Bible Baptist Church in Madison, Tennessee, believed the Authorized King James Version of the Bible was the final authority. They believed the Genesis account of creation as literal. And they believed their congregation alone would be saved following the apocalypse triggered by Y2K. Everyone else would burn.

"That shows so much about Paul's ego. He thought he was the leader of the last chosen people on this planet," recalls Cameron, who spoke with me over the phone and requested I use a pseudonym. He joined the group as a tween with his mother and older brother. "They expected planes to fall out of the sky, the power grid to go down, all that stuff. I remember being told, when I was fourteen, that there's going to be dead bodies floating in the creek around our house."

Paul Iannello had been the youth pastor at Bible Baptist Church, in Hendersonville, Tennessee, in the early 1990s when he left to start the King James Bible Baptist Church. Some of the congregation followed him, including another local boy, Will (whose name has also been changed) and his family. Will's parents pulled him out of public school and put him into a homeschooling umbrella linked to the church. "It was a gradual transition away from intermingling with the world at large," Will told me. No television or movies. No friends outside of church. Women were discouraged from working outside of the home. "Every time the [church] doors were unlocked, you ought to be there."

Sundays were twelve-hour affairs. There was an additional service Wednesday evenings and street preaching on Friday nights in downtown Nashville. Weekdays were easily filled with chores and homeschooling. The church purchased two hundred chicks and developed a garden in order to grow, prepare, and store food items. Cameron built the coops, raised the chickens, and eventually slaughtered them for cooking and canning. "That whole year was my brother and me working in the garden and going to church," Cameron recalls. "All of 1999 was just preparing for the end of the world."

In the months prior, copies of a VHS tape explaining Y2K had circulated among local churches. During the early nineties, computer programmers had sounded the alarm that software couldn't handle dates beyond December 31, 1999. From there, conspiracy theorists warned all the world's computer systems would fail at the stroke of midnight—causing, for example, planes to malfunction and crash—and toss the world into chaos. Some fundamentalist Christians reasoned that the ensuing chaos would trigger the apocalypse, leading Jesus to return for Judgment Day.

One weeknight, Will's family was invited to another church member's home without explanation. A deacon and another head of the church explained Y2K, that society would fall apart, first inciting social anarchy, and then Satan's battles, earthquakes, and the bloodshed of the masses. According to the book of Daniel, the period of tribulation before the messiah returns will last seven years. That's a lot of canned beans. Cameron says, "Families in the church started dumping insane amounts of money into preparation."

Since they'd need to protect themselves from looters and bad actors, they started collecting weapons. "It was just part of the checklist," Will explains. His dad bought a couple of rifles through someone else in the church, as almost all weapons were brokered. By point, Will and Cameron both felt completely isolated from the rest of the world. They had no friends outside of the church and rarely if ever spoke to extended families. "[Church leaders] felt like any outside person was potential to mess it all up," Cameron explains.

Pastor Paul was savvy enough not to preach doomsday from the pulpit, though. Most conversations happened in hushed tones and off church property. Also, anyone could enter the church, so he couldn't be sure who was listening. "There was paranoia," Cameron says. For example, the suspected FBI agent. "He was a single guy who just showed up one day and was very friendly to everybody," Cameron recalls. But one night, the deacons had a meeting and the next day, he was gone. "At church, Paul was like, 'We had to kick somebody out. We think they were an informant. We're going to be more careful with things like that in the future.'" Next, they turned their suspicion inward. "They started cutting people off, anyone who questioned anything," Cameron says.

Cameron's family lived on property owned by one of the deacons, along with several other families. In the lead-up to Y2K, the church scouted areas where parishioners could live together. Four properties were purchased in different parts of town, since they couldn't predict where it would be safest during the tribulation period of the apocalypse. Almost everyone moved on to one of them. "Once things went down," as Cameron puts it, they planned to join together on whichever property could be most easily protected.

One day, Cameron found a *Sports Illustrated* "Swimsuit Edition" in the garbage behind the King James Bible Baptist Church and managed to sneak it home. "I was going through puberty basically on my own because no one would tell you anything about sex other than 'Hey don't do it,'" he explains. But the magazine only brought him guilt. After a week he burned it in his backyard. The deacon who owned their property saw the smoke and investigated. Cameron confessed, the deacon talked to his mother, and they decided the teen should stand in front of church on Sunday, confess his actions, and ask for forgiveness. "They wanted me to go up there and be like, 'Hey y'all, I've been masturbating, sorry.' That whole week I was living in fear and dread."

Cameron says Pastor Paul "loved humiliating people." If he felt somebody was backsliding, he would call on them to sing in front of the church without accompaniment. "He did it to me one time, and it didn't bother me too bad, but man, I had seen other people where it just destroyed them," he adds. He describes the deacons as Paul's goons, who intimidated church members and gathered information about them. "They operated like a mafia."

Meanwhile, "people were gathering insane amounts of guns and ammunition," and had also started wearing camo, Cameron says. The church started a program for teenage boys that Cameron compares to ROTC. They marched and performed drills, wore fatigues, and street-preached in them. In spite of the ROTC-like training, Will remembers when a deacon strongly opposed a decision by one of the teenage boys to join the military. The church's leadership expected their community eventually to be in conflict with the U.S. government. Therefore, Will says, they reckoned this kid "would be on the wrong side of the barrel of a gun."

Then, Cameron's mom heard that someone had purchased grenades. The church feared that neighbors and maybe even the government would come after their food and water. They didn't want to share. By their logic, why should they? Resources would be wasted on those doomed to perish. Before the next service, his mom asked the man about it. Cameron recalls him saying, "Well, [a grenade] is a good way to disperse a large group of people."

The next Sunday morning, Cameron prepared to confess his teenage sins to the congregation. Meanwhile, his mom was called into the pastor's office. "She came out crying and was like, 'All right boys, we have to leave.' I thought, 'Man, they must've been really mad about the magazine.'" But once in the car, Cameron discovered someone had "tattled," as he puts it, to Pastor Paul that his mother questioned the need for grenades—so he kicked them out.

Fortunately, at least Cameron's family didn't have to move—because the people who owned the compound on which they lived had also been kicked out. Around that time, Cameron estimates that church membership, around eighty when he and his family joined, had been cut almost in half. "Anybody who remotely questioned anything, you were gone."

———

This story is riddled with the kind of social-norm policing we discussed earlier— tattling on those who don't play by the rules we evolved to practice in order to cooperate better when competing with neighbors—and of the excommunication that can follow. The story is also a classic case of violence escalation, specifically the kind that results from isolation.

Only a small number of cults become violent, a truth that reveals much about our understanding of these groups. First, it betrays the outsized media attention afforded to communities that do turn brutal. It also hints at the staggering number of destructive groups in existence—estimated to be around ten thousand currently in the United States alone (remember that some cults are only a few people, for example Larry Ray's group at Sarah Lawrence College).[33] And it points to how extreme and unique conditions must be for any group to cross that threshold (I'm looking at you, January 6).

Most instances of violence occur in groups that meet three criteria: they believe the end of the world is near, have a charismatic leader, and become socially encapsulated.[34] At least some degree of isolation, whether physical or virtual, is a hallmark of all destructive cults. Typically, though, isolation results in plummeting recruitment, which is in part why so many groups fizzle out and disappear.[35] However, when groups have enough people and resources to maintain themselves, isolation can hurtle them toward an ending that's less fizzle and more pop.

Members of Heaven's Gate had been living together in isolation for decades, first as nomads on campgrounds, then in a compound surrounded by a wall of dirt-filled tires stacked twenty feet high, and eventually inside a Rancho Santa Fe mansion, where Marshall Applewhite and thirty-eight of his followers took phenobarbital, hoping that a UFO trailing the Hale-Bopp comet would carry their souls to the evolutionary level beyond human. By the time Keith Raniere was arrested on trafficking charges for orchestrating a pyramid scheme of sex abuse, NXIVM followers had been living in close proximity to one another for years in a development outside of Albany, New York, and had been actively discouraged from spending time with anyone outside of the group. The tragedy in Waco, Texas, happened inside literal compound walls, and the Jonestown massacre occurred deep in the jungle of Guyana, separated not only from civilization but from the members' country of origin.

The tendency to isolate is often amplified by a charismatic leader's efforts to hold power specifically by resisting society at large . . . which engenders paranoia . . . which leads to further isolation. But social encapsulation is not merely a hallmark of destructive groups. Rather, it is a leading cause of their calamities. What happens to a group of people when they peace out together? Answers can be found not only in studies of cults, but also in forensic psychiatry, evolutionary biology, and the inner workings of our bodies' cells.

Social systems require feedback—both from within and without—in order to survive. Isolation hamstrings such natural feedback mechanisms. Sociologist Lorne Dawson explains why. First, he argues that when groups isolate, they experience a reduction of what's known as *normative dissonance*. Basically, we are accustomed to living with and navigating among different people with a diversity of values who practice varying social norms. For example, we behave differently at home than we do at the office than we do in school than we do at a baby shower. This is good because if we always behaved as if at a baby shower, possibly no one would ever have sex again and the human species would cease to exist.

According to Dawson, this kind of flux has a moderating effect on individuals and groups. "The continual need to negotiate a path amongst differences imposes a crucial moment of critical distance between the impulse to act and the actions actually taken."[36] It's as if the panel of voices moderating our innermost thoughts is influenced directly by the panel of voices surrounding us—or perhaps they are one and the same. As such, the removal of disparate outside voices results in the removal of a layer in the filter of our decision-making processes. When you encapsulate yourself within only one group of people, who have similar ideas and goals, eventually no filter remains.

Without filters, we become especially susceptible to *groupthink*, the second in Dawson's trio of isolation's effects. This is kind of like peer pressure. People in highly cohesive groups seek one another's approval, silence their doubts, and *Yes* each other until everyone on spring break wakes up with the same shark ankle tattoo. This behavior is magnified when each person also seeks a leader's approval, accepts without question a leader's message, and tells a leader what the leader wants to hear. Groupthink leads members to overestimate the strength of their morals and the soundness of their plans—and to underestimate the same in their enemies.

When normative dissonance is reduced and groupthink is in play, the conditions are primed for a movement or cult to experience a *shift-to-risk*, the third force at play in Dawson's argument. Sometimes in a group of like-minded individuals, you'll say and do questionable things you'd never say or do in a group comprised of diverse opinions. If those thoughts and actions are met with validation, you will likely be encouraged to adopt more extreme thoughts and actions—which can lead others in the group to adopt more extreme ideas and behaviors, creating a snowball effect that has the group careening toward trouble—for example, storming the U.S. Capitol carrying Q flags.

Stop the Steal marchers in 2021 may have also been experiencing *folie à groupe*, aka shared psychosis. Be careful to whom you listen, because pathological symptoms are literally contagious. They spread just like viruses except through emotional bonds, which I guess makes emotional bonds the bodily fluids of the mind. According to forensic psychologist Dr. Bandy X. Lee, three conditions are necessary for infection: an influential figure who is suffering from severe pathology, high emotional investment among group members, and an environment that fosters contagion. Mental symptoms most commonly go viral in isolated settings (think hospitals, prisons, households, and gangs). The most common symptoms to transmit are delusions of persecution or general paranoia—both of which are hallmarks of isolated apocalyptic groups. As Lee writes, "cultic programming and shared symptoms are a feedback loop."[37]

A group's power is physiological, as if we literally are each other. This is why the question "Why didn't you just leave the cult?" is absurd. When a group loses the feedback mechanisms necessary to regulate itself, and then suffers from the spread of delusions, it becomes a loop with no exit.

In those ways, isolation primes us to behave violently. But it also gives us *permission* to do so. Let me back up a minute. Remember raid teams? Because our ancestors spent millennia attacking neighbors and also defending their own communities from outside attack, we became very good at both: cooperating with and caring for members of our in-group, while also executing swift, extreme, and effective violence against those in out-groups. This dual ability of ours is somewhat contradictory. How are we able to approach our own species with both kindness and brutality? How do we know which to use when? Our brains evolved specific mechanisms that shut down our empathy in certain situations, making it possible for us to bring down the hammer without pause or doubt.

An ability unique to humans and other domesticated species is something psychologists call theory of mind. It's how we guess at what other people are thinking or feeling. For example, if someone points at the sky, I can assume there is something up there worth regarding, unless it's my nephew pointing, in which case he's hoping I'll "look" so he can punch me in the arm. Theory of mind helps us cooperate with one another as well as feel the intensity of love toward family members (except on occasion my nephew). It's how we get into each other's brains. Which means it also allows us to feel the suffering of others.

Using brain scans, researchers discovered that those networks allowing for theory of mind to operate become dampened when people feel threatened. The culprit is oxytocin. Typically, a flood of oxytocin, sometimes called the cuddle hormone, leads us to feel more friendly, loving, and cooperative. It does this by disrupting the connection between the amygdala (the ancient part of our brain that's always thinking about fight or flight) and the theory-of-mind network, thereby allowing for a more active theory of mind and increase in empathy. But when we face outsiders we deem as threats, oxytocin instead blunts the theory-of-mind network and amplifies the amygdala's threat signal. Study participants who inhaled oxytocin vapor became more likely to punish or behave aggressively toward out-groups. And adolescents "who grow up in areas plagued by chronic ethnic conflict have higher circulating oxytocin levels and reduced empathy toward the rival ethnicity."[38]

Although all of that science might be new to you, you're already familiar with this whole process. It's colloquially known as dehumanization. When our theory of mind is unengaged, we see people as less than human, as mere animals, whose desires, fears, and emotions can't be discerned and, therefore, may as well not exist. When communities—or cult leaders (or politicians)—refer to certain groups or individuals as animals, as less evolved, or as monstrous, violence against those groups or individuals almost always ticks up. This is simply how our brains operate. And the circumstance that makes people most likely to dehumanize others? When they feel *they* are the ones being dehumanized.[39] Violence is an amplification loop.

Hate is the personal manifestation of this macro indoctrination. I used to believe no one is born hateful, that people have to be taught to hate. But no matter how many heartstring-tugging Instagram posts express that, it's not exactly true. Rather, we are all born with an ability to hate. Context—fear— triggers it.

———

Certain among our elected officials have expertly manipulated these universal human responses to group isolation—to the degree that Congress hardly functions anymore. Starting in 1995, Georgia congressman Newt Gingrich launched a concerted effort to separate Republicans and Democrats from one another. As speaker of the House, he changed the workweek in Washington to three days, instead of five, encouraging representatives to spend the extra days in their districts. This discouraged friendships from developing across the aisle because Congress members weren't seeing each other at dinner parties or their children's sporting events. Fewer and fewer representatives even moved their families to DC at all.

Gingrich discouraged any cooperation with Democrats and advised Republicans to use dehumanizing language when describing the other party. Before long, Democrats mirrored their adversaries, and an amplification loop was born. In 2017, Joe Biden, speaking at the national Constitution Center, recalled his friendship with John McCain, explaining that they used to sit with one another on either side of the floor and engage in friendly debates, until "the Gingrich Revolution in the nineties," after which he says they "were chastised by the leadership of both our caucuses. . . . They didn't want us sitting together, that's when things began to change."[40]

That was basically the end of bipartisanship on the Hill. No more closed-door compromises or across-the-aisle caucuses. "Eventually the norms Gingrich introduced to the House took over the Senate's culture as well."[41] Gingrich's goal in discouraging cooperation was clear: if Congress wasn't working, then the party in control, the Democrats, would be blamed and lose power. He held

America hostage as part of a power grab. It was basically a coup. As he put it, "You have to blow down the old order to establish a new order."[42] By now, you surely recognize that classic doomsday language.

———

If you've ever been in a Facebook group and suddenly found yourself caring a great deal about, say, the keto diet, and then begun referring to people who eat carbs as "sheeple," you already understand that groups don't need to be physically isolated for the aforementioned forces to wreak havoc. The reduction of normative dissonance, increase in groupthink, and eventual shift-to-risk can actually happen *faster* in an online group than in one living together IRL. Understanding how easily we lose our inner arbiters when isolated, the statistic that fake news on Twitter spreads six times faster than truth is no longer surprising.[43]

Social media is especially powerful at spreading and indoctrinating people into doomsday ideology. One researcher described it as a "carrier wave" for apocalypticism. On platforms, bad actors easily leverage "the dynamics of social contagion and remote intimacy" in order to accelerate the spread of "beliefs that have an inherently viral appeal," for example warnings about any imminent battle between good and evil, whether that's Armageddon, an election, or the alleged persecution of misogynist stand-up comics.[44]

On social media platforms, people form focused echo-chamber communities very quickly, making them easier to indoctrinate and isolate from their IRL communities. Cult expert Steven Hassan has argued that social media platforms even engage in love bombing, showering "users with positive notifications after joining, while personalized feeds create the perception of a community 'just like you.'"[45] As we more deeply immerse ourselves in virtual groups and separate further from friends and family, we will be—unlike our counterparts in geographically isolated cults—physically alone. And loneliness makes people even more vulnerable to indoctrination by extreme ideologies. Families have no idea their child or parent is being indoctrinated in the bedroom upstairs, while watching hours of videos online, until the family member has given away $50,000 or run away to live with whichever malignant narcissist entrapped them.

Many cults have online presences now and recruit on TikTok and You-Tube. Plus, the internet has made it so easy to put yourself and your ideas out into the world that upstart charlatans and egomaniacs flood our feeds. But it is not only the unscrupulous and unwell who proffer personality and ideology online. These platforms have democratized charismatic authority, just as the Great Awakenings did, so that every person with an account is a kind of mini cult leader trying to get followers and spread their truths. Those who succeed are literally called *influence*rs.

Influencer culture feels like a continuation of what Tom Wolfe dubbed the Third Great Awakening of the sixties and seventies. I wonder now if we are actually experiencing the Fourth Great Awakening. Sixty years later, charismatic authority has not only been flattened, but atomized; previous hierarchical structures are completely shattered. We are all simultaneously salespeople and consumers, simultaneously cult leaders and followers, simultaneously posting and watching. God gave us cat videos to make us happy, and we remade them in our own image.

––––

We have explored the variety of ways isolation leads to violence, but violence is not the only method by which isolation kills. Now we arrive at the cellular-biology portion of this science lesson. Dr. Isaac Eliaz, an integrative oncologist, studies a protein in the body called galectin-3. He calls it the "survival protein," because we produce it in response to injury and illness, as well as to general stress.[46] Basically, it performs repair work at the cellular level. During a healthy stress cycle, galectin-3 is flushed from the system after it's performed its duties and once the body has calmed. However, when we experience extended stress and anxiety—for example, daily in America, where 77 percent report regularly feeling physical symptoms of stress[47]—the body never has a chance to calm. Plus, it keeps receiving signals to make more galectin-3. The proteins build up inside us.

While hanging out together in the body, they tend to connect into a kind of lattice formation. Those can then attach en masse to cell-membrane receptors. In this way, they create microenvironments within the body that are walled off from circulation, that are isolated. If blood can't reach the area, then neither can oxygen, and you wind up trapped in a cycle of inflammation, which leads to "the hardening or dysfunction of tissues, organs, and blood vessels."[48]

That's only what happens to otherwise healthy environments. Galectin-3 also creates microenvironments around damaged or infected areas. Within these pockets, "diseases can develop undetected and remain protected from drug treatments and other therapeutic agents."[49] In one study people around fifty years old were tested for galectin-3 levels and then followed for a decade. Researchers found that participants with the highest levels of the protein experienced a threefold greater mortality rate compared to those with lower levels.[50] Just as an isolated cult can exist off of society's radar for years before "suddenly" erupting into violence, so can your kidney harbor disease off of your body's radar for years before "suddenly" failing.

More alarming, infectious agents and cancer cells like to hijack galectin-3 for their own purposes, utilizing the protein's lattice formations to create shields around themselves, so they can grow and gain strength without your pesky immune system ruining everything—which sounds a lot like a con man convincing people to cut ties with family and friends and join him in the middle of nowhere so he can exploit them unimpeded. Eliaz writes often in his work that "the micro mirrors the macro." Indeed.

There's good news, though. According to Eliaz's research, we can stop the overproduction of galectin-3—and as I'm sure you've guessed, I see a metaphor between that and stopping the proliferation of cults and extremism. But we're not there yet. We are still isolated inside the loops of cultlike thinking. It's almost as if we're hypnotized by it, like it's calling to us from our deep past, whispering, "Join us."

Up until a few years ago, I believed certain things about human psychology. I assumed, for example, that we are independent and individualistic creatures, who are analytical and value reason, are concerned about fairness and have strong senses of right and wrong regardless of context, have free will and like choices and control, and are driven by self-interest. For that matter, I also believed each person *has* a self, a specific personality, comprised of certain character traits, that is unique to them and is basically the same, no matter the circumstance. I was in good company as basically every Western psychologist agreed. In fact, these character traits are not typical of the human species, but only of people born in certain societies: those which are western, educated, industrialized, rich, and democratic. These people are, as evolutionarily biologist Joseph Henrich and his colleagues coined us, WEIRD. Compared to the rest of the world, we are an aberration. Compared to all of human history, we are brand-new.

Up until less than a thousand years ago, humans lived in kin-based communities—tribes, clans, houses, lineages—that grew out of families and their networks. A person's very identity and survival, not to mention comfort and success, depended on the health and strength of their kin-based community. They lived in a different kind of culture, which caused them to develop accordingly different psychological profiles. They valued conformity and obedience, and deferred to authority and hierarchy. They were very suspicious of strangers and fiercely loyal to those within their network. They were more likely to lie for the benefit of a friend or family member. What we call nepotism, they saw as common sense. They were not much concerned about the intentions behind actions or the beliefs or mental states of actors.

Many communities like this still exist in the world. When researchers asked some of their members in Africa and the South Pacific to complete the statement, "I am _____," they were inclined to answer with relationships and social roles: I am the daughter of _____, the mother of _____, the husband of _____. When Americans were asked, they replied with personal abilities, attributes, and aspirations: I am kind, I am a mountain biker.[51] *I'm a multi-hyphenate creative but mainly a podcaster. I'm a family therapist but deejay on the weekends. I am allergic to gluten but still have a fun time.*

As we've learned, those communities that cooperated most effectively were conquered less, conquered others more, and were emulated more, all of which spread their culture, including the norms that had led to their success. Beginning generally around the sixth century, one set of norms developed which wound up—rather inadvertently—being so successful, they resulted in the creation of the WEIRD culture that has dominated the world.

After all that buildup, the norms themselves are going to sound kind of trivial, but here they are: don't marry family relations or more than one person at once. The group that spread these norms and achieved incredible success as a result, in an almost Rube Goldberg–device kind of way, was of course the Western Church in Rome, which begot the Roman Catholic Church. Here's a ridiculously abridged history of that Rube Goldberg path.

First, the rules against marrying anyone closer than a second cousin forced people to look farther and farther afield to find partners, including into neighboring tribes or clans. Plus, if your spouse died, you weren't allowed to marry anyone in their family either, meaning you had to leave the community—along with your wealth. The long-term result was the obliteration of the kin-based structure. Out of its ashes, people were forced to form new kinds of communities. More and more, they were required to approach out-group strangers.

Once this happened, modern Western society was off to the races. Markets developed, along with rules and norms supporting the efficacy of markets. We invented contracts and laws. (Without a kin-based network's imprimatur, one had to build a reputation, encouraging one to follow the rules and stick to the contracts.) Eventually, we trusted each other enough to rely on strangers, leading to the need for ever more complicated institutions to govern transactions, including banks and third-party justice systems. As we congregated together to find opportunities among one another, a new kind of community developed: cities. Within them, strangers formed networks and voluntary organizations, such as professional guilds and universities. People banded together to found their own charter towns, for which they eventually developed representative government. All the while, our psychological profiles were adapting to our new culture and environments.

Living solo made us more inclined to classify people and objects into categories, to think about the attributes and properties of things and people, as opposed to their relationships and interconnectedness to the families and clans in which they are based. Once we were all solo agents, we became less conformist (to what was there to conform?), less interested in tradition, and more individualistic. But we were still very much inclined to seek cooperation within groups in order to face other groups. It's just that now those groups in competition were guilds, monasteries, cities, universities, scientific associations, territorial states, and eventually, sororities during rush. In these kinds of matchups, as opposed to athletic trials, testosterone is lower, allowing for superior analytical skills and cognitive performance, leading to more success.[52] Whichever group/school/town got the best artisans, lawyers, and merchants became stronger and more capable. Plus, as those new people entered, bringing their disparate knowledge and skills with them, innovation flourished (just as it does in communities following an influx of immigrants).

A quick but important aside: under WEIRD culture, progress occurred at such an accelerated rate, it transformed our understanding of time itself. Previously, when not much changed from decade to decade, we understood time as circular. Then, in a state of constant growth and change, we started seeing time as linear—as if on a graph, having started from some source while heading toward some destination, just beyond the paper's edge. If life keeps getting better, surely our source was insufficient and our destination ecstatic. This paradigm feeds into the grace-nature divide, the one which claims all nature is depraved, and we are separated from it by grace, which will carry us to heaven. It's another form of separation, of isolation. And if we believe we won't return to source—whether figuratively because of technology and progress, or literally because of doomsday prophecy—why not isolate from it? Why not fell a forest, dredge a marsh, and dump in the ocean? If we are headed somewhere else, what do we care?

Humans in WEIRD society also came to believe in the idea of universal truths—whether handed down from God (religion) or the harmony of the universe (science). The result was a society less authoritarian and more egalitarian. The result was modern Western culture. This path led directly to Protestantism, which focuses on a believer's individual relationship with God, outside of community, rituals, ancestral heritage, and intermediary priests. To get into heaven, intentions and beliefs matter more than behaviors and actions. Self-reliance and personal responsibility reign supreme.

And Protestantism, of course, led directly to America. We are the apotheosis of WEIRD psychology. I'm telling you all of this because I think it's part of why Americans are so inclined to join cults: when the pendulum swings that far out, it's bound to swing back.

See, being an individual is hard. First of all, isolation and loneliness: boo. Also, self-reliance and personal responsibility lead us to put incredible pressure on ourselves . . . *while* we're isolated and lonely. A study on nineteenth-century Prussia found that counties inhabited mostly by Protestants had more than twice as many suicides a year than did Catholic counties. Second, historically, people have responded to wars and similar "shocks," as Henrich words it, by tightening their bonds with fellow villagers, leaning into religious commitments and rituals, and strengthening their participation in other voluntary associations. But what if you don't have a community? "For those lacking strong interpersonal networks, shocks will propel them to seek out and invest in new relationships and communities."[53]

As you've read several times now, people today join cults during times of incredible stress and anxiety. And as you've probably already been thinking, the kin-based networks of our ancestors have a lot in common with the cults of today (heads of clans take countless mates, as cult leaders do, and build dynasties beneath them, as MLM founders do). Is it possible we join cults because stress triggers an unconscious need to return to the kinds of communities within which we evolved? Are we unconsciously returning to the comfort of hierarchy, the relative stasis of the relationships therein (sister of, mother of, daughter of), and the cooperation from which we'll benefit?

"I mean, that seems like a plausible hypothesis to me," Henrich said when I got him on a video chat. He then explained that kinship "never really goes away and always tries to reassert itself. One of the things about a very individualistic society is you end up with a lot of loneliness and people can feel disjointed from societies unless they're able to join voluntary communities. That's why voluntary communities have been so important in U.S. history." For most of America's past, those voluntary associations were churches, which provided services for members in need. As America grew more secular, many of those services fell to the state. But our government has been eroding social safety nets ever since FDR dared to roll across the earth. Therefore, when crisis strikes, many of us, having nowhere else to turn, will take the hand of a narcissistic charlatan who promises community and purpose, but instead triggers us-versus-them thinking, isolates us, and robs us of all we have and are. This is particularly dangerous at a time when shocks and times of crisis are no longer occasional aberrations but our constant reality.

———

Even when people are separated from and pitted against another group, or are isolated from society at large, information can creep in. That happened when Dwight York sent his eldest children to school. Later in Georgia, while holding court among his newly built Egyptian icons, York probably didn't realize that would prove to have been his fatal mistake. One of his early children, Jacob, told reporters about the confusion he felt in the outside world. "You've been told the white man is the devil all your life, and then you go off to school and white men are teaching and taking care of you. And you think, 'Where is the white man being the devil?' It changes your mentality."[54]

In a later radio interview, Jacob explains that his dad told his first generation of kids that the Ansaru Allah community was the family business. "But then he felt like he lost us," he adds. "We went to private school. We went to public school. We traveled the world. We had an opinion. So we began to verse him. So the next generation, he pretty much brainwashed, and he kept them contained their entire life. He was their total education."[55]

Jacob, now a successful music producer and entrepreneur in Atlanta, declined my interview requests and has claimed he didn't bring charges and appears nowhere in the discovery documents. Around the late eighties and early nineties, one of York's sons, who was fourteen or fifteen at the time found a videotape of his fourteen-year-old girlfriend having sex with his father. He probed deeper, learned more about his father's actions, and began speaking out against him within the community. Then he and his mother left. According to the *Atlanta Journal-Constitution*, they joined one of York's daughters, who'd been banished after refusing to have sex with him.[56]

Cut to 1998, when local officials in Eatonton, Georgia, received an anonymous tip that kids were being molested at the compound (called Tama-Re). They investigated, but the breakthrough arrived in a 2001 letter that named alleged victims. By this time, Jacob had moved to the Atlanta area and turned his home into a kind of safe house for people leaving the Nuwaubians. He also began connecting victims with the local sheriff, Howard Sills. Eventually, almost thirty-five, including other of York's children, came forward to participate in the case.[57]

Around this time, their dad called a family meeting in New York with several of his older children. They hoped he wanted to make peace (he had admitted some years prior that his sexual predations were sick and he wanted to get help, though he made no efforts to do so). Instead, they claim he just needed money. He allegedly said his followers were idiots, and expressed surprise that his sons didn't want "what he had, that is, power, money, and women."[58]

Meanwhile, Sheriff Sills was moving slowly and playing it safe. The Nuwaubians seemed to be looking for a battle. "Please help us," read a flyer they posted in 1999. "We smell a Waco in the making." They published on their website that Sills was planning an attack on the group, including on its innocent women and children. When the sheriff came to deliver a court order—regarding that nightclub permit violation—armed guards blocked his car. "I pulled back," he later told a reporter. "Normally I'd never do that. But they clearly were desperate for an armed confrontation, and I was not going to give it to them if I could help it."[59]

York began preaching that attack was imminent. Nuwaubian men conducted paramilitary drills. Two years later, armed now with allegations of child abuse and rape, but still determined to avoid an armed conflict, Sheriff Sills coordinated with neighboring law enforcement and planned to move when York was absent and couldn't instruct his militia to shoot. Almost three hundred officers traveled to Putnam County and waited for York to leave the compound. After he and his "main" wife, Kathy Johnson—his handmaiden and groomer, who would later serve jail time—had driven off the property, they were apprehended, and then the officers swept into Tama-Re, surprising those inside, securing the perimeter, and moving quickly to conduct their search. Hours later, York's followers returned, doubled in force, to take back the compound. But by then,

Sills and his officers were leaving. Dwight York is serving a 135-year sentence in federal prison.

"My father did a great thing for the African-American community and still destroyed African-American kids," Jacob later told a reporter. "He's done a lot of damage to his own people as much as the good he did." He also expresses feeling conflicted. "That's my father. . . . I lived with him in his house. He poured me breakfast when I was five."[60]

Although Jacob declined an interview, I did meet another of York's children. In January 2024, I wandered the Nuwaubians' former real estate empire on Bushwick Avenue in Brooklyn. I found two remaining buildings: one with a bookstore on the first floor, and the other, an adjoining cavernous, one-story temple, its exterior painted with ancient-Egyptian-style iconography. I requested a tour, was told to return on the weekend, and when I did, I was greeted by a handsome thirty-something in ceremonial garb. He declined to go on record, citing media stigmatization, but spoke for an hour about the group's belief systems, and the hypocrisy and racism of the government's case against York. He eventually shared, if somewhat reluctantly, that York is his father. Proceeds from sales of the books and pamphlets in the bookstore, mostly written by York, purportedly support the group's efforts to secure its leader's release from jail. By August 2024, the buildings were for sale.[61]

The showdown at Tama-Re ended with much more drama than the Y2K production did at the King James Bible Baptist Church. But the latter certainly felt dramatic to Cameron and his family at the time. He believes his mother had joined the church mostly because of their dire financial situation. When his father died, the insurance company found a way to deny paying out his policy. "There was no support," he says. "Poor people need religion a lot more than rich people do." They were still broke when the church excommunicated them—just before (what they believed would be) the biggest crisis in history. "We were like, 'Well, we're screwed now. We lost our support system and the people with all the food and guns.'"

But, of course, the actual event was uneventful. On December 31, 1999, in White House, Tennessee, Will lay in bed, sick with the flu and watching the New Year's Eve countdown on TV. "The ball fell, and then the power was still on. I just shut the TV off and went back to sleep," he recalls. It wasn't such an open-and-shut case in church, though. For a week or two, leaders discussed the ensuing breakdown of society, claiming it could still happen at any moment. Eventually, Paul addressed Y2K in front of the congregation. "He basically said, *I wouldn't have done anything differently, and Praise God, it wasn't today, but it might come later*," Will adds. "He sounded kind of defeated."

CHAPTER 7

CONTROL-ALT-DELETE
ON CONTROL AND COMFORT

Former members of Love Has Won call it a cult, but it was not the sort where the leader overdoses on power, sexually abuses children, and hoards weapons until it all implodes. For starters, this group's leader, Amy Carlson, began her journey more as followers tend to: she fell down an internet rabbit hole, then ran away from her family. Before long, though, she claimed to be God and started collecting followers . . . who helped her slowly die.

"She created a monster, and eventually the monster got ahold of her, even when she wanted to let it go," Andrew Profaci told me. From 2014 to 2015, he was a member of the group and Carlson's boyfriend. Everyone called him Father God. Actually, he was their third Father God (but not the last). And the monster Profaci references was the belief system Carlson designed.

In April 2021, following a tip, police located a body in an advanced state of decomposition, wrapped in a sleeping bag and decorated with Christmas lights. Carlson had died some days earlier in an Oregon hotel. Not knowing what else to do, her disciples took the corpse to a campground. While driving, they laid the body in the back seat, wearing a hat and glasses, as if sleeping, which did trick the cops who pulled them over en route. At the campground, Jason Castillo, the last Father God, slept next to her in a tent. Then he and two other followers drove her body across several state lines, back to a home base in Colorado. Before she died, her skin had turned grayish blue. The police who found her thought she had been painted.

Her slow march to death began in 2007. Stressed out by and unsatisfied with her working-class life and three children, Carlson had descended into extreme online thought—mostly classic conspiracy theories along with beliefs about angels and ascended masters. Then she disappeared without warning, abandoned a life of responsibilities in order to join a guy she met online. Soon they were making their own rabbit-hole fodder, videos proselytizing about the deity within us all. They called themselves Mother God and Father God. But soon, as that original Father God said, Carlson decided "she was more God than other people were God."[1] She left him and found her second Father God, Miguel Lamboy, whose cancer he claimed she cured. A so-called cult was born.

The self-styled deity sold remote healings and slowly gained an impressive online audience: almost twenty thousand followers on Facebook and nearly ten thousand on YouTube. The group's videos were watched more than 1.5 million times.[2] Her followers believed (and many still do) that she was 19 billion years old and being helped by a team of dead celebrities, led by actor Robin Williams, in a cosmic battle against "the cabal." As a healer, they claimed she could cure cancer, addiction, Lyme disease, and suicidal thoughts.

Yet this healer would also, as Profaci has said, "drink herself into oblivion every single night." All the while, she convinced more and more people to escape their lives and join her alcohol- and drug-fueled party. "You were high from the moment you woke up to the moment you went to bed."[3]

As did most of Carlson's followers, Profaci found her online. She spoke of "a new earth coming," he told me, which would require everyone either to rise up into it or be left behind. But more than the doomsday preaching, he was interested in "the path forward" she provided for people who had questions such as "What is reality? What is the point of living? What am I here for?" He started dreaming about Carlson—it happened six nights in a row. In online messages to him, she said she dreamed about him too, and increasingly pressured him to join the "team," as she referred to the core group of followers, who lived together. He believed it possible she was God. But the moment he arrived—in the middle of the night to a party house in disarray—he knew he'd been wrong.

"At the first sight of the dirty dishes, when I saw the place in shambles, I knew God doesn't live like this," he recalls. "It was just so obvious to me." Then he found Carlson herself, wasted. He says she had been "drinking on top of shrooming" for two straight days. She was awake but nonverbal, drooling in her chair and unable to sit up straight. "It was the scariest moment," he says. "I couldn't believe I had gone through everything I'd gone through to get there, only to see this." Even so, he stayed. He tried to unsee the truth. "I wanted to give it a chance."

Carlson gave Profaci a large dose of psilocybin mushrooms, said he was the brightest light she had ever seen, and whenever he was ready to make love, to let her know. He wasn't attracted to her, but figured this was a challenge. Within a couple of months, they were happy. He genuinely fell in love with her. He still remembers her fondly. "She was magnetic, just a lot of fun. A life-of-the-party kind of person. But she was sweet. She had manners." He says she loved to dance and play music, and describes her as positive and bubbly. In later years, however, she developed a reputation for lashing out at members.[4]

He also recalls her uncanny ability to "spot somebody's baggage" and point it out. "She was incredible at helping people realize the parts of themselves that weren't in alignment, and how they could be better," he explains. "She couldn't see it for herself—she was absolutely blind. But when it came to everybody else, she was spot-on." Some who came sought such spiritual wisdom; others came to party. Nearly everyone was escaping an untenable life.

One specific reality in particular plagued her devotees, according to film director Hannah Olson, who scoured more than a thousand hours of footage from the group's 2,700 YouTube videos and live streams for her HBO documentary series, *Love Has Won: The Cult of Mother God*. "This is a group of people who were traumatized by the healthcare system," Olson told me. Profaci arrived after struggling with an opioid addiction. Another found the group after losing his father to that same disease. One young woman joined after waking up from a coma to discover she owed half a million dollars in medical bills. "Love Has Won exists," says Olson, "because people were searching online for how to heal their bodies and minds, because they could not afford to go to a doctor." Many, if not all, were without insurance. In 2023, the uninsured rate for American adults stood at 11 percent.[5] "Amy's ideology empowered people to believe that they could heal themselves."

In Love Has Won, unlike in most alleged cults, the core followers eventually took the wheel. While investigating the group, says Olson, "I couldn't tell who was steering the ship." This is partly how Carlson lost her life.

Love Has Won sold merch and supplements online, including colloidal silver, a tincture of silver particles suspended in liquid. Its healing properties have been touted by other outré wellness sites and hawkers, specifically its support for immune function. Though actual science has found no benefit to the oral ingestion of silver, Carlson said it could cure almost anything. A member alleges that colloidal silver has been intentionally targeted by the medical establishment: "The pharmaceutical industry banned it because healed people don't make money." As their leader devolved into alcoholism (Carlson believed and told her followers that alcohol and drugs were her "medicine"), Carlson's disciples served her more shots of silver and doses of beer. One former member estimates that Mom, as they called her, was consuming a half liter of colloidal silver a day.[6]

Meanwhile, she lost weight. Carlson also suffered from anorexia, a disease characterized by a strong desire for control and often associated with anxiety disorders. A diary entry by one of her disciple caretakers suggests the severity of her illness: "Robin [Williams] says 103.1 is maximum weight Mom can get to" in order to ascend out of the false "3D" world and into the true "5D" plane. The group believed ego entered through "two back doors": food and sleep.[7] Everyone lost weight. (And why Robin Williams? Carlson was a fan. She often played his albums in her online chat room late at night. Shortly after his death, Profaci explains, "We were on a mushroom trip and she said, 'Oh, somebody's coming through the field,' meaning the quantum field. 'Somebody's coming to join the [galactic] team. Oh, it's Robin Williams.' All of a sudden, he was there every day and he was our guy.")

Eventually, Mother God stopped moving from the waist down. It's unclear whether this was paralysis. At least one former member believes it resulted from nerve damage due to advanced alcoholism. Her devotees believed her physical deterioration was due to Carlson taking on the world's negative energy, a sign her ascension was imminent. They scoured the sky for the spaceship that would gather her. Meanwhile, her caretakers fed her tincture. A buildup of silver in the body leads to argyria, a condition that turns skin blue.

Years earlier, Profaci had tried to stop the train. On a few occasions, at night, when the two of them were alone, he'd even convinced Carlson she wasn't God. "I would say, 'You are embodying virtues of Mother God, but you are not her,'" he recalls. And she would say, "'OK. No, you're right. Maybe I'm not.'" But then, "she would talk to Miguel the next day, and he would reel her back in: 'Don't listen to Andrew. He's just trying to break down what we're doing here.' She would snap right back into it."

He's referring to Miguel Lamboy, the second Father God, whom the group called Archangel Michael. Many believe that Lamboy puppeteered the entire charade. (Carlson put him in control of all the finances and legal documents.) Others see him as a true believer. To be sure, after Carlson died, he emptied all accounts and took off with $330,000.[8] He was also the one who alerted the police of her body, although that feels fair, considering it was in his house, near his sleeping child. But his motives are unclear. Profaci isn't sure whether Lamboy truly believed Carlson was God or only pretended to in order to protect himself. He leans toward the former theory but adds, "He was very very slick."

After living with the group for about a year, Profaci, who was around thirty during his time there, uncovered a bit of fraud. A group member had developed a computer program allowing him to masquerade as four or five chat room users at once. "He was pretending to be these beings that came into our chat room, and were spitting knowledge and truth that nobody else had." Someone else in the chat room mentioned she'd lost her mother and couldn't find her will; as a result, she and her family would lose their home. "These beings said, 'Oh, it's upstairs under the floorboards in your mother's house, go and look.'" Lo and behold, there was the will. But, of course, as Profaci alleges, the "woman" was also invented by the guy voicing these fake beings.

As cult fraud goes, this is pretty light. The problem arose when Carlson backed the scheme. She told her online followers the beings were real and that Robin Williams had said so too. Therefore, if the truth came out, it would be clear that Amy's guides were false. Profaci went to Carlson and Lamboy with the information. (Reminder that Profaci and others refer to Lamboy as Archangel Michael.) "I was told I would either have to keep my mouth shut or leave," Profaci recalls. "I looked at her, I looked at Michael, I walked over to the laptop, typed out the truth, and pressed *send*." The group hemorrhaged followers. But Profaci was not excommunicated. Carlson loved him. A couple of months later, he left anyway.

"She wanted a new Father God, because at that point, I wasn't fitting the bill. That was hard for me because I had grown to love her very much," he explains. He left for Florida. Carlson followed and for a few months ran the team from a distance. "She lived with me, just me and her. She left the whole team behind. I thought I had her. I thought I had her snapped out of it. I was so close to saving her. But [Archangel] Michael just kept reeling her back in." Profaci ended their relationship. That was the last time he saw her. "Without Michael, I bet you Amy would still be alive," he told me.

Despite her occasional late-night admissions to Profaci, did Carlson really believe she was God? "I think she wanted to," Profaci says. "She enjoyed it and there was definitely a part of her that really wanted to believe it no matter how much truth I could show her."

Of the many tragedies associated with Love Has Won, one stands out: Carlson knew she was dying and tried to get help. But she was trapped by her own theology. "Her teachings came back to haunt her in the sense that she had told everybody, 'I'm Mother God: doctors can't help me; hospitals can't help me,'" Profaci explains.

In a 2018 video, a member who went by the name Archeia Faith explains that Carlson was "throwing up, diarrhea, she was shaking."[9] Faith attributed the illness to an assassination attempt by the cabal—a "sword sliced one of her hearts," Faith says—and to the metaphysical surgery she afterward experienced. At times, Carlson had even instructed followers never to take her to a hospital.

But toward the end, she asked for traditional help. "There's been moments when Mom has asked us to take her to a 3D hospital, and we were like, 'Nope!'" one of her core disciples says in a video from 2020.[10] In other reports, we learn why: her followers believed that if she entered a hospital, members of the cabal, who were trying to stop her ascension, would take over the body of someone working in the hospital and then harm Carlson.[11]

"She wanted help, and then couldn't get it," Profaci told me. Her daughter, Madi, has said, "I feel like there was something in her that was telling her to go home and then something just kept pulling her back."[12]

Carlson weighed just seventy-five pounds when she died. An autopsy determined the cause to be "alcohol abuse, anorexia, and chronic colloidal silver ingestion."[13] She was forty-five.

———

Was Carlson's death a murder or a suicide? "She created a belief system where poisons were remedies. She adhered to it. And she collected followers who adhered to it. That belief system had her death built into it. It's a death by addiction," says Olson, who comes from a family suffering generational addiction. "It has the same culpability for both the person and the people around them, that addiction has. It's just that this one came with a whole cosmology."

Profaci argues, "She had to know that she was putting herself into a grave. It was obvious."

At times, it can be hard to summon sympathy for Carlson and her followers: some of their views were deplorable. Members thought the Sandy Hook massacre was a hoax and believed Hitler was "working for the light." But using that D-word—as Hillary Clinton famously did at a 2016 campaign fundraiser—to describe the people themselves doesn't help. "It's so easy on the left to look at people as repugnant, rather than as people who have been failed by our social system," Olson says. "Reality doesn't make sense for a lot of people because of enormous income inequality. My generation has not inherited the world we were promised."

It's a kind of failure of prophecy. Olson is a millennial, the first generation to break from the traditional American pattern of children out-earning their parents. In Olson's series, another Love Has Won follower discusses the trauma she experienced and witnessed following the 2008 mortgage crisis. Millennials are also more likely to work in low-skilled service jobs, most of which offer no stability or health insurance.

The American dream is itself now a failure of prophecy. It used to come true for everyone in a booming middle class. But since the eighties, the corporate oligarchs have made that impossible. To distract us from this reality, American culture still pretends fortune and fame are accessible to all—sells and promises the dream in advertisements and political propaganda. When people can't achieve it, they feel betrayed. It's that grievance narrative again. They turn to extremism as a result. I wish our forefathers had added *security* to the list of "life, liberty, and the pursuit of happiness."

In addition to providing followers with some semblance of control in an increasingly chaotic world, Love Has Won gave them a chance to feel like they mattered. Many of Carlson's followers sensed they didn't belong in the "3D world" of everyone else's reality, that it offered nothing for them. They were, in effect, part of a surplus population, people who couldn't find a place in society and turned toward cultlike thinking for comfort. "What she really hooked onto was this feeling most people had that there's something more special here for them to do," Profaci explains. Inhabiting their thought processes, he says, "'I want to be special, or what meaning does my life have? I don't have money. I don't have fame. I don't have clout. I don't have all of these wonderful things that I see people have. So what's in it for me?'"

Trump exploits such grievances expertly. He tells his followers they've been screwed by a system of power. They have. Many politicians neglect to acknowledge it. Sure, Trump isn't totally honest about who does the screwing, since many of them are his fat-cat Wall Street friends. And worse he was lying when he said he'd help. Instead, he has screwed the average American even more, to enrich said friends. But he does acknowledge their pain. No one should be surprised by his popularity. He promised to steady their wobbling worlds. In exchange, they made him sovereign.

We seek cults when our realities feel out of control, then cede control upon joining. At their heart, all doomsday groups are autocracies—it's another kind of escape, in this case from the hard and messy work of democracy.

The core members of Love Has Won still believe Amy Carlson is God and reject the 3D world. The last Father God started a group called Joy Rains. Some of Carlson's other followers continue the mission through an organization called 5D Full Disclosure. Their story isn't over. "What happens 'afterwards' is that these are our neighbors and extended family members," Olson says. "There are people looking for these kinds of answers all over America."

The ancient Egyptians called it *ma'at*, "a principle of order so all-embracing that it governed every aspect of existence." *Ma'at* was in the harmony of the universe and in the proper behavior of humans in all relations to each other and the state. *Ma'at* was constantly under threat by chaos, lurking always in the primordial disorder out of which the ordered world emerged, and surfacing as, for example, floods, hostile armies, and unfair dealings. Those who worshiped Osiris believed they'd be judged at death in "the chamber of the double *ma'at*" (double, meaning life and death), to determine how ordered their lives had been.[14] They were judged not by good deeds done but absence of chaos introduced.

People still have a deep psychological need to understand the world as non-random. Psychologists argue we meet that need by exercising personal control. A lack of personal control fuels anxiety and leads us to compensate, which researchers call *compensatory control*. A 2009 study determined that "people respond to losses of personal control by imbuing their social, physical, and metaphysical environments with order and structure." It outlines three basic ways we do it. First, we lean on superstitions and similar ways of perceiving patterns in noise and thereby ascribing order to the world. Second, we support and defend controlling sociopolitical systems and structures, especially governments, but also other organizations, such as universities. Third, we increase belief in a controlling, interventionist God. For example, following economic depressions, interest grows in strict religions.[15]

What drives compensatory control? Anxiety, which is currently *out of* control. While 3.9 percent of people suffer from such disorders globally, that number in America is 6.2 percent. In 2019, 12 percent of American men and 19 percent of women claimed to have experienced recent anxiety. By 2023, that had risen to 25 percent of men and 32 percent of women in America. Leading causes include climate change, bills, health, and the safety of one's family.[16] Eating disorders doubled between 2000 and 2018.[17]

If this increase leads us to desire controlling, interventionist gods, that role is easily played by autocrats of every stripe. Plus, we're currently experiencing a loneliness epidemic affecting about one in two Americans.[18] As explored in the last chapter, isolation leads us to regress to cultlike communities when stressed. We're also reeling from a surge in surplus populations, specifically people shut out from stable participation in the workforce as a result of mechanization and of NAFTA pulling jobs out of America. We are about to experience another surge in surplus populations, due to work made redundant by AI. Add to that all the aforementioned classic sociological hallmarks that trigger cult increases—major technological advances, major societal changes, and crises—and you've got a nation already experiencing a cult wave that is now facing a tsunami. If you're a con artist, now's your chance, dude.

I have an idea, though: What if there's no reason to try to control who is or isn't chosen because *no one* is chosen? What if the entire premise is false? But a world without the chosen would be a world without order, and that is too terrifying to imagine, much less consider. So we keep expecting rewards, feeling robbed of them, and manufacturing thieves to punish. We continue seeking perfection by imposing our own image of it onto everyone else. We go on assuming an evil faction is out to get us and waste time and resources fighting the wrong enemy. We try and try to achieve salvation by purchasing it. To prove we finally got it, we work even harder to collect wealth, no matter its origin. And then we isolate ourselves—the true believers, the chosen perfect—from the unchosen, even though it slowly kills us to be alone. We do it all just so the world can have order. But, hey, pssst, com'ere. [*whispers*] *What if no one is chosen?* And what if that would free you to live as a perfectly imperfect creature of this earth who doesn't have all the answers, but can share in collective wonder over the utter improbability of it all? Just an idea.

Ironically, it was a search for control that created most of the circumstances now ungluing us. I'm talking about comfort and convenience. Our desire for it, and for the resources and technological innovations that deliver it, are major causes of the disorder we now fear. There is arguably no other country more obsessed with comfort, convenience, and the intersection of the two, whether that comes in the form of bite-sized, flavor-packed foods with interminable shelf lives (Cheetos), discreet life-taking implements that fit into our waistbands (guns), or disposable plastic pipes filled with cannabis extracts (take mine from my cold, dead hands). We are the engines of our own chaos.

From my perspective, all efforts to control fall into one of two buckets, either time or resources. We can't get enough of either. Our race for the comfort of time—for conveniences that save us time, whether washing machines or online banking—are efforts to achieve more life by optimizing the time-to-experience ratio. If we can't live forever, we can at least live more of now. Some conquer death by joining religions that promise an afterlife. Others do so in the Chick-fil-A drive-through line; Southern Baptists do both.

Meanwhile, our race for the comfort of resources has depleted the world and exploited workers. We seek control to maintain order, but instead, the process creates chaos. The result is nationwide insecurity and instability—*less* control and order. We are trapped in a cycle of control.

In the margins of all my research books are scribbled the words *comfort* and *control*. They appear again and again in notes I've taken over the last few years. Now I come to the end and realize every chapter is riddled with these themes. After reading the psychological study of compensatory control, I see one of its three outcomes (the desire for a controlling government) in the American Monomyth's expression of latent yearning for an autocratic strongman, and another (leaning into superstition as a way to find patterns in chaos) at play in America's dominant conspiracy theories, from the John Birch Society to the New World Order.

The Oneida experiment, and the eugenics and pronatalist movements, are efforts to control death, whether by perfecting oneself to the point of immortality, deciding who can and can't procreate, or having as many children as possible in an effort to live forever. New Thought and its descendants delude us into thinking we can control every aspect of our lives with our minds, including enlightenment, karma, or inner new Jerusalem. What is the self-help industry if not a giant economic engine of comfort achievement through the exercise of control?

Late-stage capitalism and MLMs have allowed some to indulge their desires for comfort and control, via money, to the degree that they continually create an underclass specifically in order to exploit it. When fate, that ultimate agent of chaos, tries to suggest good things don't always happen to good people and bad things to bad people, we use Perrault's fairy tales to reinforce the ordered morality myths we prefer. And when all of this fails, and we feel particularly threatened or chaotic, we seek the comfort and control of us-versus-them thinking.

All apocalyptic movements promise a time of bliss marked most especially by comfort: less pain and hardship; equanimity of resources; bounteous sex and music; and often the absence even of death. This is just as true for secular apocalyptic dreams. In Mankind United, con man Arthur Bell promised followers the Ritz: once they'd triumphed over the Hidden Rulers, he said, the Sponsors would bestow upon them surplus clothing and food, endless vacations, and homes full of appliances. Marx promised the proletariat emancipation from brutal labor conditions. Hitler promised the wealth and supremacy of an ascending Germany. Comfort is a base desire. These promises are hard to decline.

Perhaps the one innovation that promised the most control via comfort and convenience, but instead takes the most control from us, is the Internet. We have the world at our fingertips, along with its lies. Cult exit counselor Rick Alan Ross told me he had big hopes the Internet would minimize cult participation, since anyone could search the name of a group in question and find the quote-unquote truth. Instead, the Internet atomized truth. Social media, in particular, has separated us from and radicalized us against one another, thereby making us easier to exploit.

In some ways, algorithms themselves behave like cult leaders. Just as traditional destructive groups keep followers trapped, so do algorithms entrap us. They isolate us from our communities and the real world by encouraging us to stay engaged via dopamine-releasing bells and notifications, by feeding us extreme content because they've learned it has a 62.3 percent chance of long-term engagement, and by steering us into rabbit holes of ideologically similar content to deepen our commitment.[19] They spread disinformation that separates us from those who subscribe to truth. They literally mitigate our ability to control what we do and don't believe. Plus, the goal is to extract monetized resources from us, our attention and data. Social-media algorithms are maybe the most successful cult leaders in the history of humanity.

Of course, the algorithm works at the command of others—the kind of shadowy elite whom conspiracy theorists fear—and it is not their only tool. In his now famous essay, "Why Technology Favors Tyranny," Yuval Noah Harari warns of the "hordes of bots" that know how to push our emotional buttons and do so "at the behest of a human elite, to try to sell us something—be it a car, a politician, or an entire ideology." He writes, "We have already been given a foretaste of this in recent elections and referendums across the world, when hackers learned how to manipulate individual voters by analyzing data about them and exploiting their prejudices. While science-fiction thrillers are drawn to dramatic apocalypses of fire and smoke, in reality we may be facing a banal apocalypse by clicking."[20]

Even in the face of this terror, I take back my earlier assignation of the Internet as the innovation that promised but stole the most control. That designation surely belongs to the combustible engine. The largest additional increases in cultlike thinking in America will undoubtedly occur as a result of global warming–related crises. In this case, the shadowy forces aiming to exterminate us already live inside us. America alone is responsible for a quarter of global carbon emissions annually.[21] Despite our fears of doomsday-style atrocities happening *to* us, we birthed this Armageddon and brought it on ourselves. Hell on earth was a fallacy until we created it.

In addition to destroying our habitat, such conveniences—inventions and technologies—also minimize our reliance on one another. Zoom's transformation of shared office spaces into ghost towns is only the latest result. ATMs replaced relationships with local bank tellers. Televisions and radios supplanted communal storytelling and music. Air-conditioning took us off porches. And clock snooze buttons replaced humans snooze buttons, except for Werner Erhard's assistant.

Inventions of convenience are particularly worrisome when they replace the need for trust. What Henrich calls impersonal norms (for example, when someone enters your taxi, they're expected to pay at the end) are sometimes swapped for what he calls complete contracts (when someone enters your Uber, Corporate already has their credit card and y'all need not speak). "I think complete contracts are actually worse for our trust," Henrich told me. "Then, if it's *not* a complete contract, they're probably going to screw you, right?"

Con artists, who rely on the trust of their marks, arguably exist specifically as a result of WEIRD culture. Kin-based networks kept such behavior in check, and no one in out-groups was trusted anyway, so there wasn't much opportunity to practice impersonal trust, much less betray it. "But because we are this high-trust society," Henrich explains, "we can have a certain amount of parasites in the system."

So, as a result of technology, we now have fewer opportunities to develop and engage in trust, while an abundance of scams increases our skepticism—will that affect the development of WEIRD society? "Impersonal trust will just be replaced by technology, essentially surveillance cameras," Henrich opines. "We won't actually have that trust of the other person. I think that could change the direction of cultural evolution." This is a huge problem. Trust is how we achieved progress—and democracy—in the first place.

We've grown increasingly WEIRDer for the last fifteen years, but there's no guarantee that pattern will continue. Data gathered since 2008 suggests rural parts of the United States are already becoming less WEIRD. In addition, we now engage in less intergroup competition—that which has always fueled innovation and trust in WEIRD societies—as a result of tech monopolies gobbling up competition. (Trusts diminish trust.)

All of these increases in cultlike thinking are moving us toward autocracy. We want that monomythic cowboy superhero to save us and punish our enemies. Just as the guru salesman peddles packaged salvation to solve a problem of his own creation, so does the demagogue argue we're persecuted by existing power structures and only he has the solution—offered in exchange for power. The exchange feels worth it because the only thing worse than a world where only one person has control is a world where no one has control.

"There is nothing inevitable about democracy," Harari writes. "For all the success that democracies have had over the past century or more, they are blips in history."[22] If we don't find a way as a nation to provide basic security and dignity for all, extremism will spread, strongmen will take all the resources and power, and countless lives will be ruined. Somehow, I'm optimistic.

This brings us back to galectin-3, the "survival protein" our bodies produce to repair ourselves following stressors. Recall that today, due to ever-present stress, the otherwise helpful protein tends to build up inside us, where it wreaks havoc and aids in the development of disease. I told you there was a solution ... actually, there are two. Dr. Isaac Eliaz found a way to get citrus pectin to block existing galectin-3 from creating microenvironments. But I'm more interested in his recommendation to stop the production valve from making more.

"Grasping to the ever-changing as if it's permanent triggers the survival response," he writes in *The Survival Paradox: Reversing the Hidden Cause of Aging and Chronic Disease*. "In this very act of holding on to our outer and inner experiences—of trying to prolong them, to make them survive—we inhibit the constant natural change that is needed for health and longevity."[23] He calls this a *paradox*, because our desire and striving to survive often impair our ability to do so.

We humans like permanence. It provides us with an illusory sense of control. In reality of course, there is no permanence. Each second, somewhere between 1 million and 1 trillion reactions occur in a single human cell.[24] Even if we can comprehend the reality of constant flux, we struggle to accept it. Doing so requires us also to accept death. But we are hardwired to fight death, the ultimate chaos from which we seek salvation. Our drive to survive is antithetical to change. Instead, we grasp, hold, and fixate mentally, emotionally, physically, and, as Eliaz offers, psychospiritually.

In addition to integrating Western and Chinese medicines, the clinician, researcher, and practitioner is also a student of Buddhism, who has trained for decades, including under Tibetan masters in the Himalayas. He focuses especially on healing and deepening the mind-body connection and encourages the same in his patients. In this endeavor, he writes, "we have to get through the thin veneer of 'positive thinking'" and penetrate deeper.

This is not about shifting one's mindset. But the mind certainly plays a role. "Since stress, anger, and quick reactions all bring about inflammation and drive galectin-3, it makes sense that we can minimize inflammation by calming the mind," he explains. He has seen these results in his patients. He has also witnessed something more. "Grasping and fixation have a naturally contracting effect. When we finally see and recognize that we've grasped things that could not be grasped, something softens and opens within us. Our struggle and our fight fall away. It is in this place that we begin to open our hearts to ourselves and to others."[25]

Fear of change causes us to shrink and to isolate ourselves. When our ego clings to our need to survive, that "doesn't allow us to see what is so obvious, that we are all connected," he told me in a phone interview. He admits it's scary, admits that "the greatest courage is to live in the moment because if you truly live in the moment, you never know what's going to happen."

Trying to impede change can literally make us sick. It's also an effort at control that opens us to being controlled by others. If we can't learn to metabolize chaos, we will grasp at anything. If, when the world wobbles, we don't choose to body surf the waves, we will fall for the promise of a latter-day Atlas, claiming he can hold the world in place. That promise is not only impossible but, like all scams, is a lie. Atlas was actually condemned to hold up the sky.

What if we looked at that sky of stars, and instead of experiencing the terror of utter insignificance, felt wonder and gratitude for utter insignificance? What a relief not to be chosen, which honestly sounds like a lot of work. What cheer that luck exists, meaning everything isn't up to us, an impossible burden. What reprieve to no longer fear death, an inevitability no bunker or spaceship could escape. Plus, if we no longer fear death, the liars for hire lose their marketplace for false life and have to close up shop for good. We could be our own superheroes.

I've clearly become a Pollyanna.

I'm not done yet.

CONCLUSION

I told you this book is an apocalypse, but it is not prophecy. We have a choice. Our birthright is not only to be driven by doomsday dreams, but also to be the apotheosis of WEIRD society and benefit from all of the cooperation and innovation that's bred. Forgive the patriotism, but there's no problem this nation can't creatively solve. Except maybe streaky windshield wipers, but I can live with that.

When I began this project, I steeled myself for years of darkness. To live in these worlds and explore such cruelty and greed—would I need regular massage and antidepressants? It's true my viewing preferences went no deeper than reality TV (because in every other show or film, I saw the apocalypse; our culture is riddled with it). Still, to my surprise, the process of researching and writing this book was largely a consolation. Once we know how the card trick works, we'll stop falling for it.

The issue is the card trick, not the ideologies themselves. OK, sometimes the ideologies are problematic. But for the most part, the ideas explored here also have beautiful, positive, and healthy manifestations. Avoid danger, gather with people who understand you, strive to meet audacious goals. Those are helpful impulses. Healthy skepticism doesn't have to morph into conspiracy theory and ambition needn't to become Amway. But bad actors dangle some carrot that short-circuits our warning systems and overrides our common sense.

I'm not suggesting we excise these cultural foundations. That's not even possible. We can't exist without them. In the same way there's no freedom of speech without the existence of hate speech, you can't have a trusting market-based society without scam artists, and you can't have freedom of religion without wolves in guru clothing. Fortunately, we can exit the *cult of* America without leaving America itself. Unlike escaping an actual destructive group, we can ditch this cult without saying goodbye to what we love. And we must, because participating in the cult version of America is endangering actual America, its beauty, community, hope, and promise.

I found other consolations while researching and writing this book. Paradoxically, learning that we are all born of violence had a palliative effect on me. It explains so much. We evolved through millennia of one specific pattern playing out ad nauseam: of two separate groups battling, after which one was victorious and the other exterminated or enslaved. Of course we dream of doomsday, a battle between two separate groups, after which one will be victorious and the other exterminated or enslaved. Believing in our bones that war is inevitable, we develop a wish-fulfillment theory of being "chosen" in an effort to write the ending. *Of course we do.* It is harder to be scared of things that make sense. Besides, as much (and arguably more) of our deep history was spent cooperating, so our bones know that too. We get to choose.

I also found comic relief in the research. Frankly, with distance, doomsday thinking is hilarious, particularly that assertion of being chosen. We've rationalized and sanctified the behavior to the degree that we can't see we are all just toddlers who want to be line leader.

———

Look, I'm not claiming I have the answers. That would be cultlike. I do want you to listen to me, but if you're reluctant to, good, congratulations: you get it. (And not in a Werner Erhardian est-style way of there being nothing to get. There's so much to get, I dedicated five years of my life to it.) But if you do want to listen to me, I absolutely have ideas of things we can do—to reach not some promised land, but perhaps a place of compromise and problem-solving.

We do still have at our disposal that American panacea, agency. If I had a minimum ask of you, reader, it would be to identify and acknowledge Puritan doomsday ideologies, wherever they exist, so we can determine whether or not they are being used against us. Of course, there are numerous other calls to action, in a country facing mounting problems. But there won't be political will to face any of them if we don't step back and start with something more foundational. We must turn toward each other.

We evolved to develop empathy and compassion. We evolved *as a result* of empathy and compassion. It's our secret weapon. And it's the one skill lacked by con-artist, cult-leader autocrats. When we turn away from each other, those skills atrophy and we literally devolve. That's what doomsday thinking encourages us to do: mistrust and blame, isolate from, seek dominion over, disregard the needs of, and even wish violence upon one another.

Turning toward each other is easy to do. It doesn't require expert advice or government policy. It's a choice. The result can be life-saving. Following World War II, researchers collected data about hundreds of European Gentiles who had hidden or aided Jews in some way. The researchers hoped to understand why some citizens helped victims of the Nazi pogrom and others did not. But the case studies fit no demographic patterns. Helpers were young and old, rich and poor, male and female, religious and atheist, educated and illiterate, urbanites and rural, and held a wide variety of occupations. The sociologists found only one commonality: everyone who helped had a prior, close relationship with someone of Jewish descent, for example a neighbor, colleague, playmate, or stepparent.[1] Familiarity mitigates hate.

Writer Elie Robins suggest another way to help us learn to share "in the pain and the joy and the needs of other people, human and nonhuman": by battling addiction. She argues that, whether opioid, phone, gambling, or any of the "other new and rapidly evolving ways to check out," addictions numb us from feeling our own pain and joy, thereby disabling us from sharing the same in others.[2] I believe we are addicted to the comforts and conveniences of the American dream, to the consumption economy, to the salesperson-and-customer economy that leads us to consume one another, and to the mirage of control. These addictions divide us. The more individualized and isolated we become, the more vulnerable.

These addictions have also led us to extreme income inequality, the source of most current hysterias. There may be nothing that sets one's world wobbling more than a chronic lack of resources. When I asked Bandy X. Lee, the aforementioned forensic psychologist, how to combat the spread of extremism, she first recommended "fixing the socioeconomic conditions that gave rise to psychological vulnerability to these influences in the first place."

The divisions I hope we can bridge occur not only between people, but within people. Recall Jessica Joan, who was impervious to Keith Raniere's exploitation in NXIVM because she refused to silence her gut instinct. A split person is easily conquered while a whole person is not. The false separation between the analytical mind and instinctual "gut" is cult thinking, full stop. It's similar to that between the supposedly saved spirit and the evil corrupted body, the paradigm that begat the grace-nature divide. I hope we can hear our intuitions, and thereby become whole.

Moreover, may we dissolve the line separating us from plants, animals, rivers, and rocks. Robin Wall Kimmerer invites the reader "to remember things you didn't know you'd forgotten." Potawatomi stories tell of a time when plants, and humans and animals could speak the same language. As someone who enjoys talking to rocks (try it sometime), I find this validating. Imagine how much less isolated and lonely Americans could be if we treated the earth's "resources" instead as siblings, who give gifts and whom we thank in turn. For Kimmerer, practicing gratitude for what we receive and learn from the earth leads to contentment. "In a consumer society, contentment is a radical proposition. Recognizing abundance rather than scarcity undermines an economy that thrives by creating unmet desires."[3]

Communing with nature can also strengthen ties between humans because such is the effect of experiencing awe. The wonder and goose bumps we feel while witnessing the epic or mysterious power of nature—as well as beautiful works of art, exhibits of athletic prowess, and other awe-inspiring displays—have psychological and physiological effects, including an "increase in pro-social behaviors such as kindness, self-sacrifice, co-operation and resource-sharing."[4]

Paradoxically, one of the most powerful ways humans turn toward each other, at least since the birth of monotheism, is apocalypticism itself. It developed as a way to bring people together during crisis. Kim Haines-Eitzen, professor of early Christianity at Cornell University, argues that, in general, "apocalypticism explained the cause of a crisis and how people should respond to it," made sense of and gave voice to suffering, and promised a new reality that "stands in contrast to the oppression of earlier times."[5] I wrote that the problematic cult ideologies explored in this book also have healthy manifestations. Apocalypticism itself has positive side effects. By predicting an end to suffering, it gives people hope. Of course we cling to it. *Life is hard.* We just want to be safe. We just want to be free of anxiety and fear. We want "somewhere over the rainbow." In *The Wizard of Oz*, Dorothy breaks into that song because Aunt Em has just told her to run along and find a place where she "won't get into any trouble."[6]

"Do you suppose there is such a place, Toto?" Dorothy wonders in reply. "There must be. It's not a place you can get to by a boat or a train. It's far, far away. Behind the moon. Beyond the rain." In a golden city in the sky. On an interplanetary astral level. Riding the tail of a comet. At the end of a Landmark training. At the bottom of a bottle of Rogaine. In the plasma of a seventeen-year-old boy.

Of course we want it. I know I do. The allure is too attractive not to believe. You'll never win the lottery if you don't buy a ticket. But what if there's another way to avoid trouble? It won't be totally free of suffering, but it does have the added benefit of not being a lie. Just as we can keep our love for hard work without becoming cannibals, so can we keep apocalypticism's hope without subscribing to the parts that cause us to destroy each other. We can *make sense of our collective suffering* by getting through it together and striving for a future that's better for all—without believing those outcomes hinge on the destruction of an enemy, especially since that enemy is usually manufactured.

Hey, psst: [*whispers*] *What if there is no enemy? What if there is only chaos and the fear we feel in response to it, which causes us to become the enemies we imagined?* Perhaps that's naïve . . . even delusional . . . as much of a fever dream as Revelation itself. I'm clinging to it anyway.

———

We should test for malignant narcissism before putting people into positions of power. We should read literature to increase empathy, hug children more so they develop enough social and emotional stability to resist a cult leader's siren call, experience psychedelic-driven ego death in order to release control and accept impermanence, and fight overconsumption in society and the self.

Like I said, I don't have all the answers.

But I do think I can provide more of that comfort we seek. I mentioned that this project consoled me in ways I didn't expect. The biggest of those was a new belief I've developed: that evil doesn't exist. Or at least not in the way we typically understand it. Before writing this book, I thought we all had both good and evil inside us. I figured this was a pretty enlightened viewpoint, compared to believing some are exclusively good and others exclusively bad. But now I think neither idea is right.

This is the last divide I want us to bridge. I no longer believe evil is even separate from good, is even *different* from good. Our capacities for violence and cooperation developed side-by-side, literally begat one another. They are indivisible. Oxytocin enables both deep love and brutal violence via the same mechanism. Good and evil are one and the same.

Yet an assertion of their distinction is the heart of every doomsday fantasy. Because division allows for hierarchy, providing the illusion that evil can be conquered. Elizabeth Clare Prophet told Church Universal and Triumphant members that evil was in rock 'n' roll music, which could be "bound" and neutralized. Members of Mankind United believed in a group of wicked Hidden Rulers, who would be conquered by the Sponsors. The Oneida commune believed it had excised sin completely. Amway distributors saw the devil in poverty, which it aimed to punish through increased depletion. M.S.I.A. acolytes believed John-Roger could disappear bad karma dumped on them by past lives. And Love Has Won claimed to have escaped an evil cabal. At least the Puritans said *everyone* sinned and couldn't stop. Even so, they made themselves literally sick with worry about it. In all of these groups, efforts to eradicate evil made people sicker, not well—because we can't remove an essential part of ourselves. They lost their livelihoods and often the sovereignty of their own bodies in the pursuit of a false dream.

A call to accept good and evil as indivisible is admittedly a tough sell. We feel we *need* evil to be separate. Fighting it provides a form of control over chaos. But if we truly welcome impermanence, release control, and stand in chaos, maybe we can stop trying to separate and battle evil. I don't suggest we condone or submit to it. But instead of whack-a-moling it forever, we might simply acknowledge it, as it walks with us through the carnival of life. We could ask it to express its fears and desires, since that's all it is anyway. We could listen intently and reply, "It's going to be OK, evil. Let's get some funnel cake." That may not be *exactly* what psychologists and theologians mean by radical acceptance, but it's pretty close.

It sounds like I just suggested we disarm evil with the power of our minds, like some self-help, life-coach peddler of salvation. In this Conclusion, I've also recommended testing people's mental capacities before giving them jobs, like a latter-day eugenicist. And I've suggested taking acid, hugging children, and talking to rocks. Honestly, it sounds like a pretty exciting cult. Join me?

ACKNOWLEDGMENTS

Alessandra Bastagli and Abby Mohr for keen edits and insight. Nick Ciani for interest and early development. Emma Van Deun for the cover. Erin Kibby and Falon Kirby for evangelizing. Hannah Frankel, Elizabeth Hitti, and Ifeoma Anyoku for support.

Nicole Tourtelot for encouragement, challenge, expert hustling, and endless advice. Thanks also to Ali Park.

Ben Greenman for the early read and feedback.

Adam Lustick for jokes and support.

Carla Gardina Pestana for recommendations about the Prologue and Introduction and commitment to historical accuracy.

Jamil Smith for editorial advice.

Katie Kosma for proposal edits.

Lou and Marc Pons, Tucker and Wes Andrews, Maurine and Phil Halperin, Jason Reich and Katie Davis, Olivia Wingate, Moe Kornbluth, Grace Birkenbeuel and Josh Kinne, Carey Sellin-Vetter, Lauren Cook, Sunah Bilsted, Nancy Dillon, Sarah Taylor, Rachel Moscovich, Joselyn Hughes, Renee Gauthier, and Annah Bean for a room of one's own.

Susanna Ball for translation help.

Meredith Blake for a chapter title.

Ivy Pochoda and Meredith Reese for creating space.

Lou, Tucker, Mom, and Dad for unwavering acceptance and support.

Louisa for keeping me sane and reminding me what matters. You are everything.

The Los Angeles Public Library for the incredible resource. Sorry for the late returns.

NOTES

EPIGRAPH

1. Thich Nhat Hanh, *Reconciliation: Healing the Inner Child* (Berkeley, California: Parallax Press, 2010).
2. Alexis de Tocqueville, *Democracy in America* (Garden City, NY: Doubleday, n.d.).

AUTHOR'S NOTE

1. Frank Newport, "Fewer in U.S. Now See Bible as Literal Word of God," *Gallup*, July 6, 2022. https://news.gallup.com/poll/394262/fewer-bible-literal-word -god.aspx
2. There are key distinctions between the Pilgrims and the Puritans—most notably, the former wanted to purify the Church of England, while the latter separated from it (although some also accused the Massachusetts Congregationalists, aka Puritans, of separating). But for the purposes of my arguments, their ideologies were similar enough for me to lump them together and refer to them as "Puritan."
3. Philip Jenkins, *Mystics and Messiahs: Cults and New Religious Movements* (Oxford University Press, 2000).
4. Robert Lifton, MD, "Cult Formation," *Cultic Studies Journal* 8, no. 1 (1991).
5. Casey Kleczek, "How to Rescue a Cult Victim: An Interview with Rick Ross, Professional Deprogammer," *Salon*, July 30, 2022, https://www.salon.com/2022 /07/30/rick-ross-deprogrammer-profile/.

INTRODUCTION: WEEKEND AT BARTHOLOMEW'S

1. Christopher Columbus, *Libro Copiador de Cristóbal Colón*, edited by de Armas Rumeau (Testimonio Compania Editorial, 1989).
2. Samuel Morison, *Journals and Other Documents on the Life and Voyages of Christopher Columbus* (New York: Heritage Press, 1963) .

3. Laurence Bergreen, *Columbus: The Four Voyages* (New York: Viking, 2011).

4. Or, some thought the thousand years of peace had already begun and was almost over, meaning soon Jesus would be back for the Last Judgment. Others believed they were already building the New Jerusalem.

5. Norman McClure, "The Letters of John Chamberlain," American Philosophical Society, 1930.

6. Allyn Forbes and Stewart Mitchell, "A Model of Christian Charity," *Massachusetts Historical Society* 47 (1929).

7. Carla Pestana, *The World of Plymouth Plantation* (Cambridge, MA: Belknap Press, 2020).

8. Edward Winslow, *Story of Pilgrim Fathers* (Arber, 1624).

9. Stephen Innes, *Creating the Commonwealth: The Economic Culture of Puritan New England* (New York: W.W. Norton, 1995).

10. Ibid.

11. Larzer Ziff, *Puritanism in America: New Culture in a New World* (New York: Viking Press, 1973).

12. Innes, *Creating the Commonwealth*.

13. Ziff, *Puritanism in America*.

14. Ibid.

15. Michael Wigglesworth, *The Day of Doom, or, A Poetical Description of the Great and Last Judgment* (Cambridge, MA: Samuel Green, 1662).

16. Franklin Dexter, "Estimates of Population in the American Colonies," *Proceedings of the American Antiquarian Society*, 1887. Robert S. Levine, general editor, *Norton Anthology of American Literature* Vol. A (W.W. Norton, 2017).

17. "18% of Americans Veritable Potter-Maniacs, 61% Seen at Least One Movie," YouGov, accessed September 12, 2024, https://today.yougov.com/society/articles/1878-18-americans-veritable-potter-maniacs-76-seen-leas.

18. Rachel A. Packard, "Dancing Along the Tightrope of Leisure: Puritans and Dance in Seventeenth-Century Massachusetts" Digital Repository, University of New Mexico, July 2, 2012, https://digitalrepository.unm.edu/thea_etds/7.

19. Michael P. Winship, *Making Heretics: Militant Protestantism and Free Grace in Massachusetts, 1636–1641* (Princeton, NJ: Princeton University Press, 2002).

20. Samuel Morison, ed., *Bradford's History of Plymouth Plantation, 1620–1647.* (New York: Alfred A. Knopf, 1952).

21. Cotton Mather and Rachel Walker, "Documentary Archive and Transcription Project," n.d., www2.iath.virginia.edu/salem/people/c_mather.html.

22. Edmund Morgan, *The Puritan Family: Religion and Domestic Relations in Seventeenth-Century New England* (New York: Harper and Row, 1966).

23. Increase Mather, *The Wicked Man's Portion* (Boston, 1675).

24. Emory Elliott, *Power and the Pulpit in Puritan New England* (Princeton, NJ: Princeton University Press, 1975).

25. Roger Williams, "Mr. Cotton's Letter Lately Printed, Examined and Answered," *Publications of the Narragansett Club* (1866).

26. Cotton Mather, *Magnalia Christi Americana* (Hartford, 1853).

27. Thomas Hooker, *The Application of Redemption* (London, 1659).

28. Ziff, *Puritanism in America*.

29. Wigglesworth, *Day of Doom*.

CHAPTER 1: THE QUICK AND THE DEAD

1. Chris Kissel, "The Sound of Doomsday in America: How a Cult Leader Made a Cherished Tape Freak Classic," *VICE* (blog), October 26, 2015, https://www.vice.com/en/article/the-sound-of-doomsday-in-america-how-a-cult-leader-made-a-cherished-tape-freak-classic/.

2. Erin Prophet, *Prophet's Daughter: My Life with Elizabeth Clare Prophet Inside the Church Universal and Triumphant* (Guilford, CT: Lyons Press, 2009).

3. Ibid.

4. Transcript provided by Erin Prophet.

5. Prophet, *Prophet's Daughter*.

6. Ibid.

7. Transcript of the June 1990 episode provided by Erin Prophet.

8. Sean Prophet, *My Cult, Your Cult* (Northfield, IL: Amika Press, 2024).

9. Ibid.

10. Prophet, *Prophet's Daughter*.

11. Robert Jewett and John Shelton Lawrence, *The American Monomyth* (Garden City, NY: Anchor Press, 1977).

12. Vincent Bugliosi, *Helter Skelter: The True Story of the Manson Murders* (New York: Bantam Books, 1975).

13. Early Christians were often seeking ecstatic states, via wine and other vehicles, in order to hallucinate.

14. Michael D. Coogan, ed., *The New Oxford Annotated Bible*, New Revised Standard Version (New York: Oxford University Press, 2001).

15. Ibid.

16. Jonathan Edwards, *The Macmillan Book of Proverbs, Maxims and Famous Phrases*, ed. Burton Stevenson (New York: Macmillan, 1948).

17. Coogan, *New Oxford Annotated Bible*.

18. Elaine Pagels, *Revelations: Visions, Prophecy, and Politics in the Book of Revelation* (New York: Viking, 2012).

19. Ibid.

20. David Emmons, *Garden in the Grasslands: Boomer Literature of the Central Great Plains* (Lincoln: University of Nebraska Press, 1971).

21. Whet Moser, "Apocalypse Oak Park: Dorothy Martin, the Chicagoan Who Predicted the End of the World and Inspired the Theory of Cognitive Dissonance," *Chicago*, May 20, 2011, https://www.chicagomag.com/Chicago-Magazine/The -312/May-2011/Dorothy-Martin-the-Chicagoan-Who-Predicted-the-End-of -the-World-and-Inspired-the-Theory-of-Cognitive-Dissonance/.

22. Bradley C. Whitsel, *The Church Universal and Triumphant: Elizabeth Clare Prophet's Apocalyptic Movement* (Syracuse, NY: Syracuse University Press, 2003).

23. "Mike Flynn Leads a Christian Church in an Occult Prayer by Fascist Cult Leader Elizabeth Clare Prophet," Vimeo, January 20, 2022, https://vimeo.com /668318602?utm_source=substack&utm_medium=email.

24. Will Sommer, "Michael Flynn to QAnon Believers: I'm Not a Satanist!" *Daily Beast*, October 8, 2021, https://www.thedailybeast.com/michael-flynn-to-qanon -believers-im-not-a-satanist.

25. Stella Rouse and Shibley Telhami, "Op/Ed: UMD Poll Shows Republicans Support Declaring the U.S. a Christian Nation," *Maryland Today*, September 22, 2022, https://today.umd.edu/op-ed-umd-poll-shows-republicans-support -declaring-the-u-s-a-christian-nation.

26. Jewett and Lawrence, *American Monomyth*.

27. Maureen Dowd, "For the 'Can Do' Colonel, Admissions, No Apology," *New York Times*, July 8, 1987.

28. Jewett and Lawrence, *American Monomyth*.

29. John Dean, "John Dean on Ollie: The Ugly Road Ahead," *Newsweek*, July 20, 1987.

30. Robert Jewett and John Shelton Lawrence, "Captain America Takes on Iraq," *Tikkun* 18, no. 1 (2003).

31. Brendan Cole, "Lauren Boebert Challenges Wheelchair User Madison Cawthorn to a 'Sprint,'" *Newsweek*, November 24, 2021, https://www.newsweek.com/lauren -boebert-madison-cawthorn-kyle-rittenhouse-kenosha-newsmax-iternship -1652871.

32. Natasha Korecki and Christopher Cadelago, "With a Hand from Trump, the Right Makes Rittenhouse a Cause Célèbre," *Politico*, September 1, 2020, https:// www.politico.com/amp/news/2020/09/01/trump-rittenhouse-kenosha-support -407106.

33. Andrew Prokop, "Curtis Yarvin Wants American Democracy Toppled. He Has Some Prominent Republican Fans," *Vox*, October 24, 2022, https://www.vox .com/policy-and-politics/23373795/curtis-yarvin-neoreaction-redpill-moldbug.

34. Galen Bacharier, "'Poisoning the Blood' of US: Trump's Harsh Words Grow Support among Likely Iowa Caucusgoers," *Des Moines Register*, December 17, 2023, https://www.desmoinesregister.com/story/news/politics/iowa-poll/cau cus/2023/12/17/iowa-poll-republicans-not-backing-away-from-donald-trump -amid-escalating-rhetoric-2024-election/71882561007/.

35. Philip Elliott, "Startling Poll Says More Americans Open to Political Violence," *Time*, October 25, 2023, https://time.com/6328179/political-violence-jan -6-extremism/.

36. "CNN Poll on GOP Primary Voters," SSRS, September 5, 2021, chrome -extension://efaidnbmnnnibpcajpcglclefindmkaj/https://s3.documentcloud .org/documents/23936298/cnn-poll-on-gop-primary-voters.pdf.

37. Cameron Easely, "U.S. Conservatives Are Uniquely Inclined toward Right-Wing Authoritarianism Compared to Western Peers," Morning Consult Pro, June 28, 2021, https://pro.morningconsult.com/trend-setters/global-right-wing-author itarian-test.

38. Yoni Appelbaum, "Trump's Claim: 'I Alone Can Fix It,'" *Atlantic* (blog), July 22, 2016, https://www.theatlantic.com/politics/archive/2016/07/trump-rnc -speech-alone-fix-it/492557/.

39. Jewett and Lawrence, *American Monomyth*.

40. Richard Lardner and Michelle R. Smith, "Michael Flynn's ReAwaken Roadshow Recruits 'Army of God,'" *Frontline*, PBS, October 7, 2022, https://www.pbs. org/wgbh/frontline/article/michael-flynn-reawaken-america-tour/.

41. Prophet, *Prophet's Daughter*.

CHAPTER 2: FATHER KNOWS BEST

1. Robert S. Fogarty, *Desire and Duty: Tirzah Miller's Intimate Memoir* (Bloomington: Indiana University Press, 2000).

2. Ibid.

3. "Oneida Limited Annual Report, Fiscal Year Ended January 31, 1948."

4. John Humphrey Noyes, *Bible Communism: A Compilation from the Annual Reports and Other Publications of the Oneida Association* (Brooklyn, NY, 1853).

5. Ellen Wayland-Smith, *Oneida: From Free Love Utopia to the Well-Set Table* (New York: Picador, 2016).

6. Ibid.

7. George Wallingford Noyes and Lawrence Foster, eds., *Free Love in Utopia: John Humphrey Noyes and the Origin of the Oneida Community* (Urbana: University of Illinois Press, 2001).

8. John Humphrey Noyes, *Home Talks*, edited by Alfred Barron and George Noyes Miller (Oneida, NY, 1875).

9. Wayland-Smith, *Oneida*.

10. Maren L. Carden, *Oneida: Utopian Community to Modern Corporation* (Baltimore: Johns Hopkins University Press, 1969).

11. Wayland-Smith, *Oneida*.

12. Jessie Catherine Kinsley, Jane Kinsley Rich, and Nelson Manfred Blake, *A Lasting Spring: Jessie Catherine Kinsley, Daughter of the Oneida Community* (Syracuse, NY: Syracuse University Press, 1983).

13. Joseph Bellamy, *The Millenium, a Collection*, edited by David Austin (Elizabethtown, 1794).

14. Joseph Emerson, *Lectures on the Millennium*, edited by Samuel T. Armstrong (Boston, 1818).

15. Benjamin M. Friedman, *Religion and the Rise of Capitalism* (New York: Vintage Books, 2021).

16. Ronald Reagan, "Address Accepting the Presidential Nomination at the Republican National Convention in Detroit," July 17, 1980.

17. Ernest Lee Tuveson, *Redeemer Nation: The Idea of America's Millennial Role* (Chicago: University of Chicago Press, 1968).

18. Josiah Strong, *The New Era, or, The Coming Kingdom* (New York: Baker & Taylor, 1893).

19. Michael D. Coogan, ed., *The New Oxford Annotated Bible*, New Revised Standard Version (New York: Oxford University Press, 2001).

20. Tuveson, *Redeemer Nation*.

21. Benjamin M. Friedman, *Religion and the Rise of Capitalism* (New York: Vintage Books, 2021).

22. Michael Barkun, *Crucible of the Millennium: The Burned-Over District of New York in the 1840s* (Syracuse, NY: Syracuse University Press, 1986).

23. Chris Jennings, *Paradise Now: The Story of American Utopianism* (New York: Random House, 2016).

24. Sterling F. Delano, *Brook Farm: The Dark Side of Utopia* (Cambridge, MA: Harvard University Press, 2004).

25. Tim Reid and Tim Layne, "Deconstructing the Spectacle and Stagecraft of a Donald Trump Rally," Reuters, April 20, 2024, https://www.reuters.com/investigates/special-report/usa-election-trump-rally/.

26. Ray S. Baker and William E. Dodd, eds., *Presidential Messages and Addresses, and Public Papers (1917–1924)*, War and Peace, Vol. 2 (New York, 1927).

27. Tuveson, *Redeemer Nation*.

28. Charles L. Sanford, *The Quest for Paradise: Europe and the American Moral Imagination* (Urbana: University of Illinois Press, 1961).

29. Henry Cabot Lodge, "Cf. Lodge's Senate Speech, March 7, 1900, 60th Cong., 1st Session," *Congressional Record* 33.

30. John L. Motley, "The Rise of the Dutch Republic," in *The Complete Works of John L. Motley* (New York, 1900).

31. Tuveson, *Redeemer Nation*; 1st Baron Macaulay, Thomas Babington Macaulay, *The History of England from the Accession of James the Second* (n.d.).

32. Andrew Jackson, *Annual Messages, Veto Messages, Protest, &c of Andrew Jackson* (Baltimore: Edwards J. Coale, 1835).

33. Friedman, *Religion and the Rise of Capitalism*.

34. John O'Sullivan, "Annexation," *United States Magazine and Democratic Review*, July 1845.

35. Louis S. Warren, "The Lakota Ghost Dance and the Massacre at Wounded Knee," *American Experience*, PBS, April 16, 2021, https://www.pbs.org/wgbh /americanexperience/features/american-oz-lakota-ghost-dance-massacre -wounded-knee/.

36. Raymond J. DeMallie, "The Lakota Ghost Dance: An Ethnohistorical Account," *Pacific Historical Review* 51, no. 4 (University of California Press, November 1982).

37. "The Ghost Dance: How the Indians Work Themselves Up to Fighting Pitch," *New York Times*, November 22, 1890, https://www.nytimes.com/1890/11/22 /archives/the-ghost-dance-how-the-indians-work-themselves-up-to-fighting .html.

38. Ibid.

39. James McLaughlin, "Memorandum Regarding the Reasons for the Ghost Dance Uprising, November 6, 1890." Digital Public Library of America, https://dp.la /item/d04d4d5a96b47ee1b99341fdfd95752a.

40. Mark H. Haller, *Eugenics: Herediterarian Attitudes in American Thought* (New Brunswick, NJ: Rutgers University Press, 1963).

41. Wayland-Smith, *Oneida*.

42. Hilda Herrick Noyes, "The Woman's Club: Report on Eugenics," *Quadrangle* 5, no. 12 (December 1912).

43. Wayland-Smith, *Oneida*.

44. Haller, *Eugenics*.

45. Ibid.

46. Ibid.

47. Francis A. Walker, "Immigration and Degradation," *Forum* XI (August 1891).

48. Cassie Miller, "SPLC Poll Finds Substantial Support for 'Great Replacement' Theory and Other Hard-Right Ideas," Southern Poverty Law Center, June 1, 2022, https://www.splcenter.org/news/2022/06/01/poll-finds-support-great -replacement-hard-right-ideas.

49. "Trump Says Immigrants Are 'Poisoning the Blood of Our Country,' Biden Campaign Likens Comments to Hitler," NBC News, December 17, 2023, https://www.nbcnews.com/politics/2024-election/trump-says-immigrants -are-poisoning-blood-country-biden-campaign-liken-rcna130141.

50. Charles B. Davenport, *Heredity in Relation to Eugenics* (New York: Henry Holt, 1911).

51. Haller, *Eugenics*.

52. Ibid. "Compulsory Sterilization of the Intellectually Weak," Project Jurisprudence, December 17, 2019, https://www.projectjurisprudence.com/2019/12 /compulsory-sterilization-of-intellectually-weak-mentally-disabled.html.

53. Dacher Keltner, *The Power Paradox: How We Gain and Lose Influence* (New York: Penguin Books, 2016).

54. Ibid.

55. Haller, *Eugenics*.

56. Wayland-Smith, *Oneida*.

57. Julia Black, "Billionaires like Elon Musk Want to Save Civilization by Having Tons of Genetically Superior Kids. Inside the Movement to Take 'Control of Human Evolution,'" *Business Insider*, November 17, 2022, https://www .businessinsider.com/pronatalism-elon-musk-simone-malcolm-collins-under population-breeding-tech-2022-11.

58. Patrick Turley et al., "Problems with Using Polygenic Scores to Select Embryos," *New England Journal of Medicine* 385, no. 1 (July 2021): 78–86, https://doi .org/10.1056/NEJMsr2105065.

59. Anandita Abraham, "Oxford Shuts Down Elon Musk–Funded Future of Humanity Institute," *Oxford Student* (blog), April 20, 2024, https://www .oxfordstudent.com/2024/04/20/oxford-shuts-down-elon-musk-funded-future -of-humanity-institute/.

60. "Transparency and Financials," Machine Intelligence Research Institute, accessed September 13, 2024, https://intelligence.org/transparency/.

61. Anja Kaspersen and Wendell Wallach, "Long-Termism: An Ethical Trojan Horse," September 29, 2022, https://www.carnegiecouncil.org/media/article /long-termism-ethical-trojan-horse.

62. Julia Black. "Billionaires Like Elon Musk Want to Save Civilization by Having Tons of Genetically Superior Kids. Inside the Movement to Take 'Control of Human Evolution.'" *Business Insider*. Accessed September 13, 2024. https://

www.businessinsider.com/pronatalism-elon-musk-simone-malcolm-collins-un derpopulation-breeding-tech-2022-11.

63. Gaby Del Valle, "The Far Right's Campaign to Explode the Population," *Politico*, April 28, 2024, https://www.politico.com/news/magazine/2024/04/28 /natalism-conference-austin-00150338.

64. Black, "Billionaires Like Elon Musk."

65. Ibid.

66. Haller, *Eugenics*.

67. Black, "Billionaires Like Elon Musk."

68. Ibid.

69. Maureen Dowd, "Elon Musk, Blasting Off in Domestic Bliss," *New York Times*, July 25, 2020, https://www.nytimes.com/2020/07/25/style/elon-musk-mau reen-dowd.html; "Genghis Khan a Prolific Lover, DNA Data Implies," *National Geographic*, February 14, 2003, https://www.nationalgeographic.com/culture /article/mongolia-genghis-khan-dna.

70. "Elon Wants You to Have More Babies," Bloomberg, June 21, 2024, https://www .bloomberg.com/features/2024-elon-musk-population-collapse-baby-push/.

71. Kinsley, Rich, and Blake, *A Lasting Spring* (Syracuse, NY: Syracuse University Press, 1983).

CHAPTER 3: DON'T SPREAD ON ME

1. "You Need Us . . . We Need You NOW!!," Mankind United pamphlet, January 1940.

2. International Registration Bureau, *Mankind United, A Challenge to "Mad Ambition" and "The Money Changers" Accompanied by an Invitation to the World's "Sane" Men and Women* (International Registration Bureau, 1934).

3. H. T. Dohrman, *California Cult: The Story of "Mankind United"* (Boston: Beacon Press, 1958).

4. *Order to Show Cause in the Matter of Christ's Church of the Golden Rule, No. 44,128-WM in Bankruptcy*, District Court of the United States, Southern District of California, Central Division, July 16, 1946.

5. International Registration Bureau, *Mankind United, A Challenge to "Mad Ambition."*

6. Adam Morris, "Mankind, Unite!," *Roundtable* (blog), *Lapham's Quarterly*, May 13, 2019, https://www.laphamsquarterly.org/roundtable/mankind-unite.

7. *Los Angeles Examiner*, December 19, 1942. As cited in Dohrman, *California Cult.*

8. Morris, "Mankind, Unite!"

9. Dohrman, *California Cult.*

10. *Los Angeles Examiner*, March 24, 1944. As cited in Dohrman, *California Cult.*

11. Jan-William van Prooijen and Mark van Vugt, "Conspiracy Theories: Evolved Functions and Psychological Mechanisms," *Perspectives on Psychological Science* 13, no. 6 (November 2018): 770–88, https://doi.org/10.1177/174569 1618774270.

12. Rainer Zitelmann, "How Many Americans Believe in Conspiracy Theories?" *Forbes*, June 29, 2020, https://www.forbes.com/sites/rainerzitelmann/2020/06/29/how-many-americans-believe-in-conspiracy-theories/.

13. "The Economist/YouGov Poll August 7–9 2022—1500 U.S. Adult Citizens," n.d.

14. Michael D. Coogan, ed. *The New Oxford Annotated Bible*, New Revised Standard Version (New York: Oxford University Press, 2001).

15. Jonathan Kay, *Among the Truthers: A Journey Through America's Growing Conspiracist Underground* (New York: HarperCollins, 2011).

16. Charles L. Sanford, *The Quest for Paradise: Europe and the American Moral Imagination* (Urbana: University of Illinois Press, 1961).

17. John Cotton, *The Powring Out of the Seven Vials* (London, 1642).

18. Henry Ward Beecher, *Seven Lectures to Young Men* (Indianapolis, 1844).

19. Sanford, *Quest for Paradise.*

20. Cotton Mather, *The Present State of New England* (Boston, 1690).

21. Sanford, *Quest for Paradise.*

22. Albert H. Smyth, ed., *The Writings of Benjamin Franklin* (New York: Macmillan, 1905–1907).

23. Sanford, *Quest for Paradise.*

24. Ibid.

25. *Works of John Adams* (Boston, 1865).

26. Sanford, *Quest for Paradise.*

27. "The American Revolution," Open Yale Courses, accessed September 13, 2024, https://oyc.yale.edu/history/hist-116.

28. Kevin Young, *Bunk: The Rise of Hoaxes, Humbug, Plagiarists, Phonies, Post-Facts, and Fake News* (Minneapolis: Graywolf Press, 2017).

29. Jacob Weisberg, "W.'s Greatest Hits," *Slate*, January 12, 2009, https://slate.com/news-and-politics/2009/01/the-top-25-bushisms-of-all-time.html.

30. "The Other 9/11: George H. W. Bush's 1990 New World Order Speech," *Dallas News*, September 8, 2017, https://www.dallasnews.com/opinion/commentary/2017/09/08/the-other-9-11-george-h-w-bush-s-1990-new-world-order-speech/.

31. Christine Emba, "Opinion How the Idea of a 'World Order' Is Changing: A Primer," *Washington Post*, January 25, 2016, https://www.washingtonpost.com /news/in-theory/wp/2016/01/25/how-the-idea-of-a-world-order-is-changing -a-primer/; William Safire, "On Language; The New, New World Order," *New York Times Magazine*, February 17, 1991, https://www.nytimes.com/1991/02 /17/magazine/on-language-the-new-new-world-order.html.

32. Anthony Aveni, *Apocalyptic Anxiety: Religion, Science, and America's Obsession with the End of the World* (Boulder: University Press of Colorado, 2016).

33. Kit Rachlis, "The Rise and Fall of Joseph McCarthy," *Los Angeles Times*, November 7, 1999, https://www.latimes.com/archives/la-xpm-1999-nov-07-me-31153 -story.html.

34. W. H. Lawrence, "McCarthy Is Dead of Liver Ailment at the Age of 47; Wife with Senator at End—Eisenhowers Send Her 'Profound Sympathies,' Fight on Reds His Forte, It Built World Reputation for Republican—Tactics Were Censured by Senate, Nixon Issues Statement Senator McCarthy Is Dead of a Liver Ailment at 47, Up for Re-election in '58," *New York Times*, May 3, 1957, https://www.nytimes.com/1957/05/03/archives/mcarthy-is-dead-of-liver-ail ment-at-the-age-of-47-wife-with-senator.html.

35. Tim Sullivan, "In Small-Town Wisconsin, Looking for the Roots of the Modern American Conspiracy Theory," AP News, January 21, 2024, https://apnews.com /article/conspiracy-theory-government-john-birch-c3809b7ad45afc3bee5f98 81b2d9aa36.

36. *The Alex Jones Show*, December 11, 2009.

37. Karen Yourish et al., "How Republicans Echo Antisemitic Tropes Despite Declaring Support for Israel," *New York Times*, May 9, 2024, https://www.nytimes .com/2024/05/09/us/antisemitism-republicans-trump.html.

38. "Trump Hammer Stomping Red List NOW Crowd," YouTube, accessed September 13, 2024, https://www.youtube.com/watch?v=CRU1CfuFTrg&feature =youtu.be.

39. Louis R. Beam Jr., "Vietnam Bring It on Home," in *Essays of a Klansman* (Hayden Lake, ID: A.K.I.A., 1983).

40. Kathleen Belew, *Bring the War Home: The White Power Movement and Paramilitary America* (Cambridge, MA: Harvard University Press, 2018).

41. *Waco: American Apocalypse*, Episode 3, Netflix, March 22, 2023.

42. Clyde Haberman, "Memories of Waco Siege Continue to Fuel Far-Right Groups," *New York Times*, July 12, 2015, https://www.nytimes.com/2015/07/13/us /memories-of-waco-siege-continue-to-fuel-far-right-groups.html.

43. Belew, *Bring the War Home*.

44. "Colorado Man Sentenced For Assault on Law Enforcement During Jan. 6 Capitol Breach," United States Attorney's Office, District of Columbia, June 23, 2023, https://www.justice.gov/usao-dc/pr/colorado-man-sentenced-assault-law-en forcement-during-jan-6-capitol-breach.

45. Chris Cameron, "These Are the People Who Died in Connection with the Capitol Riot," *New York Times*, January 5, 2022, https://www.nytimes.com/2022 /01/05/us/politics/jan-6-capitol-deaths.html.

46. "Intel Drop #34," Q Alerts, accessed September 13, 2024, https://qalerts.net /?n=34.

47. Mike Rothschild, *The Storm Is Upon Us: How QAnon Became a Movement, Cult, and Conspiracy of Everything* (Brooklyn, NY: Melville, 2021).

48. "Civiqs," accessed September 13, 2024, https://civiqs.com/reports/2020/9/2 /report-americans-pessimistic-on-time-frame-for-coronavirus-recovery.

49. Philip Elliott, "Startling Poll Says More Americans Open to Political Violence," *Time*, October 25, 2023, https://time.com/6328179/political-violence-jan-6 -extremism/.

50. Kevin Mattson, *Rebels All!: A Short History of the Conservative Mind in Postwar America* (New Brunswick, NJ: Rutgers University Press, 2008).

51. Thomas Needham and Paul Kaplan, "William F. Buckley '50 Dies at 82," *Yale Daily News*, February 28, 2008, https://yaledailynews.com/blog/2008/02/28 /william-f-buckley-50-dies-at-82/.

52. Mattson, *Rebels All!*

53. Ibid.

54. "Activist Group Led by Ginni Thomas Received Nearly $600,000 in Anonymous Donations," *Washington Post*, March 28, 2023, https://www.washingtonpost .com/investigations/2023/03/28/ginnithomas-crowdsourcers-anonymous -donations/

55. Michael C. Bender and Shane Goldmacher. "Trump Puts His Legal Peril at Center of First Big Rally for 2024," *New York Times*, March 26, 2023, https:// www.nytimes.com/2023/03/25/us/politics/trump-waco-texas-speech.html.

56. Charles Homans, "A Trump Rally, a Right-Wing Cause and the Enduring Legacy of Waco," *New York Times*, March 24, 2023, https://www.nytimes.com/2023 /03/24/us/politics/donald-trump-waco-branch-davidians.html.

57. Alan Feuer and Zach Montague, "Former Oath Keeper Says Militia Planned to Use 'Any Means Necessary' on Jan. 6," *New York Times*, October 18, 2022, https://www.nytimes.com/2022/10/18/us/politics/oath-keepers-militia-jan-6 .html.

58. "Department 'A' Telegram," Mankind United Publication, June 5, 1943.

59. *Los Angeles Examiner*, March 20, 1944. As cited in Dohrman, *California Cult*.

60. *Weekly Message*, June 23, 1945. As cited in Dohrman, *California Cult*.
61. Dohrman, *California Cult*.
62. "From 'The Speaker' in Behalf of The International Institute of Universal Research and Administration to All Registrants Who Have Retained Their Love for, and Faith in, the Christly Vision Elucidated in the Textbook, 'Mankind United,'" 1951.

CHAPTER 4: LIAR FOR HIRE

1. Peter McWilliams, *Life 102: What to Do When Your Guru Sues You* (Los Angeles: Prelude Press, 1994).
2. Bob Sipchen and David Johnston, "John-Roger : The Story Behind His Remarkable Journey from Rosemead Teacher to Spiritual Leader of a New Age Empire," *Los Angeles Times*, August 14, 1988, https://www.latimes.com/archives/la-xpm -1988-08-14-vw-882-story.html.
3. McWilliams, *Life 102*.
4. Ibid.
5. Ibid.
6. According to Nielsen BookScan, McWilliams's 1997 *The Loss of the Love* sold over 250,000 copies.
7. Philip Faflick. "Computers: The New Hardware Made Easy, *Time*, January 24, 1983, https://time.com/archive/6883940/computers-the-new-hardware-made -easy/.
8. McWilliams, *Life 102*.
9. "Cult 101: J.R. being exposed on Geraldo's NOW IT CAN BE TOLD," You-Tube, accessed October 16, 2024, https://www.youtube.com/watch?v=mKlU-P60uhFs.
10. The term is sometimes credited to psychedelics proponent Aldous Huxley and sometimes to *Look* magazine editor George Leonard, but either way, it came out of the Esalen Institute, a California cliffside retreat center dedicated to growth and exploring the human psyche.
11. Tom Wolfe, "The 'Me' Decade and the Third Great Awakening," *New York*, September 15, 2023, https://nymag.com/article/tom-wolfe-me-decade-third -great-awakening.html.
12. Bob Sipchen, "Tracking the Mystical Traveler : The church founded by John-Roger has sparked controversy over some of its teachings, now-defunct gala awards and a peace retreat near Santa Barbara. Now it is in the news because of Arianna Huffington," *Los Angeles Times*, November 1, 1994, https://www .latimes.com/archives/la-xpm-1994-11-01-mn-57257-story.html.

13. McWilliams, *Life 102*.

14. Joe Holley, "Wealthy oilman was a U.S. ambassador," *Los Angeles Times*, July 19, 2008, https://www.latimes.com/archives/la-xpm-2008-jul-19-me-huffington19 -story.html.

15. Ibid.

16. Home page, Insight Seminars, accessed September 13, 2024, https://insightsem inars.org/us/.

17. McWilliams, *Life 102*.

18. Ibid.

19. Montgomery Brower, Suzanne Adelson, and Leah Feldon, "Cult Leader John-Roger, Who Says He's Inhabited by a Divine Spirit, Stands Accused of a Campaign of Hate," *People*, September 26, 1988.

20. McWilliams, *Life 102*.

21. "Larry King Obituary: Broadcaster Who Topped the Ratings for Decades," *Irish Times*, https://www.irishtimes.com/life-and-style/people/larry-king-obituary -broadcaster-who-topped-the-ratings-for-decades-1.4470149.

22. McWilliams, *Life 102*.

23. John S. Haller Jr., *The History of New Thought: From Mind Cure to Positive Thinking and the Prosperity Gospel* (West Chester, PA: Swedenborg Foundation Press, 2012).

24. Mary Baker Eddy, *Science and Health with Key to the Scriptures* (Boston: Trustees Under the Will of Mary Baker Eddy, 1906, 1875).

25. Gillian Gill, *Mary Baker Eddy* (Reading, MA: Perseus Books, 1998).

26. Ashley Squires, *The Standard Oil Treatment: Willa Cather, The Life of Mary Baker G. Eddy, and Early Twentieth Century Collaborative Authorship* (Austin: University of Texas, 2013).

27. Mark H. Haller, *Eugenics: Herediterarian Attitudes in American Thought* (New Brunswick, NJ: Rutgers University Press, 1963).

28. Ibid.

29. Ibid.

30. Horation W. Dresser, *Health and the Inner Life: An Analytical and Historical Study of Spiritual Healing Theories, with an Account of the Life and Teachings of P. P. Quimby* (New York: G. P. Putnam's Sons, 1906).

31. Larry Tye, *The Father of Spin: Edward L. Bernays & the Birth of Public Relations* (New York: Henry Holt, 1998).

32. Gus Lubin, "There's a Staggering Conspiracy behind the Rise of Consumer Culture," *Business Insider*, February 23, 2013, https://www.businessinsider.com /birth-of-consumer-culture-2013-2.

33. Tye, *Father of Spin*.

34. Edward L. Bernays, *Biography of an Idea: Memoirs of Public Relations Counsel Edward L. Bernays* (New York: Simon & Schuster, 1965).

35. "Dispatch from United Press," *New Mexico Tribune*, April 1, 1929.

36. Tye, *Father of Spin*.

37. Ibid.

38. Edward L. Bernays, *Propaganda: A Master Spin Doctor Convinces the World That Dogsh*t Tastes Better than Candy* (Grosse Pointe Park, MI: Adagio Press, 2020).

39. Tye, *Father of Spin*.

40. Ibid.

41. Marvin N. Olasky, *Corporate Public Relations: A New Historical Perspective* (Hillsdale, NJ: Lawrence Erlbaum, 1987).

42. *Century of the Self*, Episode 1, BBC2, 2002.

43. Ibid.

44. Tye, *Father of Spin*.

45. Irvin G. Wyllie, *The Self-Made Man in America: The Myth of Rags to Riches* (New Brunswick, NJ: Rutgers University Press, 1954).

46. James Allen, *The Prosperity Bible: The Greatest Writings of All Time on the Secrets to Wealth and Prosperity* (New York: Jeremy P. Tarcher, 2007).

47. Napoleon Hill, *Think and Grow Rich* (Meriden, CT: Ralston Society, 1937).

48. Matt Novak, "The Untold Story of Napoleon Hill, the Greatest Self-Help Scammer of All Time," Gizmodo, December 6, 2016, https://gizmodo.com/the-untold-story-of-napoleon-hill-the-greatest-self-he-1789385645.

49. Ibid.

50. As I point out some of the Protestant roots of this national pastime, I do acknowledge the irony that Protestantism was born in part as a protest against the Catholic Church's literal selling of salvation via indulgences.

51. Steven Pressman, *Outrageous Betrayal: The Dark Journey of Werner Erhard from Est to Exile* (New York: St. Martin's Press, 1993).

52. Ibid.

53. Ibid.

54. Ibid.

55. Ibid.

56. McWilliams, *Life 102*.

57. "1973—John Denver—Tonight Show Hosting, Werner Erhard Interview Only," YouTube, accessed September 13, 2024, https://www.youtube.com/watch?v=d87eqHfCpJg.

58. Ibid.

59. Claire Carter, "How a 'Sweet-but Shallow' Guy Grew Up," *Parade*, February 10, 1991.

60. Jane Self, *60 Minutes and the Assassination of Werner Erhard* (Houston, Texas: Breakthru, 1992).

61. Anne Harrington, *The Cure Within: A History of Mind-Body Medicine* (New York: Norton, 2008).

62. Barbara Ehrenreich, *Bright-Sided: How the Relentless Promotion of Positive Thinking Has Undermined America* (New York: Metropolitan Books, 2009).

63. Ibid.

64. Ibid.

65. Pressman, *Outrageous Betrayal*.

66. Marc Fisher, "'I Cried Enough to Fill a Glass,'" *Washington Post*, October 24, 1987.

67. Margaret Thaler Singer, *Cults in Our Midst: The Continuing Fight against Their Hidden Menace* (San Francisco: Jossey-Bass, 2003).

68. Fisher, "'I Cried Enough."

69. Singer, *Cults in Our Midst*.

70. Pressman, *Outrageous Betrayal*.

71. Vanessa Grigoriadis, "Pay Money, Be Happy," *New York*, July 9, 2001, https://nymag.com/nymetro/news/culture/features/4932/.

72. Mark Brewer, "We're Gonna Tear You Down and Put You Back Together," *Psychology Today*, August 1975.

73. McWilliams, *Life 102*.

74. Singer, *Cults in Our Midst*.

75. Ibid.

76. Ibid.

77. M. A. Kirsch and L. L. Glass, "Psychiatric Disturbances Associated with Erhard Seminars Training: II. Additional Cases and Theoretical Considerations," *American Journal of Psychiatry*, 134, no. 11 (1977): 1254–58.

78. Pressman, *Outrageous Betrayal*.

79. Fisher, "'I Cried Enough."

80. Pressman, *Outrageous Betrayal*.

81. Ibid.

82. Ibid.

83. "Rick Ross, '60 Minutes' Broadcast about Werner Erhard," Cult Education Institute, August 26, 2009, https://culteducation.com/group/908-est/6113-60-minutes-broadcast-about-werner-erhard.html.

84. Robert W. Welkos, "Founder of est Targeted in Campaign by Scientologists: Religion: Competition for Customers Is Said to Be the Motive behind Effort to Discredit Werner Erhard," *Los Angeles Times*, December 29, 1991, https://www.latimes.com/archives/la-xpm-1991-12-29-mn-2102-story.html.

85. Welkos, "Founder of est."

86. "Internal WE&A Memo to Werner Erhard from Art Schreiber," March 30, 1983.

87. Peter Haldeman, "The Return of Werner Erhard, Father of Self-Help," *New York Times*, November 28, 2015, https://www.nytimes.com/2015/11/29/fashion /the-return-of-werner-erhard-father-of-self-help.html.

88. Self, *60 Minutes*.

89. Suzanne Snider, *The Believer*, Vol. 1, No. 2, May 2003.

90. Pressman, *Outrageous Betrayal*.

91. Ibid.

92. John LaRosa, "$10.4 Billion Self-Improvement Market Pivots to Virtual Delivery during the Pandemic," Market Research Blog, August 2, 2021, https://blog .marketresearch.com/10.4-billion-self-improvement-market-pivots-to-virtual -delivery-during-the-pandemic.

93. Iris B. Mauss, Maya Tamir, and Craig L. Anderson, "Can Seeking Happiness Make People Unhappy? The Paradoxical Effects of Valuing Happiness," *Emotion* 11, no. 4 (August 2011): 807–15.

94. Steve Salerno, *SHAM: How the Self-Help Movement Made America Helpless* (New York: Crown, 2005).

95. Adam Michaelson, *The Foreclosure of America: The Inside Story of the Rise and Fall of Countrywide Home Loans, the Mortgage Crisis, and the Default of the American Dream* (New York: Berkley, 2009).

96. S. A. James, "John Henryism and the Health of African-Americans," *Culture, Medicine, and Psychiatry* 18 (1994).

97. Jessica Joan, *The Untouchable Jessica Joan: The Downfall of NXIVM* (Art of Being Untouchable, 2023).

98. Rina Raphael, *The Gospel of Wellness: Gyms, Gurus, Goop, and the False Promise of Self-Care* (New York: Henry Holt, 2022).

99. Ibid.

100. Kira M. Newman, "Is Social Connection the Best Path to Happiness?," Greater Good, June 27, 2018, https://greatergood.berkeley.edu/article/item/is_social _connection_the_best_path_to_happiness.

101. McWilliams, *Life 102*.

102. Ibid.

103. "John-Roger Dies at 80; Founder of Controversial New-Age Church," *Los Angeles Times*, October 23, 2014, https://www.latimes.com/local/obituaries /la-me-john-roger-20141023-story.html.

104. "Heaven's Gate: The Cult of Cults," *The Second Harvest*, HBO Max, December 3, 2020.

CHAPTER 5: NANNY NANNY BOO BOO

1. Eric Scheibeler, *Merchants of Deception: An Insider's Chilling Look at the World-wide, Multi-Billion Dollar Conspiracy of Lies That Is Amway and Its Motivational Organizations* (North Charleston, SC: BookSurge, 2009).

2. Ibid.

3. Ibid.

4. Kathryn A. Jones, *Amway Forever: The Amazing Story of a Global Business Phenomenon* (Hoboken, NJ: John Wiley & Sons, Inc., 2011).

5. Scheibeler, *Merchants of Deception*.

6. Ibid.

7. Ibid.

8. Ibid.

9. Ibid.

10. Ruth Carter, *Amway Motivational Organizations: Behind the Smoke and Mirrors* (Winter Park, FL: Backstreet, 1999).

11. Sean Munger, "The Tools Cult: The History of the Amway Motivational Scam (Part 1 of 3)," *Sean Munger's History and Culture Dispatches* (Substack blog), November 13, 2022, https://seanmungerhistory.substack.com/p/the-tools-cult -the-history-of-the.

12. Scheibeler, *Merchants of Deception*.

13. Sean Munger, "The Tools Cult: The History of the Amway Motivational Scam (Part 3 of 3)," *Sean Munger's History and Culture Dispatches* (Substack blog), November 13, 2022, https://seanmungerhistory.substack.com/p/the-tools-cult -the-history-of-the-bdc.

14. Robert L. FitzPatrick, *Ponzinomics: The Untold Story of Multi-Level Marketing* (Charlotte, NC: FitzPatrick Management, Inc., 2020).

15. Scheibeler, *Merchants of Deception*.

16. Ibid.

17. Ibid.

18. Ibid.

19. "GET RID OF THE LOSERS LIMP," YouTube, accessed September 13, 2024, https://www.youtube.com/watch?v=hbjJnkeNH_w.

20. Scheibeler, *Merchants of Deception*.

21. Sean Munger, "The Tools Cult: The History of the Amway Motivational Scam (Part 3 of 3)."

22. P. Klebnikov, "The Power of Positive Inspiration," *Forbes*, December 9, 1991.

23. Scheibeler, *Merchants of Deception*.

24. "John Winthrop: A Modell of Christian Charity, 1630," accessed September

13, 2024, History Department, Hanover College, https://history.hanover.edu
/texts/winthmod.html.

25. Stephen Innes, *Creating the Commonwealth: The Economic Culture of Puritan New England* (New York: W. W. Norton, 1995).

26. Ibid.

27. Max Weber, *The Protestant Ethic and the Spirit of Capitalism* (New York: Charles Scribner's Sons, 1958).

28. Irvin G. Wyllie, *The Self-Made Man in America: The Myth of Rags to Riches* (New Brunswick, NJ: Rutgers University Press, 1954).

29. Francis Wayland, *The Elements of Political Economy* (New York: Leavitt, Lord, 1837).

30. Benjamin M. Friedman, *Religion and the Rise of Capitalism.*(New York: Vintage Books, 2021).

31. Wyllie, *Self-Made Man in America*.

32. Abraham Lincoln, "Address to the Wisconsin State Agricultural Society, Milwaukee, Wisconsin," *Speeches and Writings, 1859-1865* (New York: Library of America, 1989).

33. Moses Yale Beach, *Wealth and Pedigree of the Wealthy Citizens of New York City: Comprising an Alphabetical Arrangement of Persons Estimated to Be Worth $100,000 and Upwards, with the Sums Appended to Each Name: Being Useful to Banks, Merchants and Others* (New York: Compiled with much care and published at the *Sun* Office, 1842), http://archive.org/details/wealthpedigreeof 00beac.

34. Barbara Maranzani, "America's First Multi-Millionaire," History, July 17, 2023, https://www.history.com/news/john-jacob-astor-americas-first-multi-millionaire; "John Jacob Astor (1763–1848)," *Wall Street Journal*, accessed October 16, 2024, https://www.wsj.com/public/resources/documents/mill-1-timeline-astor.htm.

35. "Carnegie Started as a Bobbin Boy," *New York Times*, August 12, 1919, https://archive.nytimes.com/www.nytimes.com/learning/general/onthisday/bday/1125 .html.

36. William S. Dietrich II "Andrew Carnegie: The Black and the White," *Pittsburgh Quarterly*, Summer 2007, https://pittsburghquarterly.com/articles/andrew -carnegie-black-white/.

37. C. Wright Mills, "The American Business Elite: A Collective Portrait," *Tasks of Economic History*, suppl. V (1945).

38. William Miller, "American Historians and the Business Elite," *Journal of Economic History* IX (1949).

39. Edward Atkinson, *Industrial Exhibitions: Their True Function in Connection with Industrial Education* (Boston, 1882).

40. *Ali Wong: Don Wong*, Netflix, 2022.

41. Miriam Frankel and Matt Warren, "How Gut Bacteria Are Controlling Your Brain," BBC, January 22, 2023, https://www.bbc.com/future/article/2023 0120-how-gut-bacteria-are-controlling-your-brain.

42. William Matthews, *Getting on in the World* (Chicago, 1874).

43. Wyllie, *Self-Made Man in America*.

44. William A. Alcott, *The Young Man's Guide* (Boston, 1841).

45. W. P. Groser, "Reports of the Mosely Educational Commission to the United States of America, October–December, 1903" (London: A. Mosely, 1904).

46. Friedman, *Religion and the Rise of Capitalism*.

47. Russell H. Conwell, *Acres of Diamonds* (New York, 1915).

48. Andrew Carnegie, "Wealth," *North American Review* 148, no. 391 (June 1889).

49. Andrew Carnegie, *The Gospel of Wealth* (New York, 1900).

50. Ibid.

51. Henry Ward Beecher, "Economy in Small Things," in *Plymouth Pulpit* (New York: J. B. Ford, 1875).

52. Wyllie, *Self-Made Man in America*.

53. Angus Fletcher, *Wonderworks: Literary Invention and the Science of Stories* (New York: Simon & Schuster, 2021).

54. Ibid.

55. Alissa Quart, "How the Horatio Alger Lie Helped Shape the Myth of American Upward Mobility," *Rolling Stone* (blog), March 14, 2023, https://www.rollingstone.com/culture/culture-features/american-dream-myth-horatio-alger-lie-bootstrapped-excerpt-1234695926/.

56. Tom Riley, "The Orphan Trains," Irish America, April/May 2014, https://www.irishamerica.com/2014/03/the-orphan-trains/.

57. Wyllie, *Self-Made Man in America*.

58. Orison S. Marden, *The Young Man Entering Business* (New York, 1903).

59. "Money," Britannica. com, accessed September 13, 2024, https://www.britannica.com/money/robber-baron.

60. William James Ghent, *Socialism and Success* (New York, 1910).

61. Robin Wall Kimmerer, *Braiding Sweetgrass: Indigenous Wisdom, Scientific Knowledge, and the Teachings of Plants* (Minneapolis: Milkweed Editions, 2013).

62. Ibid.

63. Robert Reich, *The System: Who Rigged It, How We Fix It* (New York: Vintage Books, 2020).

64. Ibid.

65. Robert Frank, "Soaring Markets Helped the Richest 1% Gain $6.5 Trillion in

Wealth Last Year, According to the Fed," CNBC, April 1, 2022, https://www
.cnbc.com/2022/04/01/richest-one-percent-gained-trillions-in-wealth-2021
.html.

66. Reich, *The System*.

67. Nick Hanauer, "The Top 1% of Americans Have Taken $50 Trillion from the
Bottom 90%—And That's Made the U.S. Less Secure," *Time*, September 14,
2020, https://time.com/5888024/50-trillion-income-inequality-america/.

68. Ibid.

69. "The World's Billionaires," Wikipedia, accessed September 15, 2024, https://
en.wikipedia.org/w/index.php?title=The_World%27s_Billionaires&oldid
=1245831505.

70. "Jeb Bush: Americans 'Need to Work Longer Hours,'" BBC, July 9, 2015,
https://www.bbc.com/news/world-us-canada-33469209.

71. "The Personal Responsibility and Work Opportunity Reconciliation Act of
1996," Office of the Assistant Secretary for Planning and Evaluation, August 31,
1996, https://aspe.hhs.gov/reports/personal-responsibility-work-opportunity
-reconciliation-act-1996.

72. Carl Hulse and Catie Edmondson, "G.O.P. Revolts Over Debt Limit Deal as
Bill Moves Toward a House Vote," *New York Times*, May 30, 2023, https://
www.nytimes.com/2023/05/30/us/debt-limit-bill-house-rules-committee
.html.

73. Ladonna Pavetti, "Work Requirements Don't Cut Poverty, Evidence Shows,"
Center on Budget and Policy Priorities, June 7, 2016, https://www.cbpp.org
/research/test-work-requirements-dont-cut-poverty-evidence-shows.

74. "Estimating the National Housing Shortfall," Harvard Joint Center for Housing Studies, January 29, 2024, https://www.jchs.harvard.edu/blog/estimating
-national-housing-shortfall.

75. Matthew Desmond, "Why Poverty Persists in America," *New York Times
Magazine*, March 9, 2023, https://www.nytimes.com/2023/03/09/magazine
/poverty-by-america-matthew-desmond.html.

76. Robert L. FitzPatrick, *False Profits: Seeking Financial and Spiritual Deliverance
in Multi-Level Marketing and Pyramid Schemes* (Charlotte, NC: Herald Press,
1997).

77. N. J. Demerath et al., eds., *Sacred Companies: Organizational Aspects of Religion
and Religious Aspects of Organization* (New York: Oxford University Press,
1997).

78. FitzPatrick, *False Profits*.

79. Jane Marie, "How a Dream Becomes a Nightmare," *The Dream* (podcast),
2018.

80. FitzPatrick, *False Profits.*

81. FAQs, Direct Selling Association, accessed October 16, 2024, https://www.dsa
.org/about/faq. FitzPatrick argues, however, that the DSA is essentially an arm
of the MLM industry and therefore its data may be unreliable.

82. Ibid.

83. FitzPatrick, *Ponzinomics.* Dale Russakoff and Juan Williams, "Rearranging
'Amway Event' for Reagan," *Washington Post,* January 1984, https://www.wash
ingtonpost.com/archive/politics/1984/01/22/rearranging-amway-event-for-rea
gan/b3e74482-5ce0-4d20-9f98-ebdc9b4d4918/.

84. Russakoff and Williams, "Rearranging 'Amway Event' for Reagan."

85. FitzPatrick, *False Profits.*

86. Russakoff and Williams, "Rearranging 'Amway Event' for Reagan."

87. FitzPatrick, *False Profits.*

88. Molly Ivins, "Congress Distributes a Tax Break to Amway," *Star-Telegram,*
August 1997.

89. Scheibeler, *Merchants of Deception.*

90. Dan Alexander, "Betsy DeVos Says It's 'Possible' Her Family Has Donated
$200M to Republicans," *Forbes,* January 17, 2017, https://www.forbes.com
/sites/danalexander/2017/01/17/devos-says-its-possible-her-family-has-donated
-200m-to-republicans/.

91. FitzPatrick, *False Profits.*

92. "Bloomberg—Are You a Robot?," accessed September 16, 2024, https://www
.bloomberg.com/tosv2.html?vid=&uuid=f77eb74b-7432-11ef-89f2-33fc4ad5
e0d0&url=L25ld3MvYXJ0aWNsZXMvMjAxNS0wNy0zMS9oaWxsYXJJ
5LWFuZC1iaWxsLWNsaW50b24tcGFpZC00My1taWxsaW9uLWluLWZ
lZGVyYWwtdGF4ZXM=.

93. Joe Nocera, "Opinion | The Pyramid Scheme Problem," *New York Times,* Sep-
tember 15, 2015, https://www.nytimes.com/2015/09/15/opinion/joe-nocera
-the-pyramid-scheme-problem.html.

94. Lois Greisman, "Re: Staff Advisory Opinion—Pyramid Scheme Analysis,"
March 15, 2024. https://www.ftc.gov/system/files/ftc_gov/pdf/3.15.24 Letter
(003).pdf

95. Scheibeler, *Merchants of Deception.*

96. Chris Hansen, "In Pursuit of the Almighty Dollar," *Dateline,* May 7, 2004,
https://www.nbcnews.com/id/wbna4375477.

97. Reich, *The System.*

98. Dacher Keltner, *The Power Paradox: How We Gain and Lose Influence* (New
York: Penguin Books, 2016).

99. Shane Goldmacher, Maggie Haberman and Michael Gold, "Trump at the Garden:

A Closing Carnival of Grievances, Misogyny and Racism," *New York Times*, October 27, 2024, https://www.nytimes.com/2024/10/27/us/trump-msg-rally .html.

100. Reich, *The System*.
101. Kurt Braunohler, "Capitalism," *Perfectly Stupid*, 2022.

CHAPTER 6: US VERSUS THEM

1. Bob Moser, "United Nuwaubian Nation of Moors Meets Its Match in Georgia," Southern Poverty Law Center, September 16, 2024, https://www.splcenter.org /fighting-hate/intelligence-report/2002/united-nuwaubian-nation-moors-meets -its-match-georgia.
2. "Nuwaubian Nation of Moors," Southern Poverty Law Center, accessed September 16, 2024, https://www.splcenter.org/fighting-hate/extremist-files/group /nuwaubian-nation-moors.
3. Jamiyla Chisholm, *The Community* (New York: Little A, 2022).
4. Bill Osinski, "Cult Leader Ignored His Own Rules," *Atlanta Journal-Constitution*, July 7, 2002.
5. Abu Ameenah Bilal Philips, *The Ansar Cult in America* (Saudi Arabia: Tawheed Publications, 1988).
6. Dan Baum, "Legalize It All," *Harper's*, April 2016, https://harpers.org/archive /2016/04/legalize-it-all/.
7. Dwight York, "This Is Your Message Najwa and Davina, Kirsten," November 10, 2004.
8. James Baldwin, *The Fire Next Time* (New York: Vintage Books, 1962, 1963).
9. Philips, *The Ansar Cult in America*.
10. Bob Moser, "United Nuwaubian Nation of Moors Meets Its Match in Georgia," *Intelligence Report* 107 (Southern Poverty Law Center, September 20, 2002), https://www.splcenter.org/fighting-hate/intelligence-report/2002/united -nuwaubian-nation-moors-meets-its-match-georgia.
11. Richard Wrangham and Dale Peterson, *Demonic Males: Apes and the Origin of Human Violence* (New York: Mariner Books, 1996).
12. Joseph Henrich, *The Secret of Our Success: How Culture Is Driving Human Evolution, Domesticating Our Species, and Making Us Smarter* (Princeton, NJ: Princeton University Press, 2016).
13. Richard Wrangham, *The Goodness Paradox* (New York: Vintage Books, 2019).
14. Joseph Henrich, *The Secret of Our Success: How Culture Is Driving Human Evolution, Domesticating Our Species, and Making Us Smarter* (Princeton, NJ: Princeton University Press, 2016).

15. Ibid.

16. Ibid.

17. "The Knowledge Report," accessed November 4, 2024, https://www.mikerind-ersblog.org/the-knowledge-report/.

18. India Oxenberg, *Still Learning* (Webster, TX: Audible Studios, 2020).

19. Henrich, *The Secret of Our Success.*

20. Ibid.

21. Wrangham, *The Goodness Paradox* (New York: Vintage Books, 2019).

22. Mikael Klintman, *Knowledge Resistance: How We Avoid Insight from Others* (Manchester, UK: Manchester University Press, 2019).

23. Ibid.

24. Richard Rubenstein, "Religion, Modernization and Millenarianism," *The Coming Kingdom: Essays in American Millennialism & Eschatology,* edited by M. Darrol Bryant and Donald W. Dayton (Barrytown, NY: New Era Books, 1983).

25. Philip Jenkins, *Mystics and Messiahs: Cults and New Religious Movements* (New York: Oxford University Press, 2000).

26. Many scholars count the Nazis among history's largest millennial groups. Researchers also include the Marxists in this camp. Both meet the major hallmarks: believing that a cataclysmic and total overhaul of human society and culture will soon occur and, in its wake, create a kind of paradise on earth.

27. Rubenstein, *The Coming Kingdom.*

28. "Organizations Controlled by and or Associated with Moon," Cult Education Institute, accessed September 16, 2024, https://culteducation.com/unif121 .html.

29. Lorraine Boissoneault, "The True Story of Brainwashing and How It Shaped America," *Smithsonian*, May 22, 2017, https://www.smithsonianmag.com /history/true-story-brainwashing-and-how-it-shaped-america-180963400/.

30. "APA Memo of 1987 with Enclosures," CESNUR, May 11, 1987, https://www .cesnur.org/testi/APA.htm.

31. "DIMPAC Report," CESNUR, accessed September 16, 2024, https://www .cesnur.org/testi/DIMPAC.htm.

32. Don Lattin, "Combatants in Cult War Attempt Reconciliation, Peacemaking Conference Is Held near Seattle," *San Francisco Chronicle*, May 1, 2000.

33. "How to Identify a Cult: Six Tips from an Expert," CBS News, February 24, 2018, https://www.cbsnews.com/news/how-to-identify-a-cult-six-expert-tips/.

34. Lorne Dawson, *Comprehending Cults* (Don Mills, Ontario: Oxford University Press, 2006).

35. Rodney Stark and William Sims Bainbridge, *A Theory of Religion* (New Brunswick, NJ: Rutgers University Press, 1996).

36. Dawson, *Comprehending Cults.*

37. Bandy X. Lee, *Profile of a Nation: Trump's Mind, America's Soul* (World Mental Health Coalition, 2020).

38. Brian Hare and Vanessa Woods, *Survival of the Friendliest: Understanding Our Origins and Rediscovering Our Common Humanity* (New York: Random House, 2020).

39. Ibid.

40. "Media Information | Constitution Center," National Constitution Center, accessed September 16, 2024, https://constitutioncenter.org/about/liberty-medal/media-info.

41. Hare and Woods, *Survival of the Friendliest: Understanding Our Origins and Rediscovering Our Common Humanity* (New York: Random House, 2020).

42. R. Strahan, *Leading Representatives: The Agency of Leaders in the Politics of the U.S. House* (Baltimore: Johns Hopkins University Press, 2007).

43. Soroush Vosoughi, Deb Roy, and Sinan Aral, "The Spread of True and False News Online," *Science* 359, no. 6380 (March 9, 2018).

44. "The Metronome of Apocalyptic Time: Social Media as Carrier Wave for Millenarian Contagion," *Perspectives on Terrorism* 9, no. 4 (August 2015).

45. "How Social Media Features Parallel Cult Techniques," Center for Humane Technology, accessed September 16, 2024, https://www.humanetech.com/insights/how-social-media-features-parallel-cult-techniques?fbclid=IwAR0wsF2CJ-9mGzQlpB8PBdoIy_tGKO3ZJunfHT72p14Hq24ihTbzQILwq2o.

46. Isaac Eliaz, *The Survival Paradox: Reversing the Hidden Cause of Aging and Chronic Disease* (Carson City, NV: Lioncrest, 2021).

47. "Stress in America: Paying with Our Health," American Psychological Association, February 4, 2015.

48. Eliaz, *Survival Paradox.*

49. Ibid.

50. R. A. Boer et al., "The Fibrosis Marker Galectin-3 and Outcome in the General Population," *Journal of Internal Medicine* 272, no. 1 (October 25, 2011).

51. Joseph Henrich, *The WEIRDest People in the World: How the West Became Psychologically Peculiar and Particularly Prosperous* (New York: Picador, 2020).

52. Ibid.

53. Ibid.

54. Moser, "United Nuwaubian Nation of Moors Meets Its Match in Georgia,"

55. "Jacob York: Deconstructing Dr. York and the Nuwaupian Cult," YouTube, accessed September 16, 2024, https://www.youtube.com/watch?app=desktop&v=6QcQieQbwmU.

56. Osinski, "Cult Leader Ignored His Own Rules."
57. Moser, "United Nuwaubian Nation of Moors Meets Its Match in Georgia."
58. Osinski, "Cult Leader Ignored His Own Rules."
59. Moser, "United Nuwaubian Nation of Moors Meets Its Match in Georgia."
60. "Jacob York: Deconstructing Dr. York and the Nuwaupian Cult," YouTube.
61. "For Sale: Nuwaubian UFO Cult Compound, Slightly Used," *Bushwick Daily*, August 26, 2024, https://bushwickdaily.com/real-estate/sanctuary-of-the-sabaeans-for-sale-brooklyn-cult-bookstore/.

CHAPTER 7: CONTROL-ALT-DELETE

1. *Love Has Won: The Cult of Mother God*, Episode One, HBO, November 13, 2023.
2. Virginia Pelley, "How a Former McDonald's Manager Convinced Millennial Women She Was God," *Marie Claire*, September 7, 2021, https://www.marie claire.com/culture/a37417778/love-has-won-cult-amy-carlson-stroud-death/.
3. *Love Has Won*, Episode One.
4. Christopher Moyer, "From 'Mother God' to Mummified Corpse: Inside the Fringe Spiritual Sect 'Love Has Won,'" *Rolling Stone* (blog), November 26, 2021, https://www.rollingstone.com/culture/culture-features/love-has-won-amy-carlson-mother-god-1254916/.
5. "New HHS Report Shows National Uninsured Rate Reached All-Time Low in 2023 after Record-Breaking ACA Enrollment Period," U.S. Department of Health and Human Services News Release, August 3, 2023, https://www.hhs.gov/about/news/2023/08/03/new-hhs-report-shows-national-uninsured-rate-reached-all-time-low-2023-after-record-breaking-aca-enrollment-period.html.
6. *Love Has Won: The Cult of Mother God*, Episode Three, HBO, November 13, 2023.
7. Ibid.
8. Ibid.
9. Moyer, "From 'Mother God' to Mummified Corpse."
10. *Love Has Won*, Episode Three.
11. Moyer, "From 'Mother God' to Mummified Corpse."
12. *Love Has Won*, Episode Three.
13. "Carlson, Amy Renee," El Paso County Coroner, DocDroid, accessed September 16, 2024, https://www.docdroid.net/MkW2hne/carlson-amy-renee-pdf.
14. Norman Cohn, *Cosmos, Chaos and the World to Come: The Ancient Roots of Apocalyptic Faith* (New Haven, CT: Yale University Press, 2001).
15. Aaron C. Kay et al., "Compensatory Control: Achieving Order Through the

Mind, Our Institutions, and the Heavens," *Current Directions in Psychological Science* 18, no. 5 (October 2009): 264–68, https://doi.org/10.1111/j.1467 -8721.2009.01649.x.

16. "Topic: Anxiety in the U.S," Statista, accessed September 16, 2024, https://www .statista.com/topics/5223/anxiety-in-the-us/.

17. Marie Galmiche et al., "Prevalence of Eating Disorders over the 2000–2018 Period: A Systematic Literature Review," *American Journal of Clinical Nutrition* 109, no. 5 (May 2019).

18. "Our Epidemic of Loneliness and Isolation," U.S. Surgeon General's Advisory on the Healing Effects of Social Connection and Community, n.d.

19. *The Social Dilemma*, Netflix, 2020.

20. Yuval Noah Harari, "Why Technology Favors Tyranny," *Atlantic*, October 2018.

21. Hannah Ritchie, Max Roser, and Pablo Rosado, "Energy," *Our World in Data*, October 27, 2022, https://ourworldindata.org/co2/country/united-states.

22. Harari, "Why Technology Favors Tyranny," *Atlantic*, October 2018.

23. Isaac Eliaz, *The Survival Paradox: Reversing the Hidden Cause of Aging and Chronic Disease* (Carson City, NV: Lioncrest, 2021).

24. Ibid.

25. Ibid.

CONCLUSION

1. Brian Hare and Vanessa Woods, *Survival of the Friendliest: Understanding Our Origins and Rediscovering Our Common Humanity* (New York: Random House, 2020).

2. Ellie Robins, "On Addiction," *How to Go Home* (Substack blog), January 4, 2024, https://ellierobins.substack.com/p/on-addiction.

3. Robin Wall Kimmerer, *Braiding Sweetgrass: Indigenous Wisdom, Scientific Knowledge, and the Teachings of Plants* (Minneapolis: Milkweed Editions, 2013).

4. Emma Stone, Ph.D., "The Emerging Science of Awe and Its Benefits," *Psychology Today*, April 27, 2017, https://www.psychologytoday.com/us/blog/understand ing-awe/201704/the-emerging-science-awe-and-its-benefits.

5. Kim Haines-Eitzen, "Ancient Texts Encouraged Hope and Endurance When They Spoke of End Times," The Conversation, April 13, 2020, http://thecon versation.com/ancient-texts-encouraged-hope-and-endurance-when-they-spoke -of-end-times-135639.

6. *The Wizard of Oz*, Metro-Goldwyn-Mayer, 1939.

INDEX

JANE BORDEN is the author of *Cults Like Us* and *I Totally Meant to Do That*. Her work has been featured in *Vanity Fair*, the *New York Times Magazine*, the *Washington Post*, and other publications. She lives in Los Angeles. Find out more at JaneBorden.com.

One Signal Publishers, an imprint of Atria Books at Simon & Schuster, fosters an open environment where ideas flourish, bestselling authors soar to new heights, and tomorrow's finest voices are discovered and nurtured. Since its launch in 2002, Atria has published hundreds of bestsellers and extraordinary books, which would not have been possible without the invaluable support and expertise of its team and publishing partners. Thank you to the Atria Books colleagues who collaborated on *Cults Like Us*, as well as to the hundreds of professionals in the Simon & Schuster advertising, audio, communications, design, ebook, finance, human resources, legal, marketing, operations, production, sales, supply chain, subsidiary rights, and warehouse departments who help Atria bring great books to light.

EDITORIAL
Alessandra Bastagli
Abby Mohr

JACKET DESIGN
Emma Van Deun

MARKETING
Erin Kibby
Morgan Pager

MANAGING EDITORIAL
Paige Lytle
Shelby Pumphrey
Lacee Burr
Sofia Echeverry

PRODUCTION
Laura Wise
Richard Willett
Vanessa Silverio
Hope Herr-Cardillo

PUBLICITY
Falon Kirby

PUBLISHING OFFICE
Suzanne Donahue
Abby Velasco

SUBSIDIARY RIGHTS
Nicole Bond
Sara Bowne
Rebecca Justiniano